A Quick Look Ins

As I re-engage the universe into which
me, from that parallel universe, a deep :
of ritual, the language of the sacred, and the com...
sacramental value of all life is best expressed through art, poetry,
and, most important, one's feet in the dirt. How might the beauty
that I love be what I do?

---Caroline Fairless, *A Work in Process*

Over the past thirty years I've lived a life where the beauty I love
-- poetry as healer – is what I do. I am glad to be poor at math
because I can't keep up with the blessings; I have lost count.

--John Fox, *Poetry's Call: An Exploration of Let and Letting*

I want to be a change agent. However, I continue to live divided,
and I continue to return to the Courage Community through the
years because it helps me deal with the frustration I experience
about my divided existence with my students. I know that I am not
doing what I think is best for them. My truth is that I continue to
espouse my convictions, but I bow to the pressures to
perform on the tests by any means necessary.
The beauty that I love is not what I do.

---Wanda Smith Freeman, *My Truth at a Slant*

All of these people (the Writers in the book) are participants in
what I have called the "movement model of social change."
The movements from which I drew this model sometimes have big
names—the Civil Rights Movement, the Women's Movement, the
Velvet Revolution. But at bottom, the movement I have in mind
has been unfolding in ways small and large since our species first
achieved consciousness. It is the ancient movement to fulfill
the human possibility, a movement that's forever calling us to
embody what it means to be truly human.

---*Parker Palmer, The Movement Way*

LET THE BEAUTY WE LOVE BE WHAT WE DO:
STORIES OF LIVING DIVIDED NO MORE

QUILTED TOGETHER
BY
THE WRITERS CIRCLE OF TRUST

FACILITATED AND EDITED BY
SALLY Z. HARE AND MEGAN LEBOUTILLIER

WITH

AN EMBELLISHMENT BY

PARKER J. PALMER

Pp
Prose Press

Comments: sally@stilllearning.org
or visit the website: www.stilllearning.org

ISBN: 978-0-9895042-2-5

Quilting designs by Megan LeBoutillier
Photography and book design by Jim R. Rogers

Prose Press
Pawleys Island, South Carolina
www.ProsePress.biz
prosencons@live.com

Dedication

*SZH: For Jim, who creates the space for me
to know I love my life;
BQ, who is my Other Mother;
and my Sisters:
Susan who has supported and encouraged
my Courage work in so many ways,
and Jane, who gets Courage from the inside-out
and participated in that first pilot
Courage to Teach.*

*MLeB: For Bruce, who gracefully accepts
my invitations and enlivens my life.*

The Who in the Writers Circle of Trust: Introducing the Writers Who Sit Around The Table of Contents

THE WRITERS: In a Circle of Trust, we often invite people to introduce themselves in ways other than the usual job title or geographical location, so we did that with our Writers Circle of Trust. Here are our Writers, alphabetically sitting around the Table of Contents (although they move around in the book and do not appear in alphabetical order!), sharing with you, the Reader, what makes them feel most alive or some thoughts about the Beauty they love.

Marian R. David: *The Beauty I love is allowing the 10,000-petal flower of my soul to open in its own time and supporting others to do the same. My heart is full of gratitude. I am very alive in the flow of my life /work. Despite fear, in time, I step up boldly anyway. I feel alive when I am walking and just being on the ocean, meditating, dancing, creating, and communing with others and nature.*

Marcie Ellerbe: *I believe in the power of the individual to make a difference. Participating for two years of Circles of Trust has helped me listen to myself in new ways. What makes me feel most alive? Challenging work, coming home, learning and growing, playing with my cats, hugs, warm blankets, deep breaths, family. The Beauty I love? It's making time to read the world around me, helping learners see themselves with generous and curious eyes.*

Carolyn Ellis: *I feel alive when I am exploring my spirit in the company of other seekers. Reading meaningful poetry and fiction and discussing with students and teachers of all stripes makes me feel alive. The Beauty I love is hearing the Divine in my soul and in others. I am the wife of a NCAA Division I basketball coach and live an exciting life, but my life is made meaningful and abundant by the work of teaching and advocating.*

Caroline Fairless: *Baseball is my passion, and had I been born a boy, I know I'd have played professional ball (for the Pirates). The banjo is my instrument of choice . . . if only I could play it. For several years I have apprenticed myself to a marble sculptor. After my beloved dog Missy died, I swore I would never have another dog. Now we have two. My book,* **The Dance of the Caterpillars ~ In a Time Before Texting,** *is my sweetest and most tender work. The beauty I love takes many forms, with one thread in common – that it takes me out of myself and out of time. I am in awe of the simple walk from our house to a nearby pond. It is pure magic when I can be on the water in a kayak. I love what emerges when I am still and patient; it might be a phrase on a page, or a purple finch at the feeder, or seeing what my hands can shape from a block of clay. I love to garden. I love the knowledge that, as I care for the soil, I am making it richer. I love the smell of the seasons just prior to their appearance. I love New Hampshire and the beauty of our home.*

Janet Files and Sara Sanders: *We feel most alive when we are fully present to the beauty in each moment and when we are part of a vibrant community, discovering and sharing stories of personal significance. Janet feels alive sitting on her back porch in the freshness of morning, enjoying bird songs, coffee, a good read and the delicious tonic of the sounds, smells and feels of the earth and her creatures great and small. She also feels alive when enjoying the zany, warm company anywhere, anytime of the loving heap of her four grown children, her endearing, devoted husband and any beloved friends caught up in links of loving relationships. Sara feels alive in the process of making connections (with Spirit, with people--family, friends, students, colleagues, the strangers among us--with ideas, with ingredients that will become dinner, even with Scrabble tiles). Story, travel, walking, metaphor, dreams, and the three R's of reading, writing, and romance often take her there. The beauty we love is creating spaces for story, connection and joy.*

John Fox, CPT: *I could tell you the typical starting line-up for the Cleveland Indians in 1965. What Gerard Manley Hopkins wrote in his poem God's Grandeur, "There lives the dearest freshness deep down things," is, in my experience, finally true. I try to be loyal, thoughtful and giving to friends. I feel most alive at moments, taking a single, deep breath, as if it were traveling up my spine... I remember coming very alive once when I was leaning into a person's voice, especially into words permeated with vulnerability and power.*

Wanda Freeman: *The beauty I love lies in the breadth of grandmahood. The legacy I want to leave my family is what Courage has taught me: leaning in, listening intentionally, loving without fixing, sitting quietly and hearing Silence, welcoming, with open arms, Nature and all her moods, and gifts... these things, but most important, seeking, and building the undivided life. I also want them to treasure my Rumi CDs, read by Coleman Barks, when I'm gone. That love will not dim. They will hear and feel me in them.*

Veta Goler: *I'm most alive when I'm moving. That could mean I'm moving my body, as in walking my dog in nature, walking a labyrinth, drawing or coloring, or dancing in the kitchen. It could also mean moving within the terrain of my inner landscape while meditating or chanting. The Beauty I love is accessing and expressing the divine within me and helping others to do the same. My purpose on the planet is to know my divinity, which I do through creativity, spending time in nature, contemplative practices, and listening to and following my intuition.*

Sally Z. Hare: *I am a South Carolinian by birth and by choice – and I love my life! Teaching and learning make me feel most alive -- and walking on the beach makes me feel at home. I can't separate teaching and learning; they are the two sides of my Mobius strip that seamlessly flow into each other. Teaching is how I learn best. The Beauty I love comes from creating space for others to discover joy in reading, their own words and the words of others – and creating space for others to hear their own Inner Wisdom; in the process, I often get to hear my own!*

Megan LeBoutillier: *The Beauty I love includes art, nature, and making connections that create beauty. I am brave and I am fiercely honest. I am willing to share difficult truths if I believe others can benefit from the sharing. I dislike stereotypical thinking and plan to try and expose it whenever possible. I want to blow up myths and challenge popular assumptions.*

Morgan Lee: *The Beauty I love is living into my call. I am passionate about speaking up and out in the dedication to the proposition that all people should be treated with dignity and respect. My wife, Lena, has been with me always -- and my son, Chapman, teaches me each day. From them, and from my inner teacher, comes my knowing that I must do the work to help myself and others to strive for racial and cultural understanding and to be better open to our own cultural and racial biases. I remain on a spiritual journey that has taken me to mystical places and has brought wondrous dreams.*

Sandra Jean Sturdivant Merriam: *My family is my heart, especially Olivia, my granddaughter. My husband is my best friend; we live in North Myrtle Beach, South Carolina, with our 2-year old Labradoodle Millie, who loves the beach. The energy that pulls me in this phase of my life is finding ways to ensure that young teachers see the value of claiming their authentic voices. The Beauty I love is the way simple work, done well, informs the soul.*

Patricia T. Mulroy: *I have gained courage through sitting in Circles of Trust – learning to listen to who I am and what I bring to the world. I love to learn new things, try new things and be the courageous person I appear to be! I feel most alive when I am walking in the woods – thinking and capturing ways that I can make a difference, and help others make a difference in the lives of children, teachers, and educators. Writing for this book has felt like coming home.*

Jean M. Richardson: *I love my family and the respect that we have for one another. For the last two decades, the number one joy in my life has been to be a part of the lives of my two sons. Now married to my loving partner, Pat, together we are blessed with four young adult children and two Labrador retrievers. I love to create all sorts of things: good food, a welcoming dinner table, inclusive spaces, work environments that honor each person's talents, and experiences where diversity is welcomed and difference is honored. I am a creative, caring person with lots of energy and sometimes just a bit too much passion for things I care about. I love to kayak, ski, and travel to almost anywhere. While many people think I am an extrovert, I am really an introvert.*

Anna Marie Robinson: *I work in a positive, creative, dynamic work environment with an extraordinary team of dedicated professionals. My work requires energy. To remain energized, I rely on nature. When I am not at work, I am in my kitchen creating meals for family and friends, or patiently waiting in my backyard for the return of the owls or the bobcat. I love being in a canoe on a lake and then suddenly hearing the cry of a loon break open the silence. It is breathtaking to suddenly see a wild animal turn and look directly into my eyes when I am looking at them through binoculars. The Beauty I love is creating a space of comfort and safety where people feel welcome, be it in the work place, the classroom or in my home.*

Jim R. Rogers: *My name is Jimmy Roy Rogers. After my Dad...not the cowboy. I am a movie and TV watcher always looking for stories that make me think, cry, laugh, and worry, the last one not being hard to find at all. I feel most alive when I see struggling parents feel the "ah ha" moment when they understand the importance of their relationship with their children. The Beauty I love is interacting with family, friends and clients in authentic ways, not having to guard my speech or walk on eggshells as I share my truths about life and listen to theirs.*

Sue E. Small: *I want you, my Reader, to know that I believe in love; that I love my life, after more than 50 years of loving my work in public schools and universities; that I became a Courage & Renewal facilitator in my quest to live undivided and lead with soul; that I wake up in the morning with hope of seeing the sun come up; that I always buy Rosa Parks postage stamps. I feel most alive enCOURAGEing others; walking with a friend; being with the children in my life; learning, growing, and teaching; and traveling. The Beauty I love? Seeing others learn and grow, communications beyond just words, quiet mornings.*

Debbie Stanley: *What makes me feel most alive? Teaching and learning; being loved and loving others, being in prayer in early morns, being in nature. The Beauty that I love includes working on sermons/lessons that break my heart open to new insights and possibilities and then offering the experience to others. I am an introvert and I've just begun to intentionally embrace this knowing. My Christian spiritual practices make my life worth living.*

Jacqueline Miles Stanley: *I am a student of humanity. I know that we are not to live alone, that community is the only way we can really live and be alive. Smiles come from the most unexpected places as I am beginning to love me. What makes me most alive is sharing with others, being with my children and grandchildren, enjoying music of all kinds, holding hands and feeling smiles in my heart from the words of another. The Beauty I love is laughter of children; the space in silence where the chatter of heart and head can find each other; being a friend to others and to myself.*

Kay Stewart: *After 26 years teaching health and fitness at Emory University, I founded Stillwaters Mindfulness Training to encourage mindful living, joyful connection, and wise action. In our fast-paced and noisy world we need to slow down, focus, and pay attention to what matters most in our work, our relationships, and our health. I love feeling fully alive to the goodness and grace that permeates this unfolding mystery we call life! The Beauty I love is living and teaching from the inside/out, wide open to God's amazing love and grace! I love to teach and consider it an extraordinary privilege to travel alongside others to cultivate a way of being in the world that is large enough to hold mind, body, heart, and spirit in an integrated and resilient wholeness.*

EMBELLISHMENTS: An embellishment in quilting is a special addition that is not part of the original design, but adds a special touch. We are especially grateful that the first one is from Parker Palmer. You will find several others throughout our book:

- still learning, inc.
- The Center for Courage & Renewal
- Kirkridge Retreat and Study Center

What Is The Writers Circle of Trust?

We come into the world whole.

We are born fully formed with everything we need – our seeds of true Self, our birthright gifts, our temperament. We come with a sense of connectedness to everything around us. And then the deformation begins.

Our wholeness becomes hidden. We lose sight of our gifts. We misunderstand our temperament. The seeds of true Self go dormant as they recede from the light and nurture they need to grow. We see ourselves as separate from everything around us.

This book offers the stories of 21 remarkably diverse individuals who share the desire to live into their birthright wholeness. The individuals who make up our Writers Circle of Trust made the decision to live divided no more – and that decision often brought them to a retreat, seeking safe space and community for the inner journey.

These Writers weren't all in the same retreat – or in the same location – or even in the same year. The retreats may have been The Courage to Teach® or The Courage to Lead® or Circle of Trust®. Those are all names for registered programs of the Center for Courage & Renewal's in-person retreats and programs that nurture personal and professional integrity and the courage to act on it. The retreats are grounded in the writing and philosophy of Parker J. Palmer – and he explains that in detail in his book, *A Hidden Wholeness*. You can also learn more on the Center's website, www.couragerenewal.org. Sometimes the retreat has been a unique still learning, inc, co-creation of the Circle of Trust (COT), facilitated by a CCR-facilitator, in partnership with an ally in the movement toward wholeness and healing, towards being fully human. For example, one of the Writers in this book is poet therapist John Fox. John and COT facilitator Sally Z. Hare have collaborated in a number of retreats over the past five years in which they have created space at the intersection of John's work in Poetic Medicine and Sally's Courage work.

Parker Palmer uses the image of the Mobius strip, a seamless continuous curve, to illustrate that wholeness. (You can easily create one by taking a paper strip and giving it a half-twist, and then joining the ends of the strip together to form a loop.)  He says that we all live on the Mobius strip all the time. He writes in *A Hidden Wholeness* that "we are constantly engaged in a seamless exchange between whatever is out there and whatever is in here, co-creating reality, for better or for worse." Only in our learned illusion of separateness do we convince ourselves that we have an inner world and an outer world.

One of the authors, Sally Z. Hare, first met Parker Palmer during her Kellogg National Leadership Fellowship in 1992. A few years later, Parker invited her to lead one of four pilot sites for a program he had created, The Courage to Teach. Some of the Writers in this book were participants in that pilot two-year seasonal retreat series, from 1996 to 1998, in coastal South Carolina.

Parker Palmer's voice and his writings are threads throughout this quilt of stories. His vision and role-modeling and encouragement and generosity gave us the patterns for our quilt – and even more importantly, inspired the courage to create our own designs. For more than two years, Sharon Palmer created the space of holy hospitality in which Sally and the facilitators for the other three pilot groups first listened to Parker's idea that we teach who we are – and then took his words into their hearts and let them emerge, in their own individual ways and with their own authentic voices, in those early Courage to Teach groups in the fall of 1996. Sharon is the embodiment of letting the Beauty you love be what you do.

In front of Sharon and Parker's fireplace in 1994, Judy Brown, one of those pilot facilitators, introduced Rumi's words as one of the touchstones she used in her own work:

> Today, like every other day, we wake up empty
> and frightened. Don't open the door to the study
> and begin reading. Take down a musical instrument.
>
> Let the beauty we love be what we do.
> There are hundreds of ways to kneel and kiss the ground.

The beautiful translation of the 13th century Sufi mystic by American poet Coleman Barks has become an integral part of the work for Sally, as well as one of the boundary markers now essential in her Courage Circles. Coleman's gifts of Rumi's ideas are also important threads in our quilt of stories, and he has generously given us permission to use his translations of Rumi's words.

The individuals in this Writers Circle of Trust have been invited to share their stories, to go public with their decision to live an undivided life, to name and embrace their ongoing journey, with its shadows and light, starts and stops, bridges and potholes. We encouraged our Writers to be intentional in casting off the deformation of what too many of us learned in school about writing: the so-called objectivity that says we can't use the words *I* and *we* and can't claim our own voices; the academic language and footnotes that too often detract from the meaning; even the rules of grammar that say all sentences must have a subject and a verb!

We know that words matter – and we are naming and reclaiming language throughout our stories. We have included some of the key words and phrases in our glossary at the end of this book. Places matter, too, and you will also find some information on three that are very important to us: still learning, inc; the Center for Courage & Renewal; and Kirkridge Retreat and Study Center.

Common threads mean that some things may be repeated in different words in different stories, or that several of us quote the same author or poet. We embrace all the threads that make the quilting of our stories into a whole and allow us to share them with you, our Reader.

Letting the Beauty You Love Be a Quilt

A Note from Editor Megan LeBoutillier

I am an artist and a writer. I love to make things, and I especially love learning how to put things together. Years ago I literally woke up one day knowing that I wanted to learn how to weave. Fortunately, I had a friend who knew how, and was willing to show me. For my 40th birthday I asked for, and received a beautiful floor loom. I went to town exploring what could be made with a loom. After a few years I settled comfortably into making chenille scarves. I have made hundreds of them.

The year my mother died, a close friend suggested I should buy myself an expensive gift for Christmas. I wasn't exactly sure what would be served by her suggestion, but I'd had a vague notion of trying to take my woven work to new levels, and my intuition kept nudging me to think about sewing. I'd never sewn. As a child I accidentally impaled my forefinger right through the nail bed with a sewing machine needle. I gave the frightful machine wide berth after that. So, imagine my surprise when, for Christmas 2010, I gifted myself with a Bernina 330 that I had no idea how to use. Fortuitously, the machine came with lessons.

I was exploring making buttonholes in anticipation of branching out from rectangular scarves, when I came across a small, discreet package of 40 different strips of pre-cut Balinese batik fabric. I simply had to have it. No amount of negotiation and remembering that I didn't sew could dissuade me. I had to

4

have it. I brought it home and immediately set about sewing the strips together. Then I cut and stitched some more and rearranged and sewed some more, and suddenly a quilt began to show itself to me. What was I going to do with that? Luckily, the teacher at the sewing store was more than willing to help bring me along, even though I think she thought I was faking my complete lack of knowledge about anything to do with sewing.

I like the idea of stories being stitched into quilts the way stories were stitched into quilts when women gathered in quilting bees. When Sally asked me to co-edit this book with her, she told me about going to hear Mary Whyte talk about her artwork. She heard:

> We are like scraps of fabric: some are beautiful,
> and some are torn; some are colorful, and
> some are faded. Each piece of fabric is unique,
> and not particularly useful by itself. It is only
> when we stitch the pieces together side by
> side that we have a complete quilt. Only when
> every piece touches the others is the quilt
> finished and beautiful and whole.
>
> Mary Whyte, South Carolina artist

I have a design wall in my studio, a wall covered in cork where I can tack up pictures, bits of fabric, thread, beads, various embellishments, and writing; anything that can begin to inform the process of creating a quilt. I audition shapes, textures, and colors before beginning the process of cutting and sewing quilt pieces together.

The process of putting the writings of 21 different voices together into a pleasing, coherent form is not unlike picking fabric and thread and design for a quilt. It is not unlike creating safe space for community within a Circle of Trust. It takes cutting and discernment and a careful eye to check that the

5

seams have all really been stitched carefully together, and all of the threads that shouldn't be seen are hidden, and those threads that are seen are carefully sewn.

Courage Work is powerful, and it is difficult to put into words. Creative work is much the same. It is not easy to talk about where creativity and courage come from because both contain elements of mystery and intangibility. As the stories started to come in, faint connecting threads began to show themselves. No two people have the same experience, but they share similarities and they wind and weave and interconnect around Circles of Trust.

I have had the added delight of seeing a series of quilts show up as I've been writing and editing. My right brain trying to balance the left perhaps, but these colorful quilts started to emerge as this book began. Now they are adorning the cover and will gift all of the Writers as a reminder to let the beauty we love be what we do.

It has been an honor to work with the words of the Writers in this collection as they tell their individual stories of how courage has worked on them and in them. And it has been an honor to work with Sally to stitch the pieces together into *Let the Beauty We Love Be What We Do: Stories of Living Divided No More.*

I'll Meet You in the Field:
The Intersection of Education and Community

By Sally Z. Hare

 **I** ran away from home to go to kindergarten.

My mother decided against sending me to pre-school, because she didn't want me to feel she was pushing me out now that she had two other babies in the house. So I took matters into my own hands, quietly dressed my five-year-old self one morning in October and went downstairs to walk around the corner to school with my five-year-old cousin Irwin. In those days of neighborhood schools and communities of people who knew each other, the teacher called my mother to tell her I was there and encouraged her to let me stay.

My hunger to learn to read was stronger than my painful shyness. Somehow I understood, even as a young child, that learning was social, that I needed a community to learn. Learning to read was a significant stepping stone on my life's path. Everything changed the day I became a reader. The details of the moment I realized I could read remain vivid.

Whisper of Rain

A perfect triangle
Of light
Marked the center of our circle.

Eight short solid
Wooden chairs
Plus Miss Mason's tall one.

The Robins, we were,
And it was our turn
To leave our desks for The Reading Circle.
Our turn to join
Miss Mason up front.
Our turn to decode the letters, the sounds.

We'd been at it awhile.
Long enough to learn
All the vowels, long and short,
Most of the consonants,
And a lot of the rules:
When two vowels go walking,
The first does the talking.

And we practiced
Blending.
Miss Mason, I loved you
In your yellow dress and certainty.

I wanted to please
You. I wanted to **be**
You. So my stomach
Hurt every time The Robins circled up.

Sound out the letters,
You told us. Remember
The Rules. And when
You think you know the Word,
Raise your hand
And I'll let you whisper in my ear.

Time and again I raised my hand.
Time and again you let me whisper.
Time and again you sent me back
To my little chair in the circle
While Stanley and Harriet and Hank
Stayed standing, smug with whispered
Rightness.

And then That day
The sun made a triangle on the floor
The letters seemed to slide together.
r-r-r-r, long ā (Silent *i*
when two vowels go Walking,
the first does the Talking.) n...n...n...
r_ā_nn. R *rān*, I whispered.
You smiled. And I stood,
The triangle touching the toe
Of my black patent Mary Janes.

Nothing was the same
After rain came.

---Sally Z. Hare

TEACHERLEARNER: TWO SIDES OF THE MOBIUS STRIP

For me, teacherlearner is one word. Teaching is the way I learn. Those roles are the two sides of the Mobius strip that illustrate my journey. The flow between the side that is teaching and the side that is learning is so seamless that I can't tell where one stops and the other starts.

I always knew I would be a teacher. I can't separate teaching and learning. Teachinglearning is the beauty I love. And reading is my path to that beauty. I wanted to share my love of reading. I wanted to create the space for others to discover how reading changed everything, how it opened the world. Rumi and I disagree a bit on that. When he tells us to let the beauty we love be what we do, he advises against taking a book from the shelf: *Don't open the door to the study and begin reading. Take down a musical instrument.*

Reading **is** my musical instrument.

THE INTERSECTION OF EDUCATION AND COMMUNITY

When Parker Palmer invited me to pilot The Courage to Teach in South Carolina, my understanding of the importance of community deepened as I created the space for that first Circle of Trust. The essence of the human self is that it's both solitary and communal. Embracing that paradox is essential to learning, to education.

I delight in recognizing that the root of the word **education** is the Latin *educare,* to bring forth. As a Courage to Teach facilitator, I was remembering – and learning in new ways -- that **my** role was to bring forth that which already existed within the learner. Somewhere along the way of getting education degrees and teaching in a university, I had lost sight of that.

Of Teaching
(***Inspired by Kahlil Gibran's The Prophet***
and Two Friends on A Rainy September Afternoon)

"Speak to us of Teaching,"
           they asked the Prophet.
And She spoke thusly:
What I know of Teaching
    is this:
I cannot teach anyone anything.
The way I learn best is to teach.
Teaching is a reciprocal activity with learning:
      no teaching occurs if no learning occurs.
There is sometimes a differential in our perception
of Time, so that teaching and learning
seem to occur in separate
Moments.

One cannot teach without continuing to grow
as a learner.
One never reaches a state of **being** a teacher;
one is always **becoming** a teacher.
One Is constantly in the state of **being** a learner.
It is not possible to **become** a learner. You **are**.

The way I teach
      is most often the way I learn.
The way I learn
      is too often **not** the way the
    Hierarchy, the System, the Tradition teaches.

In our society, we say
Those who can, do.
Those who can't, teach.
We devalue the art of teaching and of learning.

We see learning
as a linear event in a designated moment,
usually requiring desks in a straight line
and rigid silence.

We see teaching
as an act done unto others,
with success measured in test-scores
and letter grades.
Oh, that we will come to value
　　　learning as the soul-mate
　　　　　　of teaching,
That learning is the stuff of which
　　　　Life is made.

And as Learning is Life,
So Teaching is Breath.

　　　　　　　　---Sally Z. Hare

My passion for teaching was rekindled as I rediscovered that each of us comes into this world as a whole human being with everything we need, with all our birthright gifts. As a teacher, I only had to create a space for each learner to discover, to uncover, to bring forth, those gifts. My work as a teacher was to help each student name and claim the beauty she loves -- and learn ways to take that beauty into the world.

Learning happens in community. Humans are communal creatures, and the relationship between education and community is vital. Looking back, I realize that my awareness of the importance of community was seeded early in my teaching career, when I worked with young children. Teaching four and five-year-olds affirmed, for me, that children construct knowledge in the context of their community. The children also taught me that learning was not only much easier, but also more joyful, when they saw themselves as members of a learning community, when they identified themselves as belonging in a world of learners.

12

I resonate with the insight of the Russian educator and psychologist Lev Vygotsky that learning is social. We need the love and care and attention of others not only to learn, but to thrive, even to survive. I remember my fascination with Rene Spitz's studies of institutionalized orphans who, although their physical needs for food and shelter were met and they had no discernable problems, literally turned their faces to the wall and died. We need relationships with others; we need love; we need touch; we need community.

My mother was right: some things have to be believed to be seen. You have to **know** they exist – or you won't see them. That is certainly true with the intersection of education and community. As I stand at that intersection, I can see that Life is a dance, not a linear uphill battle. It's a dance between two poles, the poles of our role as individual and our role as community member. Life is a dance between light and shadow, between simplicity and complexity, between abundance and scarcity. Life is a paradox. It's not either/or... it's both/and. Life is not a choice about being either an individual *or* a member of a community. Life is not about right *or* wrong. It's not about being *or* doing. It's both/and.

Rumi understood that, even 800 years ago. I am very grateful for the amazing translations of Coleman Barks that allow the ancient mystic and poet to speak to me across the centuries:

> *Out beyond ideas of wrong-doing and right-doing*
> *there is a field.*
> *I'll meet you there.*

That field, for me, is the intersection of education and community. Over the past 20 years of facilitating Circles of Trust and the Courage to Teach and the Courage to Lead, I have lived most of my life in that field.

NOTICING, NAMING, NURTURING

I learned the importance of naming from the Women's Movement, coming to understand that others had named me in limiting ways. Naming is power. That power comes from the way the name of a thing – or a person – affects my lens for seeing, for knowing, for learning.

For example, the names *fireman* or *policeman* limited my expectations – and even more damaging, "all men are created equal" left me wondering what that said about women. The so-called generic "he" deformed my vision – and the fairy tales and children's literature I passionately inhaled as a young reader named for me that women were helpless and dependent on the courage of men.

So I acquired a sense of urgency about naming before someone else took that power away from me. The shadow side of that urgency was that I too often named in a hurry, giving up the time required to really **know** what I was naming. I now know that noticing is important to naming. Noticing takes time – and is the work before the work of naming. Noticing can't be rushed. Noticing is being awake. It's about attention and intention.

When I am ready to name, I use great care in choosing words to communicate as clearly and as beautifully as possible. I remember Alice's reflecting on the power of naming with Humpty Dumpty (in Lewis Carroll's *Through the Looking Glass*):

> *"That's a great deal to make one word mean,"*
> *Alice said in a thoughtful tone.*
> *"When I make a word do a lot of work like that,"*
> *said Humpty Dumpty, "I always pay it extra."*

Until I hear myself, I don't know if the word communicates the way I want it to; I don't know if the name is accurate; I don't know if it is a good fit. And I can only hear myself in

14

community.   Being in community, meeting in the field that is the place education and community intersect, is essential to naming. The deep listening and open, honest questions practiced in the safe space of the Circle of Trust community are essential to me as I move from noticing to naming.

As I grow older, I am learning that names that worked earlier in my life may no longer fit. Names often change, as I reconnect soul and role on this continual journey toward wholeness. That is especially important as I name what I want to nurture in my life, as I name what I need **now** to create the space for the beauty I love.

So naming and nurturing, as well as noticing, are about attention and intention.   And nurturing means practicing what I have named so that it becomes a habit of the heart. I love Parker's definition in *Healing the Heart of Democracy* of habits of the heart: "deeply ingrained patterns of receiving, interpreting and responding to experiences that involve our intellects, emotions, self-images, and concepts of meaning and purpose."

In addition to noticing and naming, the habit of the heart that I nurture consistently is an appreciation of the Mystery that is My Story. The Women's Movement also awakened my awareness that the word history (that is, **his** story) was quite accurate, as there were few women in the way it was taught – and they were often in so-called gender appropriate jobs, such as Betsy Ross, a seamstress, and Clara Barton, stereotypically depicted as a nurse caring for the wounded brave men. History was indeed **his** story. So women began telling **her** story, creating the word *herstory*. Now, as I hear myself and my own Inner Teacher in our Circles of Trust, I am aware of *mystery*, **my** story.

NOT ABOUT BALANCE

It's not about balance. All my life I've been told that balance is the key to the good life... Balancing work and family. Balancing material and spiritual. Balancing have-to's and want-to's. I've been trying to figure it out for over fifty years. But I can't. Because it's not about balance.

Balance implies somehow managing numbers of things that can be counted, putting them into equal piles. And as the sign on Alfred Einstein's Princeton office door stated: ***Not everything that counts can be counted, and not everything that can be counted counts.*** I realize as I name those things that matter to me, that allow me to say I love my life, they can't be counted. They're not even things.

So I've learned it's not about balance; it's about seamlessness. It's about moving between work and family, between material and spiritual, between have-to's and want-to's, in a kind-of dance. It's about understanding and seeing and remembering our connectedness. With each other and everything. It's about waking up to life on the Mobius journey, to realizing that it's not either/or.

It's not balancing **any**thing. It's about embracing it all – and learning to dance at the intersection of education and community. South African Archbishop Desmond Tutu calls it *ubuntu*—and when he spoke at Coastal Carolina University's Celebration of Inquiry, he told us that's a hard concept for Americans to grasp. We don't have a word for it -- and we can't see what we can't name.

A Short Course in Ubuntu

> This being human
> Is a Paradox.
> I enter and leave
> Alone
> and yet
> the Journey requires
> companionship.
> We are hardwired

> To connect.
> The very act of
> Learning
> is Social.
> I am I be-
> cause You are You.
>
> **---Sally Z. Hare**

A READER'S SENSE OF PLACE, SENSE OF HOME

The journey to the undivided life begins with a sense of place and ends with a sense of home. If you don't have a sense of home, a sense of place, you don't have a sense of self. You can't know who you are. As I think about my continued journey to live divided no more, I know that being awake to my sense of place **and** my sense of home is an important part of letting the beauty I love be what I do.

As a Reader, a person for whom reading is literally how I learn, why I teach, the path on which I travel this Mobius journey towards wholeness, my sense of place is immensely shaped by the words and books in my life. A reader learns very early that home is where you live happily ever after. Only as I have grown older have I come to know my sense of place, my home, is within me as well as around me.

Sense of place is a birthright gift – and with growing up in the South, especially growing up in Charleston, South Carolina, during the Civil Rights Movement, that gift also has its shadow side. Even my most loving friends and family in other places often see me –and other Southerners – as somehow less-than. I spent my childhood and teen years in the city that was once one of the wealthiest places in the United States – because of the huge rice plantations that thrived in the 17th and 18th and 19th centuries and depended not only on slave labor, but also on capturing and enslaving Africans who had the skills and knowledge necessary to grow rice in this place. Vestiges of the dark side of that wealth and of the slavery and racism and sexism

17

that allowed it to thrive are evident in the woundedness and deformation of the South today. And paradoxically, the gifts of that wealth are also evident in the beauty and diversity of the people and the culture and the hospitality and the architecture and the music and the art and the incredible landscapes.

If you don't know where you are, writes farmer-poet-activist Wendell Berry, you don't know *who* you are. Author Wallace Stegner explains that Berry "is not talking about the kind of location that can be determined by looking at a map or a street sign. He is talking about the kind of knowing that involves the senses, the memory, the history of a family or a tribe. He is talking about the knowledge of place that comes from working in it in all weathers, making a living from it, suffering from its catastrophes, loving its mornings or evenings or hot noons, valuing it for the profound investment of labor and feeling that you, your parents and grandparents, your all-but-unknown ancestors have put into it. He is talking about the knowing that poets specialize in."

Stegner ponders if a place can't really be a place until it has had a poet. I would say a place can't really be a place until someone calls it home – and loves it – and shares that sense of place, sense of home, with the next generation and the next and the next. That means teaching about that place and learning about that place and telling stories about that place and singing about that place.

Heart is Where the Home Is
(after Reading Alice Walker's *There is a Flower at the End of My Nose Smelling Me)*

My work is connecting
Being the bridge, being the thread,
Being the rope from the back door,
Helping a wanderer, lost in a blizzard,
A wonderer, lost in thought,
Find the way home.

18

Here the teacher, here the student,
Here the flower, here the seed.
    Sometimes moving, sometimes still.
    Sometimes alone, sometimes surrounded,
          Always interconnected.

Carolina wren sings the Beauty
I love. Gardenia fills
    My sense of place with Beauty,
    My heart with Home.
          ---Sally Z. Hare

THE HIDDEN WHOLENESS: RECONNECTING SOUL AND ROLE

Thomas Merton writes in *Hagia Sophia*: *"There is in all things an invisible fecundity, a dimmed light, a meek namelessness, a hidden wholeness. This mysterious Unity, and Integrity, is Wisdom, the Mother of all ...."*

I struggle, as I write, to know how to end this writing, when I am still very much on the journey to live undivided, the journey to make that hidden wholeness a bit more visible. I take heart In that very fact: that I am still on the journey, still learning, still teaching, still noticing and naming. Since I got away earlier with disagreeing with Rumi, now I'll dare to resist T. S. Eliot:

Not-Quite-So Hidden Wholeness

We had the experience but missed the meaning...
         T. S. Eliot, *The Dry Salvages*

    perhaps it wasn't so much
    missing the meaning
    as the fact, indeed the necessity,
    of having to first
    have the experience
    then to step back

to get enough distance
to stand long enough
in the tragic gap
so that we might
see the patterns
see the connections
see the whole emerge.

---Sally Z. Hare

Perhaps I'll glimpse that wholeness in the field that is the intersection of education and community. Yes, I know I will continue the journey. And I know that the journey to that field beyond the ideas of wrong-doing and right-doing is an inward journey, even as it is an outward one.

The path to the field is a path I can only travel alone – and the path is made by walking, or perhaps by dancing or skipping, with Others. Only I can see the patterns – but they are too difficult to see by myself. So I'm grateful for the community I have found in Circles of Trust.

Dr. Sally Z. Hare, Singleton Distinguished Professor Emerita at Coastal Carolina University, is president of still learning, inc. (www.stilllearning.org). She lives in Surfside Beach, South Carolina, with her husband Jim R. Rogers, and two dogs, Eleanor Roosevelt and TBO. She can be contacted through e-mail: couragetoteach@sc.rr.com

A Work in Process

By Caroline Fairless

March 2, 2004 was the day I started on the long trek back to the life into which I was born, the life that had been mine. I think of this journey as I would a scroll of paper, rolled from each end toward the middle. March 2nd occupies the center.

Spring tends to come early to St. Mary's County, Maryland, and by mid-morning of that day, the robins had arrived in disproportionate numbers. It was hard to count them, in that they hopped from lawn to woods and back, all chattering as they did, but there were dozens, perhaps as many as a hundred.

The two dogwoods had flowered, and the new leaves on the sugar maples were the color of limes, each leaf no longer than an inch, yet unfolding by the minute. A winged shadow with a span of about six feet, probably a turkey vulture, crossed the yard, and I stood at the glass door of my walkout basement office, computer humming behind my back. Although my longing to go outside was palpable, I didn't go. I didn't go because I was afraid that if I walked into such beauty, I would not be able to walk back out. The loss, of course, was mine.

THE BIG HOUSE

In the 1950's and '60's, my parents, siblings, and I lived in what we dubbed "The Big House," an old rambling ivy-covered two-story brick house with substantial acreage in rural western Pennsylvania. It was a house filled with odd little spaces:

closets, out-of-the-way bathrooms, bedrooms, a pantry, big dining room, little dining room, basement, and rooms within rooms.

It is 1953. I am six years old. My mother, with me assisting, is determined to splint the twisted leg of a female bald eagle whose broken wing is making her frantic and dangerous, enclosed as she is in the water closet of a downstairs bathroom. My job is to distract her with a hamburger-laden popsicle stick while my mother tackles the leg. "Her wing," my mom assures me, "will heal on its own." I am timid but resolute, fearing that my mom will be mauled if I fail to accomplish my job. Truthfully, I am afraid she will be shredded regardless.

This magnificent creature who has the capacity to crush bones with her beak, grips my mother's wrist, all eight skimpy little bones of it just under her skin. I want to shut my eyes, but I can't. My mother is humming now, *"My grandfather's clock."* It takes her an eternity to splint the leg, hampered as she is by the beak around her wrist. But my mom perseveres, and the eagle does nothing aggressive, not once; she simply keeps my mom's wrist in her beak.

Over the years The Big House served as sanctuary for wild animals of all kinds: the wounded, the sick, and the orphaned. My mother was the principal healer, but we all did what we could, often giving up a bedroom, a bathtub, or a closet for a turkey, orphaned possums, deer, snakes, fox, skunks, raccoons, bobcat, bugs, birds, ducks, dogs, and once, a bear cub. We kids never knew who we would be greeting, by name, as we lugged our backpacks up the long hill home from school.

My mom's love of the untamed has embraced streams, ocean corals, trees, mountains, caves, wildflowers, rocks, and prairie grasses. The learning for me has been profound, and lifelong. All life has immeasurable value, no one form of any more or less value than any other, including the humans. This has been my growing up "normal."

A PARALLEL UNIVERSE

It is 1984 in Berkeley, California. I have become increasingly desperate to reframe my life, but I don't know how. To say that the past five years have not been safe for me is an understatement, and the list is long: violence, drugs, guns - not mine - culminating in the suicide of my dearest friend. I am walking on Ridge Road, and the sidewalk takes me past a not-particularly-imposing building. The sign reads *The Church Divinity School of the Pacific*. It is the Episcopal Seminary of the Pacific Rim. I walk into the building and think, "I could be safe here," and I step into a parallel universe.

The first ten years of my quarter century of ordained ministry unfolded in the 1990's. My liturgical practices were unorthodox from the beginning, but apparently containable, even desirable, within the institutional church. My particular niche was multi-generational liturgy, and because no one was daring to move to that particular edge, I pretty much had license to design weekly services as I chose. And I did.

Ultimately, it was a four-year-old named Ian who plunked me onto the trail of the long trek back to the life from which I had emerged. Each Sunday Ian walked up the aisle to the front of the church clutching a photograph and a piece of paper written in his own hand. Each Sunday Ian chose one endangered life form and led our congregation in prayer on that creature's behalf. He laid the image and the prayer on the altar, and then walked solemnly back to his parents. Every Sunday.

IAN'S GIFT

Ian led me into the questions that would ultimately, and gratefully, propel me into what I have named *the space between*; in particular, *the space between church and not-church*. The nascent questions were these, and they accompanied me through three congregations: how can any human-centered religion address adequately not only the urgent needs of the human and non-human world, but address as well the interconnectedness of all created forms? How can a congregation gather every Sunday and give no liturgical credence to the state of the deteriorating ecosystems of the world? How can members of congregations place more energy into preserving the ancient liturgical forms of their traditions than preserving earth and water, air and creature?

RETURNING TO THE PLACE I BEGAN

It is March 3, 2004, and at last I take my first faltering step back from the parallel universe that holds the institutional church, to return to the place I began, and the scroll of paper begins its forward unfolding.

It has taken ten years to approach the question, "How might the beauty I love be what I do?"

As I re-engage the universe into which I was born, I bring with me, from that parallel universe, a deep appreciation of the power of ritual, the language of the sacred, and the conviction that the sacramental value of all life is best expressed through art, poetry, and, most important, one's feet in the dirt. I include religious expression as well, but not what is so often served up as Sunday fare. I include what is often referred to as dark green religion, the religion of the earth. I also bring back an evolving question: how do I be a priest to the earth, and what might that mean?

How might the beauty that I love be what I do?

PORTAL TO A VERY DARK TIME

In 2007, the questions I had been holding voicelessly since my time with Ian, about the infertile relationship between ecology and the church, surfaced at last. It is with some chagrin that I admit that it had taken me more than a decade to find and exercise my voice, to articulate the obvious: mine is an anthropocentric religion and the questions of ten years ago remain. How possibly can humans do the work of ecological healing from a scriptural perspective of being *called out . . . set apart. . . chosen . . .?*

On the heels of the first question comes the second: How can we honor and live out of our interconnectedness with all creation from the scriptural perspective of steward, one who *manages,* one with *oversight?*

The answer -- we can't and don't -- served at that moment as portal to a very dark time. I had to let go of much that had sustained me during my years in the parallel universe of the church. But in a strange resolution of that long ago day in early March, 2004, this time, when I stepped out the door of the church and walked back into the world, I have stayed out here.

I am blessed with many companions, a parade of them, some still living, some not: Henry David Thoreau, John Muir, Aldo Leopold, Thomas Berry. The poets are legion: William Carlos Williams, Wendell Berry, Janisse Ray, Mary Oliver, Joy Harjo, David Wagoner, Rebecca Baggett. Each of them has opened a window onto the longings of my heart. How do I be a priest to/ with the earth? How might the beauty I love be what I do?

A year ago I met Trebbe Johnson through her article in *Orion Magazine*, "Gaze Even Here." In the article, Johnson recounts a week spent in the Pacific Northwest with several women friends who camped adjacent to a clear-cut. Each day, the women wandered throughout the clear-cut with journals, paints, paper, jeweler's loupes, and hearts willing to be broken. Each evening they returned to their campsite to share their experiences and insights of the day. I imagine that their free-flowing tears helped water the roots of the once majestic trees and dribble the colors of their paints down their drawing paper.

Johnson's question had to do with healing: how can we heal one another, this beautiful earth, and ourselves if we can't learn to love what is broken?

This is a religious question. It has to do with the essential nature of lament. It also has to do with the power and mystery of ritual designed to accompany us as we wander through the wreckage of our own making. My two dogs and I often wend our way through a nearby clear-cut. These oaks and white pine, birch and maple, were downed three years ago, presumably for the building of a house. Three years have passed; there is still no house. The dogs have learned to sit more or less patiently as I build small cairns on the stumps. I bring pinecones dropped from our own trees and place them in the boreholes of the woodpeckers. I bring pole beans from our garden, kale, and unshelled peanuts. The pole beans and peanuts disappear. The kale stays put!

The knowledge that the roots of these former giants are still exchanging nutrients with the roots of the birches in the woods behind the clear-cut not only comforts me, but also fills me with a sense of awe and mystery. Life emerges from death. The facts themselves are held by the sciences; religion shapes the ritual response. How do I be priest to/with the earth? I design ritual which emerges from the intersection of biology and religion, ritual which gives form to the science, ritual which brings comfort to my broken heart, and the hearts of others. I like to believe, and often do, that the earth and all creatures, the water and the wind, even the stones, appreciate the honoring.

A few months ago I chanced upon a DVD, *The Journey of the Universe,* the story of the birth of this planet and all that inhabit it, animate and inanimate. The story was written jointly by Brian Swimme and Mary Evelyn Tucker. Swimme teaches graduate-level evolutionary cosmology at San Francisco's California Institute of Integral Studies. Tucker's dual faculty positions at Yale University serve the schools of Forestry and

Environmental Studies as well as the Yale Divinity School. *The Journey of the Universe* narrates the *science* of creation even as it partners with the *spiritual*; not surprising, as the narrative was produced by two who inhabit that same partnership, science and spirit. To me, this partnership is beauty beyond measure, and my deepest longing is to allow all that I do to emerge from this core.

One day recently, across my desk, came the gift I didn't even know I was missing. The article by Rabbi Arthur Waskow, founder and director of the Shalom Center, was titled *When the World Turns Upside-Down, Do We Need to ReName God?* How are we going to do that? And what difference will it make? Waskow writes, "We must rename God, to be truthful to the changing reality, and to teach ourselves to act in new ways . . . I have been urging us to know God in our own generation through 'pronouncing' the unpronounceable sacred by simply breathing."

Simply breathing. Waskow calls it the "Interbreath of Life . . . the interbreath that keeps all life alive, that intertwines, interbreathes, the trees and grasses and ourselves. We breathe in what the trees breathe out; the trees breathe in what we breathe out: we breathe each other into life."

BREATHING

I go outside in the morning while it is still dark. The dogs don't seem to notice that it is minus six degrees today, the weather channel promising far colder temperatures. I breathe in all that the trees are breathing out. Are the trees that surround me breathing in the breath that I have expelled? I decide to embrace this as part of what Thomas Moore calls "a personal religion." Could this be? Could this be even in winter? I lie face down in the snow. At first the dogs are unnerved by my unaccustomed behavior, but soon they lie down with me. I breathe in, the gift from the trees. I breathe out and apologize for everything toxic I am releasing from my system. I breathe in; I am grateful. I breathe out. I wonder if the trees can process my exhalations. I am in awe.

I understand, at a level deeper in my soul than I am accustomed to experiencing, that I am connected. Yes, even in the winter. I have longed for this. I rarely glimpse it, but on this and other dark mornings, I know these relationships without doubt.

How do I allow this beauty I love to be what I do? How do I be a priest to/with earth? I don't know much, but I do know I have been blessed by my years in the church. I know gratitude for those years, and I know gratitude for the fact that I have stepped back into the life I was born to, today far richer than the day I turned my back on the gifts of true compassion and healing that have been my mother's legacy.

I wish I could say I know how to do this, but I don't. I am learning. I am learning to design ritual in such a way that anyone and everyone can gather around any table. I am finding the courage to share my conviction that a loaf of bread is the sacred fruit of earth, water, air, and sun. I know a flagon of wine in the same way. Likewise, water has sacramental value, and water rites belong to everyone; they serve to foster our human interdependence with all creation. I am learning to design ritual with the deepest of memory that recalls the stars which, upon their dying, release the elements of which every life form on this planet earth is made: carbon, nitrogen, hydrogen and oxygen. I am learning to trust the immeasurable value of the arts: music, poetry and prose, paint and sculpture.

I am learning to exercise the voice in me that proclaims the sacramental value of all creation, daring me and others to awaken to our place on this earth, with mindfulness and gratitude.

To make the beauty I love be what I do continues to be a process for me, and a challenge.

As I write this, it is cold in my office. At seven in the morning, as I wrap myself in a bundle of warm things, to step outside with our rescue dogs, I look at the thermometer which reads -13 degrees F, and I hurl invectives into the atmosphere. I understand that this was my outward breath that I gave to the trees to hold, and still, with such patience, they gave and continue to give me back life, love, energy; they continue to give me back an utterly trustworthy glimmer of the sacred.

How can I breathe in such beauty and refuse to return it? I am indeed a work in process, but I am learning.

Caroline Fairless is the author of several books, most recently *The Space Between Church & Not-Church ~ A Sacramental Vision for the Healing of Our Planet,* and *The Dance of the Caterpillars ~ In a Time Before Texting.* She blogs at www.restoringthewaters.com. Caroline's vision emerges from the partnership of ecology and spirituality, and she would love you to visit her website. She has been a Courage facilitator since 2008, and a member of the Leadership Core of Courage Earth ~ Awakening to Place. Ordained in the Episcopal Church in 1989, Caroline is also the founder and co-director of The Center for Children at Worship, a non-profit organization whose mission is to provide strategies for multigenerational worship. She and her partner/husband Jim Sims have offered workshops, conferences, and consultations throughout the United States, Canada, and England.

The Movement Way

An Embellishment by Parker J. Palmer

From the moment I began writing fifty years ago, I've known that my ideas wouldn't matter much if they simply sat there, inert, on the printed page. So I am deeply grateful for people who "put wheels" on those ideas—people who find ways to take their inner work into the outer world and show up on the job and in other parts of their lives with their identity and integrity intact.

The contributors to this book have done exactly that. Here they share their stories of what it means to decide to "rejoin soul and role" and live "divided no more." All of them found support for that decision in various programs offered by the Center for Courage & Renewal: The Courage to Teach, The Courage to Lead, and Circles of Trust. Their stories offer real-life examples of the Center's mission to create a more just, compassionate and healthy world by nurturing personal and professional integrity and the courage to act on it.

All of these people are participants in what I have called the "movement model of social change." The movements from which I drew this model sometimes have big names—the Civil Rights Movement, the Women's Movement, the Velvet Revolution. But at bottom, the movement I have in mind has been unfolding in ways small and large since our species first achieved consciousness. It is the ancient movement to fulfill the human possibility, a movement that's forever calling us to embody what it means to be truly human.

I want to say a few words about "the movement way" to offer insight into what has sustained the people whose stories are in this book—and can sustain all of us—in the journey toward an undivided life. In every movement I know anything about, four distinct stages can be discerned. These stages do not unfold as neatly as the following list suggests—they often overlap and circle back on each other. Nonetheless, extracting these stages from the chaos of history not only helps us see history more clearly. It also helps us get clear about what we can do to support and sustain the human possibility in our own time:

- **DIVIDED NO MORE:** Isolated individuals make the decision to stop leading "divided lives."

- **COMMUNITIES OF CONGRUENCE:** These people discover each other and join in community for mutual support.

- **GOING PUBLIC:** Empowered by community, movement advocates find public voice.

- **ALTERNATIVE REWARDS:** Movements develop—and become—alternative reward systems, thus weakening the sanctions that are the basis of every institution's power.

STAGE ONE: Divided No More

A movement is sparked when isolated individuals decide to stop leading "divided lives." Most of us know from experience how a divided life feels. Inwardly we know the truth about who we are, but outwardly we defy that truth; inwardly we know the soul's imperative for our lives, but outwardly we respond to demands of another sort. This is the human condition, of course: our inner and outer worlds will never be in perfect harmony. But there are extremes of dividedness that become intolerable—and when the pain becomes too great for this person, then that person, and then another, a movement may be underway.

The decision to stop leading a divided life, made by enough people over a long enough period of time, may eventually have political impact. But at the outset, this decision is a deeply personal one, taken not for the sake of some political goal, but for the sake of personal wholeness. I sometimes call it the "Rosa Parks decision," in honor of the woman who decided, on December 1, 1955, that she could sit wherever she liked on that city bus in Montgomery, Alabama.

Rosa Parks' decision was neither random nor taken in isolation. She served as the secretary of the local NAACP, had studied nonviolent social change at the Highlander Folk School, and had been involved in many conversations with local activists about a Montgomery bus boycott. But on December 1, 1955, her immediate motive was not to spark the modern civil rights movement.

Years later, she explained her decision with a simple but powerful image of personal wholeness: "I sat down because I was tired of giving in." She meant, of course, that she was soul-weary of collaborating with a system that denied her humanity, that treated her as less than the full and worthy human being she knew herself to be.

The power of a movement lies less in attacking some enemy's untruth than in naming and claiming a truth of one's own. The decision to live "divided no more" is less a strategy for changing other people's values than an expression of the elemental need for one's own core values to come to the fore. There is immense energy for social change in such inward decisions as they leap from one person to another and outward into the larger society. With these decisions, individuals can set movements in motion that create change from the inside out.

But how do people find the courage to declare their personal truth in the public arena, knowing that when they do, they are likely to be punished in ways that range from ridicule to marginalization to the loss of their livelihoods? The answer, I think, is that these people have reframed the logic of punishment in a way that liberates the soul. They have realized that no punishment anyone could lay on them could possibly be as bad as the punishment they lay on themselves by conspiring in their own diminishment, in the denial of their own integrity. With that realization, the power of the human heart is liberated in a way that, properly disciplined and deployed, has the potential to change the world.

STAGE TWO: Communities of Congruence

The decision to stop leading a divided life comes from a place of profound inner wisdom and strength. But it often takes us directly to a place of profound vulnerability. As I like to say—with only slight exaggeration—we make the decision to live divided no more on a Sunday afternoon, and we go to bed that night feeling alive and whole. But on Monday morning we wake up terrified: "What in heaven's name have I done? I've put myself at mortal risk, and I stand to lose a lot!"

The decision to live "divided no more" is always made over/ against a culture that advocates dividedness as the sensible, sane, even responsible, way to live. That's why we have so-called folk wisdom such as "Don't wear your heart on your sleeve" and "Play your cards close to your vest."

So in the second stage of a movement, people who have chosen the undivided life discover their need for a community that can provide countercultural support. They start reaching out to each other and entering into relations of mutual encouragement that help them sustain their decision. These groups, which are characteristic of every movement I know about, perform the crucial function of helping the Rosa Parkses of the world know that even though they are out of step, they are not crazy. Together they learn that culturally-approved behavior can be mad, but seeking integrity is always sane.

In these "communities of congruence," people have a chance to practice the undivided life, to exercise and strengthen the spiritual muscles it requires, and to deal with some of its consequences in the company of others who are on the same path. They also have a chance to develop visions of change that go beyond the individual to the larger society, and tactics and strategies for pursuing those visions that make these communities a power for change in the larger world.

The history of all social movements makes it clear that "base communities" are vital if the inner decision to live divided no more is to be sustained in a way that allows the movement to gather steam, establish trajectory, and take the next crucial step: from the security of the communal incubator into the challenges of the public realm.

STAGE THREE: Going Public

As individuals gather over time in communities of mutual support and encouragement, they learn to translate their private concerns into public issues—and they grow in their ability to give public voice to these issues in compelling ways. To put it more precisely, in these groups of like-minded folk, people discover that their problems are not "private" at all but have been occasioned by public conditions and therefore require public remedies.

Take, for example, the women's movement. For a long time, women were "kept in their place" partly by a culture that relegated the pain women felt to the private realm, treating it as grist for the therapeutic mill. But when women came together and began discovering how widely shared their "private" pain was, they also began discerning its public roots. "Going public" for women meant a movement from Freud to feminism, from psychology to politics, from the therapeutic couch to the streets and the mass media.

This translation of private pain into public issues goes far beyond the sociological analysis. It also empowers people to take those issues into public places and demand public solutions. It was in small groups—notably, in churches—that African Americans were empowered to take their protest to the larger community in songs and sermons and speeches, in pickets and in marches, in open letters and essays and books. The support provided by communities of congruence encourages people to take the risk of exposing insights, feelings and fact that had once seemed far too fragile to survive publicity in the rough-and-tumble public realm.

I am using the word "public" here in a way that is more classical than contemporary. The public I have in mind is not to be equated with institutional politics. Instead, to "go public" is to put one's values and beliefs—indeed, one's selfhood—into the mix of communal discourse. It is to project one's convictions and commitments in ways that allow others to hear them, respond to them, and be influenced by them—and, in the process, to allow one's values and beliefs to be tested and refined in the crucible of public life. The public, understood as a vehicle of discourse, is "pre-political." It is a foundational process of communal conversation, conflict, and consensus on which the health of institutionalized political power depends.

The writers in this book are taking a step towards going public by sharing their stories. Because this activity does not have direct political impact, some skeptics may call it "mere words." But this critique comes from an organizational mentality as contrasted with a movement mentality. As movement participants around the world can testify, by giving public voice to our stories we contribute to something more fundamental than political change: we help create cultural change.

STAGE FOUR: Alternative Rewards

As a movement passes through the first three stages, it offers reward to people for sustaining the movement itself, rewards that are integral to the nature of each stage. For example, they are the rewards that come from living one's values, from belonging to a community of support, from finding a public voice.

But in stage four, a more systematic pattern of alternative rewards emerges—and with it comes the capacity to challenge the power of dominant organizations.

The power organizations have over our lives depends on a system of rewards and punishments. For example, the institutional racism that is laced through all of our dominant organizations involves an oppressor group which gains rewards by keeping another group "in its place"—while the oppressed group stays "in its place" for fear of the punishment that will come if it does not. But as members of one or both groups discover the rewards that come from alternative behaviors, institutional racism starts to lose its grip.

In the case of the Civil Rights movement, many African Americans discovered the rewards that come from acting on one's deepest needs and expressing one's deepest sense of "true self." At the same time, some whites began to discover the rewards that come from embracing diversity, which include the vitality that comes from interacting with people beyond one's "tribe," and the ease that comes from feeling more at home on the face of a very diverse earth.

Additional "alternative rewards" come with the growth of the movement itself. For example, the affirmation one fails to receive from organizational colleagues is received from movement friends and allies. The meaning one fails to find in conventional work is found in the work of the movement. The paid work one cannot find in dominant organizations is found in the jobs that need to be done to keep a movement alive. Careers that no longer satisfy are transformed in ways inspired by the movement.

"Alternative rewards" may seem frail and vulnerable when compared to the salary raises, promotions and social status that our dominant organizations are able to bestow upon their loyalists. In certain respects, they are: "integrity," as the cynics say, "does not put bread on the table." But people who are drawn into a movement generally find that stockpiling bread is not the most fundamental issue for them. If they have the bread they need, they learn the wisdom of another saying: "Men and women do not live on bread alone." In the absence of integrity, we may survive but we cannot thrive.

In stage one, people who decide to live "divided no more" realize that no punishment could be worse than living in a way that denies their own integrity. In stage four, people begin to realize no reward could be greater than living in a way that honors their own integrity. These two points of insight bring a movement full circle from rejecting conventional punishments to embracing alternative rewards, generating power for social change as the circle gains momentum.

NAMING AND CLAIMING OUR POWER

For me, parsing the four stages of the movement model is far more than an abstract, analytic exercise. When we understand how this kind of social change typically unfolds, many of us can name and claim the fact that we are engaged in some form of the ancient movement for the human possibility. Now we can see that we hold in our hands a form of power that has driven real change among real people throughout human history, and ask ourselves the question, "What is the most responsible use of my power?"

In addition, we can use the four stages of the movement model to assess where we are today in whatever cause claims our devotion—and ask what we need to do next in order to help advance that cause:

• Is this a day when I need to decide once again to live "divided no more"? We are constantly challenged to compromise our integrity, so this foundational decision needs to be renewed time and time again.

• Is this a day when I feel a need for support in my desire to live with integrity, a day when I need to look actively for a "community of congruence," perhaps creating one for myself?

• Is this a day when my friends and allies and I need to start "going public" with our commitments—risking the slings and arrows that come with that decision, but knowing that the time has come to start seeking the leverage required to create the change we want and need?

Movements for social change always meet with opposition because they challenge the status quo and slam into the inertia that comes with "the way things have always been done." But people who have embraced a "movement mentality" are neither discouraged nor defeated by opposition. Instead, they take energy from it. They read resistance as a sign that they are on the right track, and feel validated in their audacious belief that change must come.

At every stage of a movement there is both encouragement for the disheartened and the power to advance important forms of social change. Wherever we are on this journey, a step taken to renew and sustain our spirits can be a step towards personal and social wholeness—once we understand and embrace the movement way.

Sustaining the Beauty of Teaching and Learning in the Tragic Gap of Education

By Debbie Stanley

There are hundreds of ways to kneel and kiss the ground.
---Rumi, translated by Coleman Barks

I am an irrational lover of children. And to the core of my being, I am a teacher.

As far back as I can remember, I've always taught someone or something. I have had the pleasure of teaching and learning with and from various colorful, amazing and wonder-filled dolls, students, best friends, my parents, young and old people. Through these teaching and learning experiences, I have come to know and appreciate the ways in which I, then and now, "kneel and kiss the ground." However, the kneeling and kissing experiences were not easily attained nor professionally understood and, at times, were unappreciated.

There have been many significant milestones on my timeline to becoming a credentialed teacher. I was educated in the schools of the borough of Brooklyn, New York, resulting in a very culturally rich public school education. Taking "field trips" anywhere in New York was an educational experience indeed: The Statue of Liberty, The Museum of Natural History, The Brooklyn Botanical Gardens and the "oh-so-magnificent" Brooklyn Academy of Music, Midtown Manhattan and Broadway, just to name a few!

Yet with all of those precious and memorable learning and feeling moments, I had one experience, retrospectively, that changed my life's trajectory. I remember being an avid reader in third grade. My teacher even boasted of my reading abilities to my parents. In her class I felt smart until the day we received "big test" results, a day that has proven to be a pivotal one in my life's journey. On that day I was implicitly informed by the actions of my teacher that I was not smart "enough." Although I could read books (according to the standardized reading ranges) at the high school level, my score wasn't as high as my best friend's test. That best friend received a new name that day, given by my teacher: "Smart Myra." Not only did Myra receive a new name, the next school year she would be transferred to a new school for "really smart" students. I wasn't given anything; not Delightful, not Daring, not Dumb... nothing, just plain Debbie. Later in life, Myra shared how devastating that name and placement were for her (by the way, we are still best friends of 50+ years). Now when I look back and I reflect on my life, I place this event as a negative timeline notch, naming it as the beginning of my shadow journey into invisibleness and voicelessness.

After high school, I left Brooklyn to attend college in the South. I landed in the South because my mother was born and raised in the most northeastern part of South Carolina and my dad was from the most southeastern part of North Carolina. My dad made me go to a North Carolina university for my freshman year, as he felt my attending a university near the beach town close to my mother's birth-place would not have been in my best interest. I didn't dare to differ. During my freshman year, I discovered the beauty of African history, with its roots in the various countries of Africa as well as experiences (positive and negative) in America. The timeline notch-holder during this period of my life was my professor, a Caucasian man teaching African history with passion and deep respect. I loved his class because he loved and knew his content so well. I never spoke to him; there was no need. He was thorough, knowledgeable, and available if I needed assistance. This classroom experience held an important spot on my "teacher behaviors I ascribe to" list I created for future reference.

In my sophomore year I did transfer to a South Carolina college that was indeed near the beach. I became an average student with social, rather than academic, activities on my mind. My dad's concern was actualized in my exceptional party life. Although my courses were relevant and teacher education courses were content specific, I remember, very vividly, feeling invisible and voiceless in my college classroom. The invisibility that I had experienced in third grade was more pronounced in college and made more explicit through the actions of my professors. I was a lost soul in the academy of higher learning. I had neither advocate nor empathetic ear to help me process these churning feelings of inadequacy. One professor told me, "You are a diamond in the rough." To me that meant, for right now, you are useless. Other than that, not one professor ever made a positive move towards me or said anything that would encourage me to be the best I could be.

Now I have come to understand that all of these shadow experiences have a light side. These experiences had gifts! They became informing elements of my teaching practices. I would use my experiences of invisibility and voicelessness to insure visibility and astute listening from me to each person, each child, with whom I would have the opportunity to teach and also learn.

HIDING IN THE WORDS OF OTHERS

One of the shadows of invisibleness and voicelessness is hiding in the visibility and words of others. Since I was neither seen nor heard by my college teachers, I used their courses' texts to seek my emerging professional voice. In the deepest part of my psyche I pondered, "Maybe my teachers will hear me if I use the voice of another." So that's what I did -- and that's where the gift kicks in: I became a lover of wondrous words and illustrative theory.

My teachers and allies in acquiring my voice and creating my theory of early childhood literacy acquisition included many learning theorists: Jean-Jacques Rousseau, Abraham Maslow, Erik Erikson, Jean Piaget, John Dewey, Maria Montessori, and Urie Bronfenbrenner. My favorite overall was Dr. Bronfenbrenner, a professor of psychology at Cornell University in Ithaca, New York, who asserted, in *The Ecology of Human Development,* that a child's most basic need was "the enduring and 'irrational involvement' of one or more adults in the child's life who share in joint activity with the child." He explained that "irrational involvement" meant to love without conditions. I found solace in those words, and I knew I wanted to become an irrational lover of children. Not only did I find hope in Dr. Bronfenbrenner's written words but also in his spoken words. Years later, I was invited to have dinner with him when he was a guest speaker at the university where I was teaching. What a gift for my soul... true sustenance.

My early twenties mark the timeline notch when I began, professionally, to teach. No sooner had my career started than I experienced an intuitive realization, an epiphany of sorts: I was professionally stuck. I felt forced to forsake my literary allies that I had met in college, and I was miserable. My **new** literacy informants, the curriculum directors in the district where I worked, defined my teaching pedagogy with scripts for teaching, rules for pseudo-community with children, data-driven techniques and strategies all designed to manipulate my students to learn. I was in deep distress. Yet, epiphany unveils a subtle hope for something better, and my hope came in the form of graduate school.

I decided a graduate degree might help me find more meaningful ways of connecting with my students while subjecting my teaching pedagogy to the district's stipulations for classroom instruction. I now realize that the intersection of what I believed and hoped for my students and the instructional methodology I was expected to use with these same students abided in what Parker Palmer has coined "the tragic gap." Parker, another wordsmith ally, writes in his book, *A Hidden Wholeness: The Journey Toward an Undivided Life*,

"By the tragic gap I mean the gap between the hard realities around us and what we know is possible — not because we wish it were so, but because we've seen it with our own eyes."

What had I seen with my young teacher's eyes? I had "seen" the methodology of Jean Rousseau, who espoused that children were inherently good; physician Maria Montessori, who believed that "children at liberty to choose and act freely" within an environment prepared according to her model would "act spontaneously for optimal development"; John Dewey, who asserted that students should be involved in real-life tasks and challenges; Jean Piaget, who demonstrated that children construct knowledge and use it; Eric Erikson's persuasive theory on the need for positive and safe emotional environments which encourage social relationships and self-understanding; and the adult's role in irrational involvement with children opined by Urie Bronfenbrenner. Designing a classroom with these theoretical "insights" became my professional life's quest. How would I sustain myself in the quest for creating an optimal learning environment for my students without neglecting what I was required and hired to teach? What a paradox! Once again the feelings of inadequacy taunted my soul. My safety net of the literary world resounded in the deep recesses of my psyche to find resolve for this most perplexing question. So off to graduate school I went and there I met a remarkable woman, who would forever change the direction of my professional life.

Dr. Sally Z. Hare was my first graduate school teacher. Sally embodied what I felt in my freshman history class. Like my African history professor, she had such passion for her subject. But the difference was she had passion for her students, too. She saw me. She seemed to….God forbid…like me. I felt safe around her. Sally was, and remains, the teacher I wanted to emulate. When I entered her classroom, I was philosophically lost, desperately angry, fearful, distrusting, and disillusioned. Sally provided space in her course for each student to tell his/her story. I couldn't believe it; she actually wanted to hear "my voice." Sally respected my anger and did not attempt to "calm me down." She agreed with me and facilitated my thinking in ways to allow me to express my anger and bring about positive change in my teaching and most of all, positively impact my students. While in graduate school, my sense of voicelessness and invisibleness diminished some. I became more "focused" in my teaching philosophy; heretofore, my "grounding." I became more intentional in my teaching pedagogy. I found ways around the teacher-directed methodology. By God, I was realizing my "eclectic" teacher self! Through the work of Ken and Yetta Goodman, Frank Smith, Constance Kamii, Ralph Peterson, and Katie Wood Ray, to name a few of the "friends" I met in graduate courses (and in real life, as many of them came to speak at Sally's campus conferences), I became more confident in the knowing that all children can be taught well and enjoy the learning journey with a knowledgeable, informed, and loving teacher. This knowing sustains me even to this day.

FINDING THE SCHOLAR WITHIN

My graduate school experience provided more than philosophical grounding; it also allowed me a peek at the true scholar residing deep within, the one that I had hidden so many years ago when I felt I wasn't enough. I had an insatiable appetite for knowledge. I wanted to know how to be the best teacher for my students. This fed my "irrational" need to be fully present to the students who were committed to my care. Because of this appetite, I continued beyond a master's degree and earned a Ph.D. in education. Although the experience was, at times, insane, it sustained the very needs of my soul. While working on my doctorate, I taught fulltime, parented three young children, and intentionally held the paradox of what I was learning and what I was required to teach. Yes, I am patting myself on the back because that was a feat!

My students and my three babies were the sustaining influences for the completion of my doctorate. My dissertation, *Teachers' Knowledge about African American Children and*

Culture and the Development of Culturally-Inclusive Curriculum for African American Students, served as my step out of obscurity, inadequacy, invisibleness, and voicelessness. It was a declaration that redefined who I was. It also served as a statement of realized truth that I must continue to mindfully love, honor and respect others and to treat myself likewise. The fear that had bound me had lost its control, although it was still there, not as an enemy but an ally. Fear had a new role in my life, one that Haim Ginott very eloquently described in his book, *Teacher and Child*:

> I have come to the frightening conclusion that I am the decisive element. It is my personal approach that creates the climate. It is my daily mood that makes the weather. I possess tremendous power to make life miserable or joyous. I can be a tool of torture or an instrument of Inspiration, I can humiliate or humor, hurt or heal. In all situations, it is my response that decides whether a crisis is escalated or de-escalated, and a person is humanized or de-humanized. If we treat people as they are, we make them worse. If we treat people as they ought to be, we help them become what they are capable of becoming.

Holding this fear as an ally invited me to create a classroom that would showcase the beauty of teaching and learning and also demanded that I continue to have open and honest conversations with my colleagues in the school district that I had feared for so many years. Thus I began the next phase of my journey, a journey of courage... A journey continued with co-conspirators, Dr. Sally Z. Hare and Dr. Parker J. Palmer.

FINDING THE COURAGE TO TEACH

When I met Parker, he was writing *The Courage to Teach: Exploring the Inner Landscape of a Teacher's Life*. Need I say more? In graduate school I had read Parker's book *To Know as We Are Known: Education as a Spiritual Journey*. Out of the many heartbreaking-open and mind-elevating statements

I had read in the book, the one that provided the greatest impact for my journey was this one: **"To teach is to create a space in which the community of truth is practiced."** This declaration became a kind-of mantra for me. Those words called and spoke deeply to the yearnings of my soul. I wanted a classroom of independent learners who were fully engaged in the teaching/learning community. I wanted to hear them deeply into speech. I wanted to be known as a teacher who cared, who shared, and who listened. This is the beauty that I love. My classroom was the place where I loved and was loved, listened and was heard, saw and was seen.

My deepest teaching desire was to provide a classroom designed like an oasis; better yet, a refuge for the souls of children: A place where they could receive what they needed emotionally, intellectually, and socially. I had theory to support my desire, but a district mandate still required me to teach in ways that contradicted my teaching style. Parker's work supported my quest to find ways to hold this paradox. Instead of fighting the system, I decided to become more informed of **the who** and **the why** behind my district's decision-making process. Sadly, this proved to be less fruitful than I anticipated; the politics and bureaucratic meanderings of my school district required more energy than I had to give. I did, however, learn enough to make the difference in the one place that I could, my classroom. My district also supported my participation in Courage to Teach retreats which were grounded in Parker's ideas. I applauded my district's attempt to help me become a highly qualified practitioner.

The principles and practices that I experienced as a Courage to Teach participant, facilitator, and Center for Courage & Renewal (CCR) board member were and still are extremely valuable, both personally and professionally. CCR, of which The Courage to Teach is a registered program, provided the "soul-food" needed to sustain me in the tragic gap where I have spent my entire professional life. In the tragic gap, I have learned that there are indeed many ways to "kneel and kiss the ground."

One way is to have open and honest conversations with trusted colleagues. How do I define true colleagues? True colleagues are those who embrace the beauty of teaching and learning; those who help me (and themselves!) explore the struggles and joys of being a teacher. This e-mail exchange concerning a district-mandated teaching program illustrates this point:

Teacher One: *I think fear is a good term...but also I fear that I have become "passion-less"- a word I had to make up because I could not find another one to name it. I have a lack of passion because I don't OWN what I am doing. I don't OWN my time or the words I use. I am told that a computer will "do all of the thinking for me" about MY people that I am entrusted with. We have helped inspire good learners in the past. Everything we have previously done CANNOT be wrong. Why does school make me sad lately??? I went yesterday to work and just left after a little while. I simply could not embrace it!*

I attended the funeral of the mom of a former student yesterday. This beautiful lady died at the age of 42 from a horrible cancer that could not be treated. She had only 3 months after her initial diagnosis. What would I choose to do with 3 months? I would absolutely tell you how much you mean to me. I would absolutely tell you how fortunate I feel to work with some of my VERY favorite people in the world. I would absolutely tell you that I love you with a deep and grateful heart. So, I am assuming that I have only 3 months and telling you.

Teacher Two: It is guided reading plans. It is not THE solution. We have taught successfully for years without them in an official format. We have not and will not teach successfully without joy and passion. I am suggesting that we focus on joy and passion and let the other things work themselves out. And they will, because they aren't lasting or transforming. Joy and passion, shown to our children and to each other, are absolutely lasting and transforming. I will step off of the soapbox now. :)

My Response: *Thanks for your matching responses...I do not feel alone...I met with Janet last night... and Sally...and Sandie...and other loved ones from the Center for Courage & Renewal... Janet started it...she is deeply saddened by our plight (she had met with a very sad K teacher... who remained unnamed and had told Janet about the script in (unnamed reading program)...earlier that day...I shared what happened during our collaborative meeting and how I quoted the piece from Haim Ginott...* **I've come to the frightening conclusion that I am...** *and how after reading Ginott's statement, I was all but ignored...well...after more discussion around the Dalai Lama's statements this past week on compassion...the whole group named the culprit of our plight as...FEAR...I guess if we are all doing the same thing...then we can be tracked and held collectively responsible...I will hold the paradox of fear and trust and compassion in the coming days... Remember at the beginning of the year I sent us a poem? Here it is again...for the children, our students, and my precious K colleagues...I want to be of use...Just as poet Marge Piercy writes about in her poem with that name:*

> **I love people who harness themselves, an ox to a heavy cart,**
> **who pull like water buffalo, with massive patience,**
> **who strain in the mud and the muck to move things forward**
> **who do what has to be done, again and again.**

WITHOUT FEAR I WOULDN'T NEED COURAGE

Sharing Marge Piercy's words helped convey the unresolved fear in my heart: that my colleagues and I were undervalued and of little use in our district's unwavering use of resources that seemingly did not support the eclectic and creative nature of veteran teachers. Once again, the feeling of invisibleness and voicelessness attempted to seep into my professional life. With all of my knowledge, and all of the training, I had now been reduced to a script-reading teacher...again. How could this be? I resolved to use my gleanings from The Courage to Teach, so I "turned to wonder."

I revisited the voices of my literacy allies. Frank Smith, in his 1986 book, *Insult to Intelligence,* propounded that reading should be kept whole "as a joyful, humanistic, intellectually challenging alternative to deadening phoneme drills -- one that turns the classroom from a factory floor into a nurturing environment in which children naturally blossom." Ralph Peterson, in *Life in a Crowded Place: Making a Learning Community,* insisted that "creating a community -- bringing students together and keeping them together -- is the most vital aspect of a teacher's work. Without it, real learning cannot take place, as even the soundest philosophies and techniques amount to little without a community to bring them to life." With the help of these two of the many informed and respected voices in the field of education, I garnered my philosophical strength and put into practice what I knew to be true: it really takes courage to teach.

Each day, to maintain the beauty of what I love, I recited this mantra: "Would I want to be my child's teacher?" To sustain beauty in teaching and learning, robust yearning must reside within the practitioner; a love for knowing and showcasing what is known. The Courage to Teach, perhaps not considered education theory in some academic circles, informed my instructional practices.

Let me provide a concrete example of how my Courage work has impacted my classroom setting: to sustain beauty in teaching and learning, I held the Courage principles as the informing element for setting up and designing the physical and emotional environment for the students in my/our classroom. The practices serve as the vehicle for my professional interactions with my students and colleagues. I teach the practices as the ground for how we will be with one another in our classroom. For example, the practice of *asking honest, open questions to hear each other into speech* is used when comprehending text. In the kindergarten setting, I would ask my students questions such as "Have you ever felt like this character?" The students would be invited to ask me questions similar to the ones I asked them. I used many quotes from noted mystics, such as Rumi's **Let the beauty you love be what you do...** to establish my discipline parameters. I asked my students, "What is the beauty you love and would you like to share with others?" I would then ask, "How would each of you love to use your hands that would be considered beautiful?" That question led us to writing beautiful poetry, using our hands gently with others, and so many other rich responses. I also used evocative books like Jon J. Muth's *The Three Questions (Based on a story by Leo Tolstoy)* to help deepen my students' understanding of how to be more humane, whether at school or at home.

I used my Courage approach as I followed the district's mandated curriculum. As Parker had helped me see, I could make the program "more real and rewarding" for the students and me. My design, which held the required curriculum without annihilating it, offered more challenge, literary explorations, more rigor, and brilliant insights. I created the space for authentic learning that did not deny the need for the phonemic knowledge, but made the learning community more enriched and vibrant, or one can say...a refuge for the young learning soul. My work has been seen as valuable not only by me (which is most important!), but also others: my students and their families, my colleagues, and the Center for Courage & Renewal. The Center affirmed my work by investing in a videographer to "catch the wonder" of the learning that happened in the room I shared with five-year-old people. (You can see the result in **Inner Work and the Life of a Teacher,** http://www.youtube.com/watch?v=pf2dcNmjd2I.)

I TEACH WHO I AM

I teach who I am. My professional self began (by default) in the third-grade classroom. All of my educational experiences -- the good, the bad, and the complicated -- have assisted in my growth as a professional educator. I resonate with May Sarton's words in her poem *Now I Become Myself* to describe my journey thus far:

Now I become myself. It's taken
Time, many years and places;
I have been dissolved and shaken,
Worn other people's faces

To share my story is an act of responsibility to pre- and in-service teachers. My journey has taken years and, hopefully, there are more to come. Being given the opportunity in this Writers Circle of Trust to go public with my journey is liberating and strengthening. Being able to tell the truth "slant," as the poet Emily Dickinson says, helps others to hear my journey and to see if it might "be of use" for **their** journeys. Being able to acknowledge that I had seen inappropriate teaching methodology was a gift; without that opportunity, how would I have known appropriate? Every step of my journey has led to the next. I have now retired from public school teaching but not from the power and beauty of teaching and learning. I still have my family, cosmetics business, and work for the Center for Courage & Renewal. These contexts have provided and continue to provide wonderful paradoxes from which to glean strength and wisdom in the beauty of teaching and learning.

Maslow's theory of motivation, leading to self-actualization, has sustained me in holding the beauty of teaching and learning in the tragic gap of education. Maslow describes a hierarchy of needs; for me, the needs are not "hierarchical," but are integrated. In a sense, my journey has been and continues to be about self-actualization. As I have stood in the tragic gap, my safety net has been provided by the voices of others, including the learning theories I knew and put into practice; my colleagues in many settings, as well as my family who provided love and friendship; and the completion of my Ph.D. and the affirmation from my students and their families (which placed my esteem off the charts!).

Langston Hughes' words in his poem *Mother to Son* affirms my theory:

But all the time
I'se been a-climbin' on,
And reachin' landin's,
And turnin' corners

That's exactly what I've been doing all of these years. Hughes affirms my knowing of what has sustained me in the tragic gap. My true self knew what was right, and true, and good.

And sometimes goin' in the dark
Where there ain't been no light.

My soul knows this very well. The splinters of invisibility and voicelessness were catapulted into strong planks of mindfulness, integrity, and humanness. I am so grateful for my life's path and the tenacity of the human spirit...**my** spirit.

'Cause *I'se still climbin'* to the place of self actualization.

Debbie Stanley, a retired early childhood educator, has 32 years of experience in the field of education. She has been a teacher in the PreK-12 public school setting and an assistant professor of education at Coastal Carolina University in Conway, SC. Debbie is a founding Courage & Renewal Facilitator, and recently served as a member of the CCR Board of Directors. She is now a member of the Leadership team for the Center's Facilitator Preparation Program. Her doctorate is in Elementary Education with an emphasis in Early Childhood and Administration. The mother of three adult children, Christina, Matthew, and Debora, Debbie lives in Little River, SC, where she is an ordained minister at Grace Christian Fellowship Church in Little River, SC. She is providing care for her mother and two dog children, Carolina and Dondi Brutus, and Carson Z. Cat. You can reach her at joyfulone120@gmail.com

Now I Become Myself

By Megan LeBoutillier

*"Hell, in my opinion, is never finding your true self
and never living your own life or knowing who you are."*
---John Bradshaw, *Healing the Shame that Binds You*

The wallpaper in my childhood home had cream-colored raised patches of fuzzy fabric in the shape of flowers on a lustrous flat background. I used to run my index finger over these patches as if I were secretly petting a tiny animal. I was infatuated with the surface texture of our walls until one day a friend of mine disapprovingly sniped, "Only *your* family would have velvet wallpaper." My infatuation turned instantly to shame.

MY LIFE BECOMES DIVIDED

There were countless moments throughout my childhood and young adulthood when the difference between how my family lived and my friends' families lived caused me to unconsciously disapprove of myself in subtle ways. Looking back, I can see my life becoming divided. I judged myself harshly through the imagined eyes of others, rejected my self and my circumstances, and began to mentally participate in my own diminishment.

Flocked wallpaper, live-in help, club memberships, new cars, travel vacations, the heady re-examination process of the 1960's, and a mother who repeatedly let me know that I was undeserving made for a confusing developmental brew. In trying to find my way into an adulthood that mirrored my sensibilities, my family and my school were not helping much. Without knowing it, I discarded crucial aspects of who I was in order to "fit in," or rather, to **not** stand out.

At age 18, just as I thought I'd successfully rejected most of my privileged familial trappings and gone into hiding, I was plunked down in front of my family's financial advisor and warned to never trust anyone's motives for knowing me because some day I was going to inherit money and people would be wanting to take it from me. My response, rather than losing trust in others, was to lose trust in myself. I feared I would become disdainful, privileged, removed and uncaring. I'd seen money used as a way of separating oneself from the "real world." By the time, three years later, I inherited the trust created by my grandparents, I was so riddled with guilt and a sense of being undeserving that I was well on my way to self-loathing.

A SLOW PROCESS

I have a friend whose son is gay. One day she told me that her son informed her that he "hates gay people." I was shaken by the idea that someone could hate the very thing that they are, and then I snuck up behind myself and realized that I do the very same thing, just for a different reason.

Inherited wealth is not a sympathetic topic. My discomfort with my circumstances could find no outlet. Therapists were not interested in the subject and I was too ashamed to share my feelings with friends. I carried my guilt in isolation.

In my late twenties I learned about a workshop offered by the Community Foundation in Atlanta on "Women and Wealth." One year I called and asked for an application to attend. The second year I actually filled out the application. The third year I sent in the application but did not attend. The fourth year I filled out the application and drove three hours to the location of the workshop and turned around and drove home. The fifth year I actually attended the workshop. I met other women who shared my financial circumstances and many of my feelings.

There were various workshops offered throughout the weekend, but I was in such a terrified state of mind that I was barely hovering within the group setting. I remember talk of how to deal with dismissive or condescending financial managers, but more than strategies I heard complaint. I particularly remember one woman who asked me to help lead a panel discussion on class. I told her I knew nothing about class and couldn't possibly. Her response was, "Have you ever looked into a mirror?" Shame rushed in again to taunt me that I'd been unsuccessful at hiding all along.

Some of the women described carrying guilt that spanned generations due to how the family money had been acquired. They spoke of slavery, colonial oppression, natural resource ravaging, land grabbing, financial philandering, and toxic manufacturing. Some seemed to feel personally responsible. I remember having a brief instant of relief where I rested into the thought, "Well, at least I don't have to contend with that." Other women spoke of strife between siblings based on differences between what boys and girls in the family had been taught about inherited wealth. As for my own story, other than being taught to distrust everyone, the only education I received about money was, "Never a borrower or lender be." The lessons started and ended there and didn't prepare me well for the circumstances that were to become mine.

Most of the women lamented the divide between friends and loved ones created by financial disparity. There was a great deal of conversation about the difficulties with finding suitable life partners because of financial or vast value differences. I could detect no difference between what the lesbian women shared from the straight ones. No one seemed comfortable with her circumstances. For the first time I'd found some like-minded, though equally unsettled, peers. I was beginning the slow process of trying to sort out who I am, how I feel about who I am, and how to live in the world **as** who I am. Believe me, it has been a slow process.

NOW I BECOME MYSELF

Nearly twenty years ago I was invited by my friend Sally Z. Hare to come to a weekend workshop in a Myrtle Beach oceanfront hotel to hear from her mentor, Parker J. Palmer, about work he was calling The Courage to Teach. I couldn't identify any personal intersection with the topic of public school educators, but my boyfriend's parents were in town for a prolonged visit, and I desperately needed an excuse to get out of the house.

While I am not a teacher, I **am** a human being trying to live a conscious and engaged life. For two days my soul resonated with the invitations to nurture my own identity and integrity, to identify and honor my birthright gifts, to resist the pressures and projections of others and to acknowledge the lifelong process of unfolding.

Two years later I found myself in graduate school and asked Sally to serve as a member of my doctoral committee. When I needed an Internship to fulfill part of my academic requirements, Sally once again put Parker Palmer and The Courage to Teach in my path. She was beginning a two-year pilot program, funded by the Fetzer Institute, and inviting K-12 public school educators to apply for eight three-night seasonal retreats over two years. Sally wanted a scribe to take notes of the conversations that took place when the group sat in their circle. I needed an Internship and thus the relationship moved to a new level when I agreed to attend the eight weekend retreats she was facilitating.

As the one participant who knew nothing of the public school system and the inherent stresses upon teachers, and as the one participant who did not speak within the large group setting because I was there to listen and notate, I sometimes fooled myself into believing that I was not really a member of the group. In order to adequately take notes I had to listen in an uncharacteristic way. I listened in order to catch words, not to construct an answer or response. Often I wasn't really aware of what I'd heard until days later when I was transcribing my notes.

As I typed the notes I'd taken in the circle, I knew whose voice was whose, and for the first time the impact of what was being said was getting through to me. I was stunned by the sadness, stress and frustration that the schoolteachers and administrators were voicing. And I was struck by how Sally's gentle invitations allowed participants to go deeply into their souls and risk sharing themselves in the larger group. She used poetry as a way to invite people to go inward. One of the first poems that really spoke to me was May Sarton's "Now I Become Myself." Those words struck me as powerful, scary and completely necessary. I was nowhere near where I needed to be with myself, but I didn't quite know it yet. I just had a gnawing sense of guilt that interfered on a regular basis with my well-being and my decision-making process.

I found Clearness Committee to be the most powerful ingredient of a weekend retreat. Out of our twenty-four participants, four were offered the opportunity to present themselves as focus persons at each retreat. Amazingly, four people always came forward to share some personal or professional issue with which they were struggling. Sally was always extremely careful as she prepared the group to move into this process. The boundaries and confidentiality of the Clearness Committee verged on the sacred. The members of the committee who were not being focus persons were given careful instructions to ask only open and honest questions. We were not to try and fix the other person with suggestions or solutions we thought they might use. We were to ask only questions for which we did not know the answer, and which were carefully designed to help the focus persons to hear their own inner wisdom.

I came out of my role as scribe for Clearness Committee and thus could fully participate as a committee member. The first few times as a committee member, I was struck by how truly hard it is to ask open and honest questions. I realized how much of my "regular" conversation was often designed to give suggestions and intrude on another's journey. While I had to work hard to be a good committee member, I was surely not going to risk the vulnerability involved with being a focus person. Then came the summer retreat of our first year, our fourth retreat in the two-year series. Every time someone asked me how I was doing, I burst into tears. I'd just broken up with yet another boyfriend, but something else seemed to be trying to push itself into my awareness. Quite to my surprise I put my name forward to be a focus person and then I wondered, "What am I going to talk about?"

I deeply trusted the entire group and especially my committee for clearness. I decided to risk it. They were instructed to never broach the topic with me again, and this felt like the assurance I needed to tell my story. I left the cottage where we met for three hours with the burden of twenty-one years of guilt completely lifted from my psyche. For a while I kept looking behind to make sure it wasn't still lurking, and eventually I stepped into the light of my release. Generosity, shyly and ever so slowly, began to take the place of guilt.

After the two-year program concluded, I asked Sally what was going to happen with The Courage to Teach and she told me that the Fetzer Institute was going to fund the training of future facilitators so that the program could grow. I applied and was accepted into the first facilitator preparation program in 1998.

Transformation is a very slow process. It took me twenty-one years to gracefully accept and step into a birthright gift that I tried to disown for a long time. Once I shed the debilitating guilt I carried, the question became, "So, now what?" The changes took place so slowly that one could scarcely detect them, but subtle changes began taking place. I made a decision to focus my philanthropy into a more concerted and hopefully effective strategy. Instead of responding to many requests with small amounts of money, I decided to choose three to five charities or organizations I wanted to support in one year, and make significant contributions to them. I was delighted with this first step until I realized that with a larger donation, I was drawing more attention to myself as a donor and I was attracting more requests from the very places I'd chosen to support. I didn't particularly like either outcome, but I chose to simply take notice and learn how to respectfully decline solicitations. I was learning how to be different in the world, not trying to make others treat me differently.

More time passed, I matured, and the divisions between classes grew wider. Happily, the guilt stayed away, but awareness of the divisions within our society became impossible to ignore. Greedy people, at the horrifying expense of others who could not afford to fight back, caused the financial meltdown of 2008. My heart ached as people lost their savings and their homes while fat cat bankers and business people padded their already burgeoning bank accounts.

When my mother died in 2010, another weighty installment of the family wealth passed to the next generation. While I qualify nowhere near the "one percent," I cringed whenever I walked by the Occupy encampment on our downtown mall. I feel an increasing responsibility to contribute somehow to causes I care about, or to help remedy injustice.

Miraculously, just when I had almost completely lost hope that I would ever sustain a love relationship, I met and fell in love with a man from my background, who is actively engaged in his own life, who shares my core values, and who is willing to share with me as an equal partner. It took me a long time to realize I needed to raise the bar to this level, but I finally managed to do so. We married in 2011.

I suppose I will always be in the process of becoming myself, but since I shed the guilt of being me, I am left with the question of how to align my broad material capacity of choice with my spiritual capacity of character. My question becomes how to turn money into meaning. My process of late has been how to become a strategic philanthropist. I am living my way into the question of how to align my spiritual desire and will to benefit humanity with how I choose to allocate my wealth. I read a quote from Nelson Mandela recently that is illuminating my journey. "What counts in life is not the mere fact that we have lived. It is what difference we have made to the lives of others that will determine the significance of the life we have lived."

From my current vantage point of 58 years, I see two aspects of myself that I have fought hard to reclaim. Generosity and creative expression are currently avenues through which I channel my birthright gifts, but it was not always that way. School silenced my voice and any other form of creativity and shame hid my light under a bushel. Graduate school and the publication of two books convinced me that creative expression could be recovered, and with that discovery an otherwise unknown aspect of myself emerged: my inner artist, what a surprise. Circles of Trust help me and hold me as I step into conscious philanthropy, and as I move more fully into living divided no more and letting the beauty I love be what I do.

 Dr. Megan LeBoutillier lives outside Charlottesville, Virginia, with her husband, Bruce Gordon, and Chance, their Weimaraner. She is an artist with a doctorate in creative non-fiction and a national Center for Courage & Renewal facilitator.

What is the Clearness Committee?

By Sally Z. Hare

As we quilted our stories together, the editors noticed the thread of the Clearness Committee throughout much of our book. So we decided to add this embellishment about the Clearness Committee, a practice that has been used in the Quaker community for over three hundred years.

I wanted to write it, because the first time I was introduced to the practice, it changed my life. Or perhaps it would be more accurate to say that with the help of the Clearness Committee, I changed my life. The basic idea behind the process is that each person has an inner teacher, and with the help of our communal resources, we can more clearly hear that inner teacher. That certainly happened for me as I struggled with a career decision.

As Parker J. Palmer so insightfully writes in *The Clearness Committee: A Communal Approach to Discernment*, "On the one hand, we know that the issue is ours alone to resolve and that we have the inner resources to resolve it, but access to our own resources Is often blocked by layers of inner 'stuff' – confusion, habitual thinking, fear, despair." The Clearness Committee process allows us to tap into our inner wisdom by using the community to run interference, to help us through our own inner maze.

Parker adapted the traditional Quaker clearness process for our use in Circles of Trust, and it quickly transformed the nature of our being together. Participants report taking the Clearness Committee to their organizations and families, their offices and corporations, their schools and universities.

I admit to being awed by the power of the process of the

61

Clearness Committee. It is a simple process – and a sacred one. Parker cautions that the Clearness Committee is not for everyone – or for every setting. The process invites a level of vulnerability that requires a space of safety and trust. It is not a process to be entered into lightly.

Entered into with care and intentionality, the process offers a valuable means of finding clearness in a world that often feels muddy and chaotic. The rules of the Clearness Committee are critical to its success. They create and hold the boundaries for the safe space. Even when group members are familiar with the Clearness Committee process, I teach the rules at the beginning of each session. I want to remind myself, as much as anyone, of their importance, because the behavior required in Clearness Committees is counterintuitive. The Clearness Committee demands that we suspend our normal ways of doing business, our typical ways of being in our society, in order to be in community in a way that is virtually unknown to us.

Perhaps the most crucial rule is that of confidentiality. In our first Courage to Teach group, we called it deep confidentiality, meaning that committee members would not only never speak to each other or anyone else about the issue when the Clearness Committee ended, but they also would not speak with the focus person about the problem, unless she or he requested the conversation.

In our retreat settings, the facilitators invite persons who seek clearness on some issue to volunteer to serve as focus persons. Committees of five or six people are carefully put together by the facilitators, with important input from the focus persons.

Time is critical to the process. The committee meets for two to three uninterrupted hours. It's important to allow the process to take the entire time; we don't end early. During that time, committee members practice the discipline of giving the focus person their total attention. They are fully present to the person and his or her issue, listening deeply, creating a space of deep respect. The function of the committee is not to "fix" or give advice, but to help the focus person hear her own inner wisdom, claim his own authority (to literally be the author of her own story).

The committee begins with the focus person sharing his or her issue for about ten minutes. *That is when the other critical rule comes into play: Committee members are forbidden to speak to the focus person except by asking open, honest questions.* Since authentic questions are not the norm in our society, the practice of asking open, honest questions requires discipline and self-monitoring. We so easily slip into advice disguised as a question, judgment disguised as a question, sharing our own experiences disguised as questions. "Have you thought about seeing a therapist?" is NOT an open, honest question. Neither is "Have you ever tried to lose some weight?"

What is an open, honest question? Perhaps the best answer to that is that it's a question to which the questioner could have no idea of the answer. The pacing of the questions is as important as the wording of the questions. The Clearness Committee is not a grilling of a suspect or a dissertation defense or a cross-examination; questions should be asked at a gentle, humane pace. Time to reflect on the answers, moments of silence, "wait time" are vital to inviting in the focus person's inner teacher.

The focus person usually responds to the questions. The questions — and the answers — then often lead to deeper questions. The focus person should be brief but full in her answers, resisting the temptation to tell his entire life's story. Sometimes, for whatever reason, the focus person may choose not to answer a question or may ask to have a question reframed. *The focus person always has the right NOT to answer a question.*

The exception to the rule of asking only open, honest questions may come about ten minutes before the end of the Clearness

Committee. At this time, a committee member asks the focus person if he or she would like to have the "question only" rule suspended and to invite committee members to mirror back what they have heard from the focus person. Mirroring is exactly that: the committee member serves as a mirror, holding up for reflection the focus person's own words or body language. Mirroring is not an opportunity to give advice or pronounce judgment.

For the last five minutes, the Clearness Committee members share affirmations and celebrations. As with the other aspects of the process, this is important, as the focus person has been very open and vulnerable with the group. Group members find much to celebrate after a glimpse into the gifts and grace of a human soul.

I said earlier that the behavior required in Clearness Committees is counterintuitive. This means suspending our normal ways of being together – no small talk, no jokes to break the tension, no noisy laughter, no attempt to fix or reassure or comfort the focus person, no patting or touching. The only task for members of the Clearness Committee is to listen deeply and ask thoughtful questions. They are not trying to impress the others by their grasp of the situation or by their ability to ask clever questions. They are charged with holding the space for the focus person, not filling that space with their own egos. The reward for the committee members is often being surprised by some clearness on their own issues, by some insight they weren't expecting, as well as the sense of hopefulness that often comes from seeing that the focus person truly has everything he or she needs and the hope that comes from seeing the resilience of the human soul.

The Clearness Committee is not about fixing anyone or solving anything. In fact, with a good clearness process, the answers, the insights, continue to come for hours, days, even weeks after the actual meeting. In my own case, I find that I sometimes go back to questions from that first Clearness Committee more than 20 years ago; sometimes I review the notes and have yet another "ah-ha."

Parker first introduced me to the Clearness Committee during a weeklong retreat on leadership and spirituality. I will never forget Parker's charge to the committee members: he used the metaphor of holding the focus person (me) as if she were a small bird. Your responsibility, he told the group, is to hold the bird safely in your cupped hands rather than giving in to our all-too-human tendencies to either suffocate the bird by closing our hands too tightly or by putting the bird down prematurely or pushing her to fly before she is ready. The success of the clearness process, he told us, is not measured by whether the bird flies, but in how we hold the bird.

Doing Simple Work Well: The Beauty I Love

By Sandra Jean Sturdivant Merriam

There are hundreds of ways to kneel and kiss the ground.
---Rumi, translated by Coleman Barks

My mother often said that doing simple work well is an act of worship. To my teenage mind, my mother, Katherine Juanita Pinson Sturdivant, said that way too often. I wondered where she came up with the *stuff* she would say when I complained about the mundane tasks required of a teenager. Looking back, I am now grateful for the repeated touchstones that were my family's way of pointing me in the direction of humility and collaboration; that is the form of worship pulling my energy now.

I have recently retired from a lifetime of teaching, work that I loved. I love being with my granddaughter, Olivia Clare Merriam, who is ten years old. I also love being with the young teachers who feel called to today's complex and difficult world of public education. This is the work I want to do now, the work of an elder who creates space for Olivia and for the teachers coming along behind me, space for finding their authentic voices and the energy that pulls them to show up in the world. Simple work. But not easy.

I am a link in the chain of integrity that connects my small work to the larger work in the world. Tending my link is my life's work. I am still a teacher - and I want to hold a space for hope now that I am retired. Theologian Reinhold Niebuhr speaks to me from decades past: "Nothing that is worth doing can be achieved in our lifetime; therefore, we must be saved by hope."

I know I can't accomplish all that needs doing in my lifetime, so I must have hope -- and I am called to offer a safe space to nurture hope. My intention is to reach out to my granddaughter and to the young teachers who are the next critical links in this chain of integrity – a chain strengthened by authenticity, personal willingness to convert energy to agency, and the courage to identify rewards that are transcendent. The space I envision will require a steadfast and patient partnership between what is and my own hope for what could be. The energy of that space will be charged with the knowledge that what we seek to find there is deeply personal -- a space of discovery, not fixing. Holding that space faithfully is the simple work I seek to do.

My own 35-year journey toward authenticity and resilience began with my discovery of Virginia Satir's therapy model for helping her clients make changes In their lives. In the 1960's, Satir created one of the earliest models of *family* therapy, and, in 1970, she founded The International Human Resources Networks to support mental health workers. I learned of her work through my own mental health colleagues, who were struggling to cope with their conflicted feelings about standardized approaches to families and children living with the life-long disability known as autism. Blame paradigms were pervasive and surrounded the diagnosis and treatment of children with autism. Satir's approach focused instead on helping families find the possibilities for family unity and guided practitioners away from pathology thinking and the language of pathology models. Her model suggested that change takes place in stages and involved chaos. It was the first time I had ever encountered the idea that learning took place at the cellular level. But it was her explanation of *The Change Process* that taught me the value of the chaos that was a reoccurring theme in my life – a theme I was convinced I was smart enough to avoid. Satir's model for change became, for me, a way of fixing myself, as I took her ideas from the *outside-*

in to attempt to shape my response from the *inside-out* to the world around me.

My outside-in paradigm shifted with my participation in a two-year program, The Courage to Teach, grounded in the writings of Parker J. Palmer. Then in my forties, I felt myself withdrawing, feeling reluctant to speak up, moving inward. Trusted colleagues called it burn-out, but I knew in my heart it wasn't. My journey in The Courage to Teach helped me to name my withdrawal and silencing of my own voice as the path of least resistance, a way of conserving my energy. I came to understand that my voice and my birthright gifts were stifled by not having a community that shared my longing for a deeper connectedness to true self, for knowing the Who that was teaching in my classroom.

You could easily conclude that finding The Courage to Teach, finding a community of trust, a community that would hear my thoughts and ask questions that did not carry the weight of judgment or ego, would have fixed me and satisfied my longing. Nope! No quick fix! In fact, those two years were the beginning of my journey, of my living into these gifts for many years, before my longing turned to the strength of action that is with me today. Parker Palmer's writing of his own story in *Let Your Life Speak* helped convince me that this journey required a lifetime of inner work, of reflection; that the only catalyst that would bring back both my voice and energy would be the one, as Parker wrote of his own journey, that "pushed me down onto ground where it was firm enough to stand." Accessing the energy of that catalyst would require the humility and collaboration of the simple work that my teen-aged self had dismissed as *mundane*. In order to make the shift from outside-in to inside-out, I would be required to show up. No one could do that for me; it could not happen without my active participation.

The Courage to Teach was an invitation to the most difficult work of my life.

GRATITUDE FOR THIS WORK
Inspired by David Whyte's *Deciding*

In a world where I am accosted
by the notion that others
know best what I need,
I am grateful for work
that is an invitation.

In a world talking **AT** me,
I am grateful for work
that values deep listening.

In a world that marginalizes and trivializes
what it does not understand,
I am grateful for work
that challenges me to hold the growth potential
of paradox.

In a culture of positional power built on the
shifting sands of conformity, isolation, and fear,
I am grateful for work
that calls me to move but not, as Rumi says,
in the way that fear makes you move.

With my gratitude to guide me into this work,
I will carry your voices in my head and heart.
I will remember Australian Aboriginal Dreamtime
where, quite literally, past and present and future
exist simultaneously.

I will choose to live intentionally and courageously
toward a time when God, world, and gold can also
exist congruently
in the spaces you and I co-create.

                              ---**Sandie Merriam**

NATURAL METAPHORS

The use of the natural rhythm of Earth's seasons in the Courage work initially drew my attention. Metaphors from nature are the ones that speak most eloquently to me when I am trying to reach deep inside, trying to find what will be lasting and portable as guides for my growing belief system. I am moved by my understanding that everything in nature is exquisitely tiny and a masterpiece of collaboration – the interconnectedness of every atom. The seasons themselves are paradoxical in terms of the flow of their collaborative energy. American economist Stuart Chase reminds me that the natural world will never embrace either/or thinking. Instead, he points out, chaos is the natural world's way of being: every bit of energy in service to the collaboration and the chaos of strange attractors.

Nature was an early and *strange attractor* in my life. My favorite definition for this term is the one that comes from the study of physics, which defines a strange attractor as one for which the approach to the final set of physical properties is chaotic. That would be me. I'm smiling now because this is the perfect way to describe my love of nature in all its perfection! In their *Canadian Manager* article in the summer of 2012, authors Michele Vincenti and Matthew Jelavic shared my current favorite explanation of this concept as I would apply it to myself (still smiling!): "The transition from attractor to strange attractor is the difference between settling into a constant, predictable equilibrium, and continually seeking another trajectory that constantly seeks to find this stability (equilibrium)." The explanation itself is the chaos I feel in my gut when I understand that my perspective is shifting. Naming this transition has always been difficult; I think of it as a kind of longing, an intense desire to understand. And that is the encouragement I need to continue to engage my thinking.

In the 1980's, as the diversity of the faith traditions became more visible, and I felt encouraged by new organizations like the Institute of Noetic Sciences that did not hold science and spirit as either/or, I began to explore my own belief system that underscored my love of science and the natural world. As a science teacher and student of natural history, I was conflicted in what I had always understood to be my religious solid ground. When I entered The Courage to Teach program, I was ready to explore a deeper understanding of my desire to embrace all forms of diversity. I resonated with Stuart Chase's words: "For those who believe, no proof is necessary. For those who don't believe, no proof is possible."

What did I believe? Chase reminded me that I must spend my energy in service to the work of holding on to the edges of paradox. In order to hold paradox, I realized I would need a different vision and a more sophisticated ability to see inside what appeared on the surface to be difference. I was living into the awareness that I would need, to quote the German philosopher Arthur Schopenhauer, "not so much to see what no one yet has seen, but to think what no one yet has thought about that which everybody sees."

I remember reading an article in *Science Daily* a few years ago in which biologist Todd Palmer described his research into ants protecting trees in Africa. I was moved by the notion that tiny ants could form a community around a tree and protect it from the huge plant-eating elephants that drive so much of what happens on an expansive African Savanna. Palmer wrote elegantly about the tiny work of the natural world: "It really is a David and Goliath story, where these little ants are up against these huge herbivores, protecting trees and having a major impact on the ecosystems in which they live. Swarming groups of ants that weigh about 5 milligrams each can and do protect trees from animals that are about a billion times more massive."

I love knowing that the energy in each drop of water in a waterfall is part of the collaboration that results in the spectacular display that stuns humanity. The work of each drop is exquisitely tiny.

There are countless examples of nature's understanding of the paradox between what human beings see as casual observers and the lessons we are able to learn when we see the deeper collaboration of energy flow under the surface. That is the kind of work that I hope will fill the remainder of my life.

MAPLE SYRUP MEMORIES AWAKEN ME

I have come to understand that, just as a tree's existence is mostly underground, so it is with much of my own identity, who I am and the beauty I love. Each time my work takes me out into the world, each time my energy is pulled toward some idea or project, I sincerely want to bring my best self. But there is real risk involved with these journeys from inside to out there. The risk has never outweighed the reward of going, even with the self-doubt and painful reflections that come back to me. I am aware of a growing ability to access the power of these doubts and painful reflections in ways that can shift my energy to agency.

I love real maple syrup! Pancakes, too, but it is the maple syrup, the real-deal maple syrup, that takes me back to a time when I was at ease. The disequilibrium of my adult life has not erased the awareness of the childhood feelings of transcendent comfort and freedom. When the delight of maple syrup reminds me of that comfort and freedom, I also awake to my new-found awareness that I have now begun to live in a different way. I am no longer oblivious to the knowledge of my own light and shadow. I understand dark, the terrain of sadness, and the comfort of rest; I understand light, the joy and the energy and compassion of my own birthright gifts. I am also aware that these seeming polar opposites coexist; that one cannot be understood without the other.

Maple trees live this paradox throughout the year and offer me a metaphor for my truth about the simple work that calls my energy. In the late summer and early fall the maple tree begins to save some of the carbohydrates that run the power house that is the tree's photosynthetic food source. These saved carbohydrates remain above ground as the rest of summer's carbohydrates travel to the roots, where they are stored for the tree's next year of growth. But in the dead of winter, late in January or sometime early in February when the nights are still very cold, the maple tree releases the food it has stored above ground, and maple syrup experts gather the tree's energy-wisdom in the delightful form of maple syrup. The maples are my teachers in how I want to focus the way my energy flows from the inside-out.

WINTER GIFTS

How then, do I winter through?
Is there a wisdom in me that will guide
My pace and purpose for going in and storing up?

The Maple tree understands winter's design
And saves something back for the journey *in*,
And knows the pace of its own existence,
And practices its unique wisdom in
And between every season's melody.
Holding to the rhythm of true self,
It releases its energy at just the right moment.

What has been carefully held in silence
Is now given in gracious hopefulness;
A renewed stream of sweetness
Allows a moment to savor
Understanding.

---Sandie Merriam

SELF-TALK AND JOURNALING

The attempt to understand my inner complexity is a well-worn path. Over the years, self-talk has become an old friend. As I talk in my head, I'm able to label and categorize events and feelings in ways that are not readily available to me any other way. My mother often said that "we hear ourselves best when we share our thoughts with someone who will not throw us away for crazy." I now understand that in a deeper way, as a guide for reflection.

In 1996, when I entered The Courage To Teach two-year retreat series that would move me from withdrawal and insecurity toward a more confident knowing and accepting of my authentic voice, I was invited to journal as a reflective practice. I tried to write as though a wise critic stood at my shoulder, and my writing felt artificial, overly wordy and stilted. I realized that I would have to establish the habit of being with my own thoughts on a regular basis, not just during time in retreat. I shared with Mom how odd it seemed to put what I thought on paper, and I invited her to journal with me to help me learn this new practice. She loved the idea of this partnership. As we wrote, I came to understand the ways my authentic voice had been deformed by school. As a student who did not spell well, my thoughts were trapped inside me, because to put them on paper would have meant illuminating my inability to spell. In my childhood world, there had been no letters to my grandmother, no thank you notes without at least two rewrites, no helping with the grocery list, no captions on my art. Mother and I finally worked out a system so I could succeed in school: I would memorize speeches for assignments after she and I had researched the topic together; then she would type what I dictated, and I would copy everything in my own handwriting.

We had always been a team, my learning-differently-than-the-school-system-taught Self and this woman who tirelessly created ways for me to express myself and feel successful. Now we were a team again. We accepted all opportunities to write and share. Her declining health gave us the gift of quality time in the hospital emergency room, often in the wee hours of the morning. Mom hated her handwriting, and I was hard-pressed to read it. "Shorthand ruined my penmanship," she would say.

Jotting lists worked better for me as guides for my thinking. Mother's tool was stream of consciousness with no punctuation, but easy enough to hear when we shared. Some of the things I wrote were worthy of being "thrown out for crazy," but she never rejected anything, and I was able to hear myself through my writing. Mother's journaling of her childhood memories has now become a family treasure, providing her great-granddaughter Olivia with precious first-source history and family stories. (Those spelling errors are still with me but fortunately, technology has come to my rescue. Curiously, Spell Check has improved my spelling ability – go figure!)

THE POWER OF POETRY AND SILENCE

Throughout The Courage to Teach, I grew to appreciate the poems used as third things – and especially the guiding questions and silent reflection connected to those poems. I discovered a love of poetic form, as I uncovered my authentic voice that seemed to strengthen from using words to create a thought picture. These thought pictures gave me energy and drove me to deeper reflection. I found comfort in the economy of words. There was something about the effort to get to the essence of a chain-of-ideas that appealed to my quest for a freer voice. While I do not claim to be a poet, I find this form of reflection and silence helpful. Parker Palmer encourages us to think about holding conversations with what he names as "at least a small community of people living inside each of us." I have come to know myself through these poetic conversations with my inside not-so-small community. Knowing that community deeply has resulted from my growing understanding of the power of silence.

I WELCOME SILENCE

When the noise
Of rushing is so loud that
My inner voice cannot be heard,

When I receive a thought
That connects me to my soul
So deeply that only silence respects
My soul's longing to respond,

When my gratitude
For the unexpected begs me
To spend time with that gift,

When a thought of another
So conflicts with my own
That wonder is food
For growth and grace,

When joy unbounded
Breaks me open to the possibility
That each small gracious act
Is energy for Beloved Community,

When despair is so profound
That my heart's voice
Is the only voice capable
Of renewing the promise of a future,

When disappointment
In my own response to the world
Causes my heart to ache
For the memory
Of my deepest values,

I welcome silence.

---Sandie Merriam

EMBRACING DRAGONS

Early map makers drew intricate arrows and ornate dragons at the edges of their maps, with the words: *"Beyond this point there be dragons."* These dragons are a stern warning against the risk of journeying beyond them into the unknown. I am understanding more about the dragons lurking on the map I follow in the pursuit of an undivided life. They are my personal teachers about the chaos of thinking differently in institutions searching desperately to be the right solution for today's issues and the challenging demands of society on education. These are the dragons that have captured the broken hearts of those who attempted to move beyond them without the armor of self-knowledge. I want to embrace those dragons by intentionally equipping my heart to grow larger, to break open and to move beyond the limits of old maps. I want to be of use as I hold space for my granddaughter and the next generation of teachers as they choose to live undivided in their personal and professional lives, with their hearts broken open to the possibilities beyond these edges, as they learn to embrace their own dragons.

In addition to dragons, ancient explorers attempted to go beyond the maps of their day by sailing into unknown water using only the navigational technology of nature. They collaborated with the natural world to determine their location and the depth of the water around them. As I travel beyond the edges of the old maps, the image of the Mobius strip is important to my understanding of my own location and the depth of my understanding. Aware of my own hopes for being useful in this last part of my life, I am struck by how often this image comes to my consciousness. I doodle it and position myself as a stick person on its surface in various locations. I use it for determining my understanding of the big picture. It is my safety net, my go-to tool when I am confused or when I am trying to understand my own anxiety or anger.

The Mobius strip has become my navigational tool for each new challenge in my pursuit of personal congruence. I am increasingly aware that this tool of map-making is one of those strange attractors. The image that comes to mind is a conduit of sorts, helping my unique energy flow into the world beyond edges and dragons, and then returning, strengthening my sense of personal agency as it provides feedback from out there. I want to work toward being of use as a new generation gives birth to its dreams. Perhaps this is the work that will allow my own learning of authenticity to create spaces where my granddaughter, young teacher leaders, and other educators can become aware of the agency of an informed and undivided life – agents of the change that will give hope to the communities they inhabit. Can I use the Mobius image to shift beyond dragons and old maps with either/or boundaries?

It is my experience in professional development that leads me to an understanding of how institutions drive the parade of the next big idea. A common complaint in the world of teachers is the yearly changing of the way pedagogy shows up in the classroom and the increasing notion of sameness in the delivery of that pedagogy. Great teachers know and have always known that the rebellious act of giving up either/or thinking allows us to understand that authentic growth comes from holding paradox, requiring that we take responsibility for our energy in the world and that we change our perspective to focus on an understanding of the ground on which WE stand. Only then do we have the possibility of finding our voices in a way that others are able to hear as authentic and hopeful.

If sustainable freedom comes from knowing ourselves, then systems change when those inside the system understand who they are and why they have chosen to invest themselves in a particular work. Purposeful silent reflection is active and takes time, just as seeds take time, and sometimes fire, to germinate, to come to the surface, to find food, and to send roots ever deeper. This pattern from the natural world provides a pattern into the unknown territory of an individual and transcendent reward system. Parker Palmer describes the *movement model* as having four steps. I am always drawn to the fourth step -- the adoption of alternative rewards, but the word alternative troubles me; in my mind, it suggests second-best. So I am offering the word *transcendent* as I reflect on Parker's movement model. For me, this is a small but important difference; transcendence is what I seek in the final stage of the movement model. The 2012 edition of the Merriam-Webster dictionary tells me that *transcend* means extending or lying beyond the limits of ordinary. I want to be beyond those limits of old maps and old reward systems.

TEACHERS' VOICES: MY SIMPLE WORK

As I approached my last years of teaching, I wanted to create simple ways to gather teachers to spend time in The Courage to Teach. I realized that the pace of life, and particularly school-life, would not allow for the great luxury of eight seasonal four-day retreats over a two-year period that I had experienced, so I created *Teachers' Voices*, Courage work in a different format. With an intentionally small group of ten teachers, we met monthly for three hours, preceded by a pot-luck supper, for the nine-month school year. Sally Z. Hare and I, both national facilitators prepared by the Center for Courage & Renewal (CCR), co-facilitated the circles, grounded in the CCR principles and practices. We committed to creating safe space where each teacher could hear her own inner wisdom and re-discover her own personal identity and integrity.

I invited teachers who resonated with Parker's writing in *A Hidden Wholeness* and wanted to live with integrity as we faced our daily challenges and opportunities. Our time together included much of what I had experienced in The Courage to Teach. My feeling was that this work could offer important support for the newest teachers among us and had the potential to create supportive communities across our county for dedicated teachers to, as Parker puts it, "be heard into speech." I knew, from my own experience, that as we do this work, we meet ourselves again, remembering why we were called to teaching, hearing our own hopeful voices of commitment that come from "knowing the ground on which we stand."

Teachers' Voices has continued now for more than five years. The program and the format continue to be flexible, and we add participants each year. As we continue to hear each other into speech through our stories, our deep fear and mistrust and woundedness bubble to the surface, this time inside a community committed to deeply listening and equipped with practices that can be relied upon to respectfully honor authentic voices. Such communities foster hope and offer the renewal that comes from love. I want to add my energy to these spaces.

THE SACRED SPACES BETWEEN US

The space between us is real
Indignities, anguish, guilt, and blame
Travel that space on horse-back
While our collective story is ground into
The foot-path by our failure to speak it.

The mud between us is messy
Confusion, pride, ignorance and anger
Lay on that path that we've allowed
To languish unseeded while our hearts
Break in the self-imposed silence.

The silence between us is audible
Self-doubt, diminishment, emptiness and fear
Warn against traveling through the ruts
and mud.
Heeded, the soul grows despondent and
Cannot illuminate the path it knows is there.

How then, do we begin to move in the space
between us?
Are words the antidote for the muddy, rutted
silence?
It is true that words not lived are hollow.
And there is no value in a story of hollow words.

How then, do we begin to hear the story

Of self, of other?
   To tell the story of self, of other?
      To honor the space between us,
         To lift the truth between us,
            To co-create the story between us,
               In the sacred space between us?

---Sandie Merriam

Doing simple work well is an act of worship, Mother told me.
Rumi says there are hundreds of ways to kneel and kiss the
ground. And Parker writes in *The Courage to Teach* that when
we are teaching at our best, "*It is because of the grace of
great things... We invite diversity... We embrace ambiguity...
We welcome creative conflict... We practice honesty... We
experience humility... We become free.*"

I can think of no greater conduit for the energy I want to invest
in this next phase of my life than creating the space for Olivia
and the teachers coming along behind me to hear their stories
of self and other – and to tell the story of self and other. Rumi's
admonition to move, but not in the way that fear makes you
move, rings in my heart as I think about the work of freeing my
own voice and helping others free theirs.

As I think about my granddaughter Olivia and the teachers whose hearts are breaking in public education, I know my simple work will not be easy. But this is the Beauty that I love – and my best chance for transcendent rewards is to do it well.

Sandra Merriam, M.Ed., is a retired middle and high school teacher who taught special education and science in South Carolina schools for 39 years. She is also a national Circle of Trust® facilitator with the Center for Courage & Renewal in Seattle, Washington. She lives with her family in North Myrtle Beach, South Carolina, and can be contacted by email at smerriam@sc.rr.com or sandiemerriam@gmail.com .

Connecting Me

By Jim R. Rogers

 T ime seemed to stand still for many months. Many. Like a child in solo activity who, in place, spins around and around with arms outstretched, feet shuffling up dust on fresh socks, eyes slammed tightly shut, making a wish for something else. I twirled in place so long that I bore deeper into a hole that became an abyss totally unfamiliar to me. The darkness engulfed me and I stayed there much too long, and yet, some say we stay in those surprise places only for as long as we have to, and then something happens.

My seed was sown in a small southern town surrounded by tobacco farms and sweet potato fields. It's where my education began. We didn't have kindergarten back then. When we were six years old, we started first grade. Before that, our education was Sunday school and church and lots of active, adventurous, and unsupervised creative play in a safe and nurturing community where we were children of all the residents who constantly graded our behavior, always a reflection of our parents.

Perhaps they did, but I have no recollection of my mother or father ever reading to me. Neither had a high school education. I never saw them reading anything except picture magazines, the newspaper or the Bible, so I know they could read. How well, I can't say. But, that lack of reading material didn't seem to hinder their lives, at least not to me. But, how could I really know that? My parents kept their intimate lives secret, almost always putting on the faces of positive living and giving us a strong sense of self and value. They were honest to a fault, and affection from mother and integrity from father have served me well except when they didn't. They certainly seemed happy, were successful citizens, and they treated me kindly. And they bought my brothers and me a new set of the *Encyclopedia Britannica*. Not a bad resource if only I had liked to read.

My formal education was one of basal readers, memorizing, cramming, finishing homework before home, being told what and when and how to think, reading as little as possible and having no fun with the learning process. The only pleasures in school were social and athletic activities and chorus. Knowledge-growing was pretty much limited to those activities and whatever else surrounded them. We didn't have TV. I watched radio. Its imagination, entertainment and drama captured me. It launched my passion and my earliest career pursuits.

I learned how to get along with people very well. School was my first real experience of connecting with others in good ways, even though I wasn't sure what that was called then. Book learning was just too tedious and time-consuming. One very memorable teacher, Mrs. Woody, my first meaningful connection, did teach me that the world was there for the taking and that it encompassed a far larger area than my home town. She encouraged me to go for bigger bites of life and gave a lot of support to my natural abilities in the areas for which there was applause waiting in the audiences of external approval. She recognized that I was eager to take my talents as far as I could go.

With a solid Norman Rockwell-like foundation, I began my real life when I entered the University of North Carolina in Chapel Hill, which was the only UNC campus at the time. We had no SAT's back then. My good fortune. We took entrance placement tests and I ended up in two remedial courses which gave me some things I had missed in the secondary years. After those two years of struggle through "general college," I began courses in my major of Radio, Television and Motion Picture Production, a field of study which is now called Mass Communications. Masses indeed. I became one of them.

What had been an active social life in high school, where I excelled, dwindled down to a mere trickle among a much larger group of peers, more sophisticated, much more educated and better able to play the role required in the system as university student. I managed to keep my rather inflated sense of self-worth intact by being involved in areas where I felt comfortable, safe, connected: voice study and a music fraternity, church choir member and soloist, and dating my high school sweetheart who was in nursing school thirty miles away.

RIGHT ON TRACK

We would marry before my senior year. We would graduate. I would fulfill my military obligation of three years as a radio announcer communication specialist in the Army, training at Roosevelt Island in New York City, then serving with the Armed Forces Radio and Television Network in Korea, and as a hospital bedside network programmer in Alabama. And we would have children. Three. And I would begin my full-time career working in my chosen field of radio and television. To my pleasant surprise, I advanced rapidly, totally committed to it, to the point that all other parts of my life took back seats on the priority bus. I was right on track with the societal formula designed for young men of the times: Go all out with your work, move forward, bring home lots of bacon even if it took working two or three jobs. I had no idea what I was doing to myself, my wife and my children.

I was to learn that hard lesson later.

There were job changes. There were two geographic moves. There was career advancement. There was applause. There was affirmation. There was even adulation, which, as it turned out, was unfortunate. And there was loss. All parts of the life of a family rooted in small-town USA began to come apart at the seams from pushes and pulls of making it in the world then; super glue for dysfunctional marriages had not yet been invented, nor had couples therapy been un-stigmatized. The big, bad divorce came and we never really knew why. After nineteen married years, it was just over. We all managed to get through it in what we thought were positive, mature adult ways. Maybe for wife and me. But the children were to suffer damage. Not from the splitting of their parents, but from the loss of stability, continuity, supervision, encouragement and the oh-so-needed attending that was unknowingly allowed to slip from their hugs, because the caregivers were so distracted by their own ignorance, selfish seeking, discontent and disconnecting.

The seeking, which vacillated between being a blessing and a curse, took me away from my "shallow" southern roots and the firm foundation of comfort, assurance and self-confidence to the risky mysteries of New York City, where for all practical purposes, I had to start all over. Making new and effective connections once again, I made that start with head held high in pride and knowledge of competence, leaving behind three teen children whose emotional heads were held low from feelings of abandonment and playing roles of second place, a fact that eluded my sensitivity until years later. High level achievement in "the big time" whetted my appetite for more. A new romance, a new connection, produced a new wife and a new partner in our own TV production company, and when it felt right, we uprooted ourselves and our corporate papers and re-settled in the show biz mecca of Los Angeles.

The vibrations had been strong and the decision felt right. There were above-average successes and achievements; more valuable as well as disappointing connections unique to life in

Los Angeles, but there was also the beginning of the dark place, the shadow side of life that would creep up and blind-side me and my wife/partner. As the unlearned, simple "doer" from the country, I found myself in a quagmire of legal, financial, domestic and business messes, one after another, building on each a wall that would eventually prove more than I wanted to surround me. I knew I was in the wrong place, doing things that seemed wrong inside. The toxicity oozed from my pores as I was pulled apart in many directions. None seemed to be right.

I worked to find a new way of thinking about choices. I knew there had to be change. I knew that something terrible had distracted my path and that I was way off track, traveling down the wrong road way beyond the speed limit. I felt like two distinctly different men, that little boy from the country town and the pseudo-sophisticated big city professional, neither of whom was making much progress living life well.

A NEW DIRECTION

I began looking for a new direction. But, without a real goal. I just knew I had to begin something. Something else. Each time I made a move it seemed like the exact right thing to do. And each time, after a while, settled in the move, it was time to move again. The moves were major uprooting and most difficult for someone who took his first real risk only after age forty. Most of the time a change did happen. But there was no growth. I remember dramatically labeling the feeling as having a hole in my soul. As the vise of circumstance turned tighter and tighter, my need for new directions became clearer and clearer. And then, one day, quite from out of nowhere, that new direction appeared.

My talents as a director/producer were solicited by an independent group to consult with them about making a video on the subject of "parenting." My research introduced me to Dorothy Corkille Briggs, Ph.D., child psychologist, who authored the book *Your Child's Self Esteem*. That book and that time spent in research changed the course of my life and cemented in place the subject on which I would choose to spend the rest of my productive years.

As I dived deeply into the project, the reality became clear to me that the vast majority of the ills that were growing in society, from violent crime down to children "sassing" the parents with disrespect, had their roots in the early childhood experiences with those creating the environment. Most of the "ills" bantered about in the media were those that were obvious to people who had any awareness at all. Murder, rape, robbery, drive-by shootings, and so much more, were major concerns of the day, even before cyber-bullying and school horrors from guns and mental challenges appeared. I was concerned about the increases and I had a pretty good layman's idea as to the causes.

I decided to direct myself to the area of prevention, to try and help parents who were in crisis to keep their children and **their** children from stepping into the same potholes; to help break that "cycle of errors" that kept throwing good children who couldn't swim into a raging river. I wanted to go after those lesser "ills" that kept people from functioning in life in positive, constructive, productive, and contributing ways. There were human problems that kept love from growing, denied good relationships, both personal and professional; killed mutual respect; ignored responsibility and ethics; guffawed at trust, loyalty, honor, honesty and accountability. I felt the deterioration of life values I had known and been taught. I had modified some of those to fit my own modern ethical situation and to justify some of my questionable actions, but I still maintained a basic and firm belief in the genuine goodness of people and felt the driving need to in some way do my part to restore some of what I perceived had been lost. I continued to be a "touchy-feely" person, as I had been called in high school and the Army and in my first professional jobs in television and advertising; I had been rewarded time and again for my productive connections with people, inside organizations and outside. At the same time I had also often been criticized for being *too* people-oriented.

That was my first exposure to paradox. I realized I couldn't change that. My DNA included caring about others. It appeared that I was now moving in that direction, away from those who were totally self-absorbed and self-centered with little regard for others in their lives, near or far. I had tried that, and it rubbed me against the grain. There had to be a place in the world for us "touchy-feelies."

I was not making this new plan as some altruistic "do-gooder" on a mission to make up for a lifetime of errors. I wanted to try and make these small efforts because I was directed to do so by the events in my life and the acceptance of who I was beginning to see and feel as my real self, the one I had been denying and ignoring. I was beginning to face my fears of not knowing what to do, not having the answers and realizing that I could live a meaningful life without external approval, even though I knew it would be a continuing challenge, since I felt that I was most likely addicted to the applause drug and wanting to be in the spotlight of "being special." Events do not go in the life book as mistakes, but rather as lessons to prepare us for what is to be. I was determined to make these changes because I needed to. It felt right; scary, but right, and being in it, as I later came to understand from my life-changing experience in the cutting-edge Courage to Teach retreats, made me feel "most alive."

A NEW CONNECTION

I had watched television, in my years of living and working in the very foundations of my professional existence, turn from a tool of great promise and expectation for learning and growing into a gimmick for making money for just another pool of power people. Only in very select instances was this most powerful communications medium being used to inform and educate, and yes, entertain: the three primary purposes for which it was created. I wanted to be a part of all that, the good parts, but I was road-blocked by what seemed to be graft, selfishness, favoritism, nepotism, clique-ness and "good-ole-boy-girl-clubs," and by not having the right personality or character capacities.

That was what that external approval, or disapproval, did to me. I was led to believe I was not valuable...contrary to who I had always been. I was told that I didn't yell enough and lacked the fighting instinct to win. Emotionally damaged, my instincts and research for some healing balm led me to a book by James Kavanaugh, *There Are Men Too Gentle to Live Among the Wolves*. Stepping outside even an attempt to be humble, that book spoke loudly to me and affirmed that I was not born to run with the wolves. My life had turned into one of frustration, confusion, despondency and depression. I knew in the deepest part of my being that I could find at the time that I was at least moving in the right direction. I embraced it with enthusiasm and welcomed a new connection.

Graduate studies came first, a return to formal learning. My fears of the venture were grounded in the fact that I had not had a solid foundation back in that country high school, and my initially poor book learning sense that I managed to improve only slightly in my undergraduate years would indeed be rusty, perhaps even beyond the oil of desire, dedication and hard work. I was wrong. My life experiences had counted for something! I had to apply myself completely but the new beginning was an absolutely exhilarating experience. I sponged up knowledge and information as fast as my brain would take them in, which caused it to expand and process. The grey matter actually began to work again, perhaps better than ever. Perhaps for the first time. Or, maybe it was the first time my brain came into sync with the birthright gifts of my heart. It worked so well and it was so clearly right that I boldly took myself out of the graduate program where concentration had been on psychology with the aim of becoming a clinician. After a year plus, I knew I was still slightly off-kilter. I wanted to become a preventionist, working with parents and caregivers *before* problems were created or worsened.

A NEW FIELD

I found training at the Center for the Improvement of Child Caring in Los Angeles, a series of intense programs for over a year, and obtained credentials for conducting workshops to speed up my preparation and entry into my new chosen field. Within the next months I became a certified parenting instructor, with over 90 hours of training and 80 hours of facilitating workshops, working with indigent parents in crisis in the most unlikely location of inner city Hollywood, in a second floor social services meeting room on the corner of Hollywood and Vine.

What I once again found in myself as I began the new journey was confusion, frustration, despondency, and yes, even depression. Old familiar tunes, all resulting from my newness in a very different and challenging arena with unfamiliar but essential connections. Fear of not knowing, not being the man with all the answers, I struggled to find the right combination of me and them and how to forge a working relationship. The "them" included both the clients I tried to serve and the administrative teams who were in charge. The difference between what was found and what had been was that now there was hope and some encouragement. The new connections became positive in time. There were days of great satisfaction along with those of feeling a total failure.

I made an incredible discovery in connecting with the help of the workshop members. When I stopped trying to emulate my schooling instructors and allowed the class to process based on what the members needed to do, within limits, and what they wanted to talk about; when I allowed myself to be real and authentic and honest and all the characteristics that had always meant a lot to me and worked for me in other places, then, the relationship seeded and grew and grew beyond my expectations.

I began to be me.

I was working where I knew I should be. Well, not exactly. Not yet. But I didn't know that. More, bigger, unexpected treasured connections were on their way. What wasn't working were other parts of my life. I was pleased with my decision to change. I was pleased with the new direction, the nubile career, the new connections, the feelings of interest and excitement that had been lost for years. I felt affirmations of who I was coming back gradually. But the slow dismantling of my old career and my old relationships were dragging me down and back to the black hole from which I was emotionally kicking and screaming to escape.

My second marriage ended. The reasons were complex, but once again, the collapse forged for me a strength and resolve that would not have come had my wife/partner chosen a different way to live her life. For all practical purposes, the production company that we still operated together dried up from a lack of business in a time of recession and unhealthy managing of the shortages. It became impossible and impractical to try and sustain a business for two people living in Los Angeles.

Another factor had been gnawing at my heart for a long time. I sorely missed having a sense of place. For almost 20 years I felt in transit, like I was on a temporary journey of sorts that would someday end and bring me back to start. I decided to go back to that start, back to my home state to see if I could re-boot, find that sense of home and community and work on developing parenting workshops and getting my new career seriously launched. Not only did I return to my home state, I also returned to my home town, the one surrounded by tobacco and sweet potato fields and to my family home to rest, recuperate, reflect, plan and take action. I was lucky. I had a home place to which I could return. And the sense of coming home a "failure" never entered my mind.

A NEW BUSINESS

I created a one-man business I called *ParentsCare* which was the foundation for the parenting workshops and much more to come: *ParentsCare,* caring for parents who care, with the motto, Putting Parents and Children First Through Family Enrichment Programs.

My home county was not ready for parenting programs. I did get invited to do whatever I wanted for the continuing education department at the county junior college with the help of a couple of old friends: one, the longest serving North Carolina state senator, who was my childhood neighbor and one of the jungle people when my brother and I played Tarzan and Cheetah in our abundant wooded community (I, of course, was Tarzan); and the other, the running back on our high school football team for whom I blocked would-be tacklers and who had become a leading citizen with an impressive portfolio of success. The invitation seemed based on political favor, and the officials offered no support and not much interest and seemingly very little understanding of what I was talking about and why. The few who remembered me seemed glad to have "one of theirs" back home, and wanted to keep me there as a new contributor to the community, but most of what they were looking for was in the areas I was trying to avoid. I was interested in something else.

I didn't know much about how the education system worked. I knew there were public schools, private and parochial. I knew there were technical schools, or trade schools, and there were community or junior colleges, and I knew there were institutions of higher learning like four-year colleges and universities. I came to know from the pursuit of work in education that the educators in place for some time were very protective of their turfs. Indeed they were defensive. Although, in most cases, the people with whom I came in contact were pleasant and polite, they were suspicious of an older male from years in the outside world who now wanted to be in theirs. Needless to say, I was surprised and befuddled. I had zero illusions of ever being the credible persons they were; I simply wanted to try using my years of experience and my new-found knowledge, fueled with passion and desire, to help educate a segment of the community in an area that no one else seemed to care about.

LOOKING FOR NEW CONNECTIONS

Discouraged with the response in my home county, I began to look beyond for more connections. I found Coastal Carolina College (in a few years, it would become Coastal Carolina University) in nearby Conway, South Carolina, the county seat of Horry, which was about 40 miles away. Perhaps the last place I ever imagined that I would look for work was Horry County. In my youth, Horry was not considered a very progressive county, fraught with corrupt government and "red-neck" mentality. We, of the North Carolina Columbus County elite, looked down our noses at all but the area of Horry called the Grand Strand, the magnificent beaches of Myrtle and North Myrtle Beach. It's amusing now to think that that attitude existed. Time and growth and a hospital and a campus of the University of South Carolina, Coastal Carolina College, obviously had had positive effects. Horry, as I came to find out, had in many ways outdistanced Columbus, not only in population and financial stability, but also in education, government and sophistication.

I was introduced to a neighbor, another important connection, a professor at the college who said he would connect me to the vice chancellor to explore possibilities. The neighbor felt that perhaps my media background would be useful in public relations projects, and that maybe I would be able to arrange something for my parenting work.

I was clearly told that I did not have the credentials or qualifications to teach at a four-year college, but maybe something could be worked out in continuing education. I did not have great expectations. I felt that old protectionism creeping in there. I would not get my hopes up, but I felt a glimmer of encouragement.

I set up an appointment, hoping for the next connection to be *the* one. The vice chancellor was gracious and generous. He gave me over two hours of his time, a campus tour, and lunch in the faculty dining room. He introduced me to other professors who all appeared to be down-to-earth real people who did not offhandedly dismiss me, who talked with language I could understand and who made me feel welcomed and comfortable in their private room.

The vice chancellor felt sure that some doors could be opened and that there could be a place for me to work in some way with Coastal. The person I had to meet, he said, was the dean of graduate studies and continuing education; he said she was one of the busiest administrators on campus and wished me luck. "Dr. Dean," as I would come to call her with great respect and admiration, was booked solid for all of the near future, but her efficient secretary found me a spot on her calendar in two months. I learned that Dr. Dean was a very popular, in-great-demand person, and I also learned not to call her "administrative assistants" secretaries.

The hyper-connections begin!

As the next few weeks and months unfolded, I knew as I had never known before that my release from the abyss, my return to the light, my escape from the shadow, had begun in earnest. Now the desperate search for answers and reasons for all of the trials and errors, the twists and turns the gains and losses of my before-life seemed to be coming to a conclusion; it was all about preparing for this time.

I had needed to go through all of those discoveries of connections to prepare me for the now and the rest. Properly connecting can be most tedious and precarious and tiring. It needed a lot of training and aging and mellowing and becoming and being. The time had come. I was allowed to experience the miraculous results of connections.

After two months of worry and hand-wringing, I finally met Dr. Dean, who had been winding down her three-year Kellogg Fellowship and was returning to Coastal Carolina College with a changed agenda. She welcomed me and my passion, my idealistic and naive approach, and my spirit. She gave me a peek into an entirely new and exciting world. From the beginning, she encouraged and guided me into countless networking endeavors, connections that are still, to this day, unfolding. It took awhile, but she did assure me of her interest in my workshops and her intention to try them in continuing education. She was even positive about my media background and encouraging about ways to put those talents to use as well. Then, she went beyond that. She planned to resign her position as dean to devote her full time to her newest dream, the Center for Education and Community, a vision that had emerged from her Kellogg study of community. She even hinted at the possibility of my eventually becoming a part of that. I had no idea what it was. But I would learn. I had stepped onto the campus of Coastal Carolina College. I was elated. It wasn't parenting but I was being asked to work on a meaningful project by people with whom I now hoped to be working for a long time to come. I was getting more than my foot in the door.

My first assignment was to be the creative consultant for the editing of a video from the recent Calling All Colors conference, a program on racism that was developed and planned and executed mostly by children. It blew me away; I never saw anything like it in New York City or Los Angeles. Working with Calling All Colors fired up a part of my brain and my heart that I didn't know existed. How exciting that there were educators who were going out into the community, engaging children and inviting them to gather on the grounds of a college to talk about an issue as critical as racism. Having lived in a bubble for so many years, it was an issue about which I knew very little. In retrospect, as I got to know more about Dr. Dean and her associates and their important work, I realized what the adult supervisors were doing. They were not *speaking to* the children; they were *listening* to the children! It was a concept and activity of active parenting which I covered in great detail in my workshops. I would come to realize that the exhibited respect of listening was one of the real cornerstones of what was to be the Center for Education and Community's philosophy of what teaching is all about. It was my first indication that teaching and parenting were closely related. I was being offered an opportunity to work with educators who believed in children, and who were solid proponents of teaching with tools of behavior and communication and respect and authenticity, which I now wanted everything to do with! Working on the project was most gratifying and I was actually paid for it. Albeit an important one, it was only one project.

PAYING THE BILLS

Unfortunately, I still needed work that would provide some regular income, so I continued to try and find one of those jobs that would allow me some dollars but not take me from my new pursuits. I wasn't successful, and my financial condition deteriorated. I was not deterred. I mounted a massive promotional mailing to all the area churches and to prominent businesses announcing the presence and intention of ParentsCare with hopes of producing several workshops for congregation members and employees. The slow response and eventual negative answers were most discouraging. I went to work for a temporary service stocking shelves in a grocery store just to pay some bills.

Three times in Los Angeles I had taken on what I considered to be menial work to help keep the bill collectors away; I knew I could do it again. This time, however, the menial work turned out not to be menial. It was very similar work, but it was different. No, it was I who was different. My reasons for doing the work were the same but it was not all that I had.

And, I related to the other people involved in different ways, actually talking with them and sharing and learning about their lives and gleaning from their experiences correlations to my life and to the new career I was undertaking. Life had become a wonderfully equipped laboratory where I studied each day, trying to put together pieces of an emotional and intellectual puzzle called "how life works."

I actually enjoyed the process of finding out that I was not the center of the universe.

That job was just temporary; I knew that. So, I was able to interweave it with my contact with Dr. Dean and our efforts to develop what we both seemed to want, my parenting and media skills used to their fullest. I kept working and studying and preparing. She kept thinking and being and making things happen. The continuing education department was planning April Seminars, and I was invited to conduct a two-hour mini-workshop on parenting. We called it "Children, Why Don't They Come With a Manual?" I was conducting my first workshop as ParentsCare. I could not stop smiling!

After giving me several other opportunities to do my work on campus and in community, she invited me to join her new center since I was offering something she didn't have but knew she needed, parenting education. But, she insisted, I had to finish my graduate degree, started a few years earlier at Antioch University in Marina del Rey, CA; she directed me toward early childhood, not the psychology I had thought would be the right course of study.

A year later, at age 57, I received the first master's degree from the newly independent Coastal Carolina University graduate program. During the next thirteen years I was involved in countless Center projects, from parenting classes for the community and schools, graduate classes for teachers, race-relations conferences for young people, and parenting and family life education for social services and family courts.

Everything was new and exciting as I was learning about the real world and the real people who populate it daily, surmounting incredible odds to survive and thrive. We created a family resource office, *Home in The Center,* where information and materials as well as workshops were offered to the Coastal faculty, staff, and students, and to the community at large.

The connecting kept growing even more connections, and the days and months turned out even more surprises of increasing importance and meaning for me. The ParentsCare company remained the base of my teaching, made even richer by the discovery of teacher formation work that came through Dr. Dean's vision for using Parker Palmer's book, *The Courage to Teach.* She invited me to participate in the first South Carolina two-year Courage to Teach program, and that was the mother of all connections and my main vehicle for learning and growing that I have been riding for a long and fruitful time. I developed a parenting curriculum and began to write a monthly column for a regional parenting and family life specialty newspaper, Parent News. We created a certification class for ParentsCare facilitators and trained 43 more parenting instructors over the next two years to serve as resources for parents and schools. I also became a member of the National Council on Family Relations, and through it, a Nationally Certified Family Life Educator, a CFLE. I also signed on as a charter member and eventual council section head for the National Parenting Education Network.

So much learning. So much change. So much finding, naming, owning, and nurturing the me I had lost so long ago. And it all came about because of the magic of connecting and my journey to those connections and to my new life and loves.

HOME IS WHERE THE START IS

Looking back, I began laying the groundwork by knocking on doors, literally and figuratively. What is now popularly called networking became my operating tool as I realized the changes had to come, and only the right connections could help those changes take place and take root. As I found my entry into the rest of my life, I discovered that I wasn't alone in my pursuits. In fact, on the national scale, parenting and family life was becoming a subject to talk about and to which attention had to be paid. Interest had even begun to grow in Horry County and other parts of the state. My supportive and mentoring Dr. Dean believed in the work wholeheartedly and encouraged and affirmed at every turn of the trip. Other seekers were also out there looking for allies and directions. So the connections started to take hold, fertilized in growth by a cadre of advocates and early childhood education proponents who knew with me that Home is Where the Start is!! That has become my battle cry, and I don't hesitate to make it loudly known as I advocate for parenting education in high school at the latest, and for effective parenting engagement programs in all grades at all schools.

Growing chronologically older and feeling the results of my intense learning, it took a lot of energy for me to stay the course and stay undivided in my unyielding attempts for public and government and educational understanding of the needs for parenting education. I learned about Parker Palmer's "tragic gap" and how deeply I was submerged in it, knowing that on one side of the gap there is What Is, and on the other there is What Could Be. I had to develop my own method of staying focused for commitment and pursuit, head-clearing stuff, and reminders of the signposts and guidelines on the new road on which I planned to stay until I was finished. The reminders became my reasons for being and staying on track, staying true to my self, remaining undivided during the search for more and more support from believers. They were all about connections and that was the key term and process that I used...because it was connections that brought me home, to my heart.

Standing in that open door at Coastal Carolina University, seeing all of the possibilities that were ahead, some of which I could not have imagined, I realized that I could not accomplish anything important by myself. I knew it would take a herculean team effort. Even though I was handling not being the star pretty well most days, I still had the drive to want to give my best, even in a team effort, so I had to create personal reminders and supports that would keep my awareness high and my sensitivity keen. I had to prepare myself to connect with others and I had to connect in the most effective ways.

I wanted others to know about my guideposts, my stepping stones that helped me find my way and stay on the path; my guides for maintained stability and survival while living in the "tragic gap" of what is and what could be.

So I named them:

Connections of the Heart...where abides caring, empathy, involvement, empowerment, discovering those kindred spirits who shared with care, concern, efforts.

Connections of the Mind...where there is gaining knowledge, learning, growing, making contact, connecting to the close community of associates in organizations of fellow travelers.

Connections of the Body...where there is personal health, taking care of the physical self to be able to effectively make connections to all the links outside of self, outside of the comfort zones of knowing to unknowing, finding new links to resources.

And the necessary fourth...

Connections of the Soul, the inner part of us all, with which it is necessary to be connected, giving life to the inside's being undivided from the outside, showing the world the current truths we hold dear and call our own until they're not.

Then, to keep me remembering my path, proceeding as one undivided, the one I am, the one I came to be, I named my Four Pillars of Effective Connections:

INTRACONNECTIONS: Those that we must have inside our organizations with our fellow workers, inside our families and our circles of friends...Connections of the Heart.

INTERCONNECTIONS: Those we have to have in our neighborhoods and communities where we connect in common purpose and interests...Connections of the Mind.

OUTERCONNECTIONS: Those outside of our comfort zones to the other world of knowledge and education expanding our effectiveness as we go...Connections of the Body.

And the most important because without this connection all the others will suffer:

INNERCONNECTIONS: The inner self work necessary to maintain the desire, the energy, the commitment in the most healthy and undivided way...Connections of the Soul.

A CHANCE TO TRY AGAIN

I'm sure fate and possibly some type of divine intervention intersected at the grace point as I, and the work and Coastal Carolina University and Dr. Dean with all of her vision and a long list of treasured connections, found union with each other. Becoming acutely aware of needing connections and being open to all possibilities I know led me to my first steps when discomfort with self and place pushed me, shoved me into a waiting world; a world that allowed and encouraged my self-nurturing which most recently gave me the desire and energy to publish two books: *The Incredible Importance of Effective Parenting: Plain Talk About Raising Children from a Concerned Field Worker*, a compilation of over 17 years of columns from the specialty newspaper; and a thematic collection of free verse poetry on the process of aging, *Starts and Stops Along the Way: Sharing Some Stuff From the Road Most Travel.* One of the poems from the collection has become my daily mantra and I offer it to you:

Good Morning!

I love the way a new day feels.
Those few moments when
Yesterday's memories
Are slept into a docile file for later.
When rest gives birth to new eyes
That see a life
With energy and hope
And a chance to try again.

Outside and inside, NOW, I am connected.

 Jim R. Rogers. Long on the journey, non-believing of the speed of time passing. Father of three, grandfather of four, former husband of two, all of whom I love, and the husband of one who continues to enrich my life and hold my love tightly and lovingly as we move along together, smiling. M.Ed., CFLE, Certified Family Life Educator, member Directors Guild of America, National Council on Family Relations, National Parenting Education Network. You can learn more at www.stilllearning.org or e-mail me at parentscare@sc.rr.com .

My Truth at a Slant

By Wanda Smith Freeman

Tell your Truth, but tell it slant.
Listen without fixing.
I hold you in the Light.
Honor boundaries and deep confidentiality.
We just hold the bird in our hands, not restricting its flight
and not helping it to fly.

---What I still remember, 20 years later, from my
first Coastal Courage to Teach Retreat

Tell your Truth, but tell it slant. Well, what Emily Dickinson really wrote was "Tell all the truth but tell it slant," but this is the way I remember it. I heard these words, as if they were speaking directly to me, in my first-ever Coastal Courage to Teach retreat in the fall of 1996.

When I received the invitation in the mail, I knew this was something big. Somebody whom I did not know, but was really important, wanted to honor teachers and thank us and pamper us while we explored our inner spirits that, more often than not, we had to check at the doors of our schools, thus separating who we are from what we do. Courage to Teach was the beginning of a journey that has spanned nearly twenty years, on which I have explored my truths, light and shadowed, of the professional and personal me.

It was a time when the education system was blamed for every

104

failure of society and teachers were the whipping posts for those failures. Good people were walking away and young people were choosing other professions. My career, my teaching was stagnant, my children were growing away, and so was the life I had built. Courage was the shelter from this storm, and Parker J. Palmer, who created the program, and the Fetzer Institute, which funded it, were the parents with the warm towels and hot soup. From Thursday dinner through Sunday lunch, four times a year for two years, I relaxed... just relaxed, ate good food, participated in Circle, listened, talked, laughed, cried, and hung out with educators from every level from all across the nation.

I read books that celebrated teachers and teaching. I discussed the shadows of No Child Left Behind legislation and its negative effects on the children who would be left behind. I reexamined many things about my life and teaching and tried, for the first time in a very long time, to find the connection between the two. I spoke of and lamented my waning zeal for teaching and a deep longing for being in deep confidentiality with those who mirrored my inability to explain the depth and beauty of Courage.

When Courage was new and I was new in Courage, it was difficult to explain the premise to my friends and colleagues, who often thought I had gone on a religious retreat. I could not put into words the power of daring to decide to live an undivided life, to let the spirit inside guide the being outside. For most of my life I have lived divided. I lived inside myself, checking everything that I let the world see.

When, at 12 years old, I integrated the schools in my hometown, I literally, almost, became two people, the inside me and the outside me. I watched myself be forced to navigate through that new and strange and loveless world, different from what was my familiar, as I searched for acceptance, desperate to show that my spirit was not better or worse, just molded differently. Watching one's self navigate through life as though someone else is living it is quite tiring, burdensome, and limiting. Choices are made with half the insight and commitment. Creativity is harnessed. Truth is gray.

Emily Dickinson tells me, "Tell all the truth but tell it slant." Courage gave me the chance to explore my truth, put it out in the open, hold it in my hand like a small bird; not too tight, but not too hollow. I could study on it or let it waft through the voices of the group and the beat of my heart. Examining my truth helped me to begin to think that I would one day live an undivided life. I knew that my inner survival depended on voicing that choice.

Courage has given me permission to take my time, make arrangements for the journey. This has been so important because I continue to live divided in areas of my life. I struggle with living other people's idea of what my truth should be, which accounts for my deep sorrow and commitments half-done. For this reason I continue to accept any invitation I can to sit in a Circle of Trust, to spend time in a Courage retreat. The welcome I enjoy is continuous, unbroken like the Mobius strip.

Between Circles, I struggle with division in my work. My Courage work has enabled me to continue the journey for nearly twenty years. From the beginning, I have been conflicted about how the work I had experienced in Courage could be replicated in my classroom, in public education. Early on, I took what I enjoyed about the Circle of Trust to my students. Trained to be the center of instruction, I found facilitating to be off-putting, but worth the effort. My students appreciated the experience of the unbroken circle where I was sharing what I loved, who I was, with them, building community and trust. We were learning without boundaries.

Though I was alone at my school and Courage was new, I liked the way I felt in my classroom, even though I could not quite put into words that skills and strategies were second to helping students and teachers find, and embrace, their spirits and their truths. My principals had signed off on professional days and substitutes for my absences, and they were expecting in return more than feel-good words and activities for teachers and students. In the wake of standards, I didn't feel Courage had a chance. When the restraints of No Child blanketed the system, Courage retreats gave me hope that we, the educators from every level in the public system, could infuse, infiltrate, inundate the principles of teaching from the spirit of our beings and make a difference.

I want to be a change agent. However, I continue to live divided, and I continue to return to the Courage Community through the years because it helps me deal with the frustration I experience about my divided existence with my students. I know that I am not doing what I think is best for them. My truth is that I continue to espouse my convictions, but I bow to the pressures to perform on the tests by any means necessary. The beauty that I love is not what I do. Among the Courage Community there is no judgment, no fixing, just holding me in the Light.

Life just reiterates that there are no quick fixes. I have been on this quest for over twenty years, and I have been held as I have made some hard and necessary choices to experience and grow toward an undivided life. Having now moved through one major divide in my being, I continue to return to the Courage Circle for support and to bask in the presence of lives lived undivided, as I continue on the journey.

Wanda Smith Freeman teaches English and language arts at Forestbrook Middle School in Myrtle Beach, South Carolina. The Coastal Writing Project and the Courage to Teach have been important stepping stones on her teaching journey – and in helping her remember her passion as a writer.

BOUNDARY MARKERS for our Writers Circle of Trust

To Create a Circle of Trust with Clear Boundaries for Safety and Hospitality

"every circle of trust, regardless of size, requires that everyone in it help hold safe space..."
--Parker J. Palmer

1. Be here. Be as present as possible.
2. Extend welcome and receive welcome.
3. Invitation only. It's never demand... Never share or die!
4. Write your Truth, your Story of letting the Beauty you love be what you do, in ways that respect the Truths of others. No fixing!

> *Tell all the Truth but tell it slant—*
> *Success in Circuit lies...*
> --Emily Dickinson

5. When it's hard, turn to wonder.
6. See others – and especially yourself -- with "soft eyes." Allow your "soft eyes" to come through your words.
7. Welcome silence.
8. Let the Beauty you love be what you do.

> *Today, like every other day, we wake up empty and frightened. Don't open the door to the study and begin reading. Take down a musical instrument. Let the beauty we love be what we do. There are hundreds of ways to kneel and kiss the ground.*
>
> --Rumi

9. Protect confidentiality; honor the idea of deep and double confidentiality.
10. Believe that it's possible to emerge from this work with more energy, more openness, with grace, with "soft eyes," with going public with our stories in ways that open space for our own and others' hearts to break open into greater capacity and healing.

> --Adapted by Sally Z. Hare for the Writers Circle of Trust from various versions of Courage & Renewal touchstones and boundary markers, with gratitude to Judy Brown for her original Touchstones

Swimming with Courage: Re-Claiming My Underground River

By Jean M. Richardson

There is a quiet courage that comes from an inward spring of confidence in the meaning and significance of life. Such courage is an underground river.

---Howard Thurman

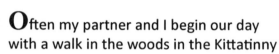

Often my partner and I begin our day with a walk in the woods in the Kittatinny Mountains of Pennsylvania. Known as the endless mountains, this ridge is believed to be the place where the world first crested some 285 million years ago. We walk the well-worn paths with our dogs in all the seasons of the year. We are blessed to observe the landscape move into rest as the sun wanes come fall, and to witness the rebirth of the forest as the sun lingers longer over the horizon come spring.

Many mornings we find ourselves walking the same path, because we enjoy crossing over a footbridge that spans a small creek bed. We have learned not to always expect water, knowing that the flow of water can vary greatly from a roaring stream to a dry bed, depending on the day or season. Over time, I have come to honor that the presence of rain or sun is not always a predictor of the water flow. In all my explorations of the woods, I have never found the source where the water rises to the surface. Like courage that flows from an inward spring of confidence, the source of water that nourishes the forest floor comes from an underground river deep within the earth.

When I was young and naive, I knew such confidence and, in turn, such courage. I was reared in a family where courage was a value. We were taught to think education was important and service to the community an expectation. The youngest child and only daughter, I listened well to the lessons that my father carefully taught to my older brothers. My father was full of courageous stories that came from his adventures as a young man on a two-year expedition to the South Pole in 1939. His adventures were told and re-told around our dinner table as dishes were taken to the kitchen. Courage was also taught by my mother, who rarely backed down from a challenge and was determined not to pass small-mindedness on to her children. She engaged in daily acts of kindness to others, even when they raised the eyebrows of our neighbors. And while I am not sure my hometown church ever planned on teaching me to stand up and question, it was hard not to take into my heart the Calvinist hymns while singing, *Once to every man and nation, comes a moment to decide.* From my youth, I was taught that Christian words were meaningless unless they were paired with action. With all of this said, the courage I was taught was lived out in a small conservative town, and while it took me awhile to recognize, was to be exercised differently for sons and daughters.

I was reared in a small river town northwest of Pittsburgh, and in my early years, was insulated from the outside world. Even though we were surrounded by steel stacks and mining, union strikes were seen as manipulations of big labor, and I remember many cars in my hometown displaying Barry Goldwater for President bumper stickers. But the times they are a-changin', as Dylan wailed, and each evening our small black-and-white TV told of a very different world outside of our river valley. How I remember watching Joan Baez sing at The March on Washington and bemoaning the fact I was too young to live in either Berkeley or Washington, D.C.

During my early years, the country was in turmoil, reeling from the assassinations of John and Robert Kennedy, Malcolm X, and Martin Luther King. In 1968, I followed the trial in Pennsylvania of two Catholic priests, Dan and Phil Berrigan, and seven others known to the world as the Catonsville Nine, charged with breaking into the office of the Selective Service and burning draft files with napalm. Months later I remember sitting with my mother as she listened to the numbers of the draft lottery being read, knowing all too well her two oldest sons' lives were at risk for a war no one understood.

During high school, my guitar playing began to transform from purely Christian Young Life music to protest songs and songs of the union. I learned of The Weavers and started following the likes of Phil Ochs, Judy Collins, Joan Baez, Woody Guthrie and Pete Seeger. For me, there was no conflict carrying a *Good News Bible* along with Pete Seeger's autobiography, *The Incomplete Folksinger,* through the halls of my small-town school.

WHITE GIRL FROM THE NORTH

When most kids my age were talking of boyfriends and summer tans, I traveled to the South with the blessings of our church during the summers of my high school years to work with migrant farm workers in the Bootheel of Missouri. As a white girl from the North, I learned of a history of struggle and social apartheid that I never knew existed in my own country. Over the course of three summers my life down river from my family home was transformed, thanks to the patience, generosity, and hospitality of the women of Haiti Heights and the work of a small community-organizing effort called the Missouri Delta Ecumenical Ministry.

Looking back, I realize now it was a true act of courage for the women of that community to welcome a white girl in her teens into a segregated rural black community in the South. As

112

a teenager, I never really understood why, in the early morning hours when walking down the dirt road to the day care center, I heard doors gently close when I came by. In my ignorance, mixed with a bit of homesickness, I thought perhaps I was not welcomed in their homes. It was so far from the truth. As an adult, I now recognize that it was an act of kindness to be carefully watched as I walked by, each woman in kindness taking time from her busy mornings to assure this stranger safe passage as she walked down their road. The women of the South offered me true hospitality, caring for me in a way they could only dream that someday others would care for their daughters.

My work in the South planted deep seeds within my soul. At the time I did not know I was walking in history as I sat and sipped sweet tea with Fannie Lou Hamer in her home in Mississippi and shook hands at a local rally with Cesar Chavez, the leader of the United Farm Workers Union. And when by chance I waded in the same water at a public fountain with Mary Travers of Peter, Paul, and Mary, I knew I was being baptized, truly born again into a different world of ideas and convictions.

My world exploded when one of my brothers was drafted, and, in a matter of months, went from graduate school in Wisconsin to the rice paddies of Vietnam. Without cell phones or the benefits of e-mail, Walter Cronkite and the CBS news had a regular place at our evening meal around the kitchen table.

Social activities of pep rallies, parties and football games made little sense to me as I found my way to having conversations regarding the social turmoil of the day with the assistant minister of our small town church. Ben was the first adult who spoke truthfully to me and answered my questions as honestly as he could. He treated me with respect, as if I had a brain in my head. It was then I heard "the call" to ministry. While it was still rare for a woman to become an ordained minister, the first wave had gone through, and it seemed safe enough for the second wave to step into the same denominational waters.

Believing in justice and the values I had been taught through the church, I was blind to the fact that the senior pastor of my hometown church was finally paying the price for his participation in the March on Washington and sermons on Vietnam. His colleague, my mentor, had also been asked to leave our congregation because of his great sin of requesting a divorce from his wife. He left in the dark of night, never saying goodbye to anyone in the congregation, including me.

Majoring in social work, college came and went, pretty much a blur for my eyes were set on going to seminary and changing the world. In my junior year, I met the man of my dreams, a good Irish Catholic who loved poetry, followed Dorothy Day, and went to medical school, because he too believed in working with the poor. One night, he asked me to join him in the Commons where a feminist singer was having a concert. I obligingly went, even though at the time I had no idea how a feminist folksinger might relate to me. She sang a song entitled, "Sometimes I Wish," and the chorus went like this: *Sometimes I wish my eyes had never been open, sometimes I wish I could no longer see, all of the pain and all of the longing of my sisters and me as we try to be free.* After the concert he asked me what I thought of her music and I said, I thought it was fine. While I had experienced the divisions of race, to that point I had never allowed myself to believe that opportunities ahead for me as a woman just might be different than for my brothers. Patrick did much to open my eyes and lead me down a road I was not prepared to walk.

Our first and last overnight date was to Provincetown, Massachusetts, known to everyone but me as a true social sanctuary for the GLBT community of that time. As Patrick and I rode over on the ferry from Boston, my world turned technicolor and I literally thought I was going crazy. Men were wearing tee shirts proclaiming "Squeeze a fruit for Anita Bryant," and when the women removed their over shirts, they revealed blazing tattoos. Not only were my eyes beginning to open, they saw clearly for the first time as Patrick, forever a good Catholic, signed us into the bed and breakfast as "Mr. and Mrs." When finally my eyes did open, I knew the path he hoped we would walk was not the one I would come to claim in the days and years to follow.

DEEP DIVISION

The division in my life was deep and vast, not dissimilar to the split of the Grand Canyon. I had dreams of seminary, of being the youngest moderator in the Presbyterian Church, and working for the national division in New York City. Now with eyes open and a broken heart, I had to deal with the fact that I was a lesbian. Having heard the rhetoric of hate both in and out of the church walls, having witnessed the agony of my parents when I came out to them, I dove back into the closet. Fear of rejection dried my riverbed of courage. Little did I know at the time, it would take decades for me to reclaim my courage and cross the division of my own Red Sea.

I decided to move to the western edge of the continent and drive as far as Interstate 80 would take me without driving off a cliff. I arrived at San Francisco Theological Seminary in the fall of 1978; within a few weeks, Harvey Milk and Mayor Moscone were murdered in City Hall, and the tragic events of People's Temple, headquartered in San Francisco, took place. I was not in Kansas and I certainly was not in Pennsylvania anymore.

I had two driving questions all through seminary. The first was theological: if we followed this man called Jesus, how could we not read Scripture through the lens of justice and work for radical change in our world? The second was far more personal, an ethical one: how could I, a lesbian, at the end of the road in seminary ever stand up before a Presbytery and truthfully answer the ordination question that made me lie about who I was at the core of my being? Like a juggler at a circus, I survived seminary, and I managed to balance all the balls with highest honors, become ordained, and at the end of the road, even employed.

It all seemed to be working. Stay in the closet, work hard and cover all the bases, including always hiding my personal life. For years I never talked with my parents about my partner; I went home by myself on all holidays, and as far as anyone knew, I was single. Professionally, I was seen as a rising star and was rewarded for long hours and late nights. I found a passion for working with the homeless and runaway youth of San Francisco, not ever making the connection that I, too, was a runaway in my life. I learned to ignore the rashes that periodically broke out all over my body and chalked them up to allergies. While some in my congregation might have suspected I was gay, we all simply held a deafening silence that was deadly.

For a while, life got a bit easier, and I knew I was more at home in my second congregation, when on my first Sunday, they threw pink balloons over the balcony and proudly proclaimed, "It's a girl." Having endured some very tough times at my first call, the deep acceptance of this congregation truly loved me back into ministry. The problem remained, however, that all the love and acceptance from others could not heal the pain that was deep within, caused by the fact that I truly did not love or accept myself. For far too many years, more than I would ever like to recount, I carried deep grief relating to disappointing my parents and living a lie to the larger church. My own river of worth was a dried aquifer and no matter how many buckets of water got poured in from the outside, my own riverbed remained dry. Not speaking the truth, standing silent when words were called for, living in daily fear of losing my job, ate away at my soul and created a poison soil in my being where courage could no longer grow. I felt abandoned by my parents and the church that taught me the values of acceptance and justice.

As a pastor, I lived in San Francisco from the beginning of the AIDS crisis to founding of the "cocktail." Serving a welcoming congregation, we were often called to sit with parents and loved ones who had "no idea" about the lives of their sons and brothers in my second congregation. The sad truth was, that while I found the courage to fight and speak on behalf of others in pain, I did not have the courage to fully live life undividedly. I never came out with my brothers and sisters who walked that early walk. No one but me felt the brokenness in my life, nor did anyone know or guess the cost I was paying for the division in my soul.

It was toward the end of my second pastorate, when I was in deep emotional pain that I decided to take a few days off from work and attend the spring Earl Lecture series at The Pacific School of Religion. The year was 1992 and the keynote was to be delivered by Parker Palmer. He was unknown to me. I had never been asked to read, decipher or critique any of his work throughout all my years at the masters or doctorate level of seminary. I listened well that evening, and by the end of the night, I said to myself that this was most honest and true lecture I had ever heard. Besides bringing down the house with his famous story about being asked to be a seminary president, Parker Palmer spoke openly and honestly of his depression and of the man who ministered to him in his depression, not by shoring him up with praise or quoting Scripture, but rather by keeping silence and rubbing his feet.

A SEED WAS PLANTED

I wish I could say that my life was forever changed in that moment and that the light of the spirit moved me instantly to a place of wholeness and clarity. That would be a lie. However, a seed was planted that night, and that seed offered me a lifeline and a promise. It was not only possible but also truly necessary to find the courage again in my life to speak truth in public spaces and to myself.

There are times in all our lives when our wells run so dry that if we are going to live, we need to dig to a deeper place within. In these moments we are left with a choice to live with courage, or not live at all. It took sitting in silence by the bedside of my mother six years later, caring for her in the room I grew up in, that broke my heart open. My mother, Sara, died in February, the month of the year she hated the most, days after I returned from Siberia with my newly-adopted son. Even though my mother had been sick all fall, she encouraged me to continue my quest to adopt a second son and valiantly held onto her life until my return from halfway around the world. After flying a straight 26 hours with my newly adopted 14-month-old son, my father greeted me with the news that my mother had slipped into a coma that morning. However, my mother, the strong courageous Scot, was to have the last word. I had not even hung up my coat when I heard from my room, "Jeannie, is that you and do you have the baby?" I laid my infant son Peter on her stomach. She greeted him by saying, "He's beautiful." Twenty-four hours later, my mother slipped into a coma for the last time. The woman who wore herself out caring, who set her feelings and dreams aside for years to care for my ailing father; who would say on the phone to me almost before she would say hello, "What can I do for you today?"; the woman who was my biggest cheerleader, even though she often did not understand "my choices," was gone.

The loss of my mother shattered my heart into pieces. In my brokenness and pain I made personal choices out of deep grief, including a series of decisions that not only separated me further from myself, but made the hard situation in my life much worse. For years, I had been rewarded for focusing outside myself in an effort to try and fix people, organizations and situations far beyond my control or responsibility. After my mother's death I honed this skill to a fine art and ramped up every effort to focus outwardly, avoiding at every turn the signs of a growing inward tsunami.

After having lived in the West for over 25 years, I found my way back to Pennsylvania. I returned to be the director of Kirkridge Retreat and Study Center, a place well known for having a wide-open welcome to GLBTQ individuals and for its commitment to peace and justice. After years of trying to find my way in the Presbyterian Church USA, I finally found home in a small retreat center with roots to the Iona Community of Scotland. It was during the first months of my arrival, still cleaning out drawers and going through piles left by my predecessor that I came across a letter sent by Rick Jackson, the co-director of the Center for Courage & Renewal, inviting the previous director of Kirkridge to consider attending a "Courage Circle." I carefully read the letter, picked up the phone, and called Rick. In my mailbox before the end of the week was an invitation to apply for the first clergy Courage Circle.

My slow walk toward wholeness began with the first Circle. I remember crying alone in my room at Fetzer Institute before the opening reception. Safe places in the church are rare for a lesbian person, and for the next few days I was going to be surrounded by clergy. Many gay and lesbian people had been betrayed by their straight colleagues, and I was no different. Far too often clergy colleagues had proclaimed that the ground of confidentiality was safe to walk. I, like many GLBTQ persons, had slipped on the soft ground of broken confidentiality and experienced the shameful splattering of mud on my face. It took courage to walk into my first Circle, courage that came from the seed planted by Parker Palmer so many years before in Berkeley.

Feminist theologian Carter Heyward, one of the very first out lesbians to be ordained by the Episcopal Church, writes of faith this way, "Faith is not knowing where you shall land, but believing you shall land." I had no idea where I would land when I finally dared to come out onto the balcony of my own life. Truth be told, I had just enough faith to believe that in this place there would be solid enough ground that I could finally begin to speak truth in a public space and truth to myself. That afternoon, I chose to follow the ancient adage found in the Old Testament Scripture of Deuteronomy, "...therefore, I set before you life and death, choose life." That day I was in such pain I had no choice but to choose life and seek the truth that was, for the first time, "beyond my fear."

A HIDDEN WHOLENESS

No one offered me a "seven steps to success" manual or a "Google map" to personal wholeness; not on that day, or in any subsequent Circle experience. Instead, I was offered the gift without judgment from the outside to hear my own voice; I learned to follow, for the first time, my own roadmap. I found each time in a Circle that I was on a life raft with other survivors committed to learning new skills of welcoming silence, honoring the holy and absolute confidentiality, and listening deeply to all of our stories, including my own. From our common boat, over and over we practiced rowing together toward Thomas Merton's belief that "there is in all things ... a hidden wholeness."

It took time, but finally I started to drift into believing that "all things" included me. My wounds and patterns began to heal as I began to trust that my inner voice indeed had something to say, if only I would take the time to listen. Equally important, as I began to believe in the trust-worthiness of my companions, I realized that in each Circle I could risk speaking the truth both publicly and to myself. Slowly I came to believe that I was no longer on this journey alone. I had found trustworthy companions who, by their presence, offered the gift of life to one another.

For the last few years I have been actively working to integrate the work of Courage and Renewal in my workplace, and I use the principles and practices to guide my life as the director of this small retreat center. Kirkridge Retreat and Study Center for years has danced on the Mobius strip between being an organization and a social and spiritual movement. Over the years Kirkridge has hosted such speakers as Virginia Ramey Mollenkott, William Stringfellow, Dorothy Day, Parker Palmer, Dorothee Soelle, and Archbishop Desmond Tutu. Phil and Dan Berrigan of the Catonsville Nine, the priests whose trial I had followed so many years before, found home on these very mountains where I work. At Kirkridge, as with Courage work, we deeply believe that one's inner spiritual journey informs and enables our outer work for justice.

> Kirkridge is one of those rare, and increasingly,
> indispensable places where the struggle for
> justice and a heart can be cultivated together,
> as they must be for either to endure.

> --- Carter Heyward,
> *Go Tell It on the Mountain*

It took me decades to move deeply into my center, to honor the wisdom of my inner voice and regain the courage I once had in my youth. Like others I walk with now, I believe the Mobius strip of life calls us with each breath we take to continue to go deeper on our journey in relationship to ourselves, others and the wider world. In this moment of my life, I live as undivided as I have ever known.

While I admit I am frightened to put this all down on paper, I am also honored. The challenge into which Sally Z. Hare and Megan LeBoutillier invited us has been daunting and a true gift. Like every Circle, this Writers Circle of Trust has taken me on a journey that has provided personal insight and clarity on my present path.

I live life differently these days. Each morning I begin my day with my partner Pat, who is now my wife. We read poetry, write and walk. Together we live in a household of three young adults, ranging in age from 17 to 23, and two Labrador pups. One of our sons is autistic, and the others face the normal challenges of finding their footing in the world. We are different parents these days as we have learned to honor silence, let some pieces lie, and try as best we can to ask open and honest questions.

Blessed with a loving relationship and a workplace that affirms the deep values of my life, I have found new energy and creativity for my work. I am daring in new ways to push my work at Kirkridge in vast new directions that call me to draw once again on my inward stream of courage, so long forgotten in my life.

With my colleague Jean Haley, another Courage facilitator, I have begun to take "courage work" to new places. We have hosted retreat circles for young adults living with autism, along with those who love them. This work has pushed me to new edges and allowed me to deeply affirm the true courage of my son who lives with autism. Out of the retreat a local grass roots organization named TIP, Together It's Possible, was born. Through my work in Courage circles I have moved from the pain of isolation to truly believing that we are all in this together. In addition, along with a supportive and courageous Kirkridge

Board, we are dreaming our way into launching a democratic school for children. Moving against the tide of testing and state mandates, this school promises to honor the creativity and nurture the souls of all children.

We live in a world that values the rights of individuals and places those rights above those of the whole community, as if it were either/or. Just recently I was sitting with a professional person talking about my son Alek. She said to me, with all good intent, "Jean, you need to separate what is going on for Alek and what you see as systemic problems with the system." I fudged for a moment, and simply said, "I cannot... They are one and the same. The challenges I face as a parent are faced by other parents, and the grief I face is the grief they face." We are all in this together. We are one body, and as it says in the New Testament books of Corinthians, "When one member suffers, we all suffer ...when one member rejoices we all rejoice."

In 1976 I was gifted with a book entitled *Tears of Silence* by Jean Vanier, with this inscription: "I am giving you this gift because you will understand it." Truth be told, the book now has ragged edges and post-its on many of its pages. It has taken me years to appreciate and even more to understand the depth of Vanier's message contained in this small book:

> an encounter
>   is a strange
>   and wonderful thing
> presence
> one person to another
> present
> one to another
>   life flowing
>   one to another...

---Jean Vanier, *Tears of Silence*

As the founder of the worldwide L'Arche Communities, Vanier speaks directly to me with special meaning as the parent of both my sons. Each day with Alek I try to learn again about being and patience. I try hard to let go of my Calvinist ethic of doing and enter into a world very different than my own. With Peter, I long for him to know and love a wide and broad world that values and affirms difference. I want to affirm for him much earlier than I was able to for myself that he is worthy of love because of who he is, not what he does or accomplishes.

Courage work and its principles and practices have changed the core of my life. In this work, I have come home to myself in ways I never dreamed possible. Over the recent years, I have formed around me a tenacious community of support, individuals who know my true name and support my emotional well-being. Like the women of the South so long ago, women and men of Courage circles now watch me from their own doors and have become my new cheerleaders as I walk down my own dusty path. They are the ones who have encouraged me to drink deeply from my own inner spring and swim with courage as I reclaim the mysteries of my underground river.

Since 2005, Rev. Jean Richardson, D. Min., has served as the director of Kirkridge Retreat Center in Bangor, Pennsylvania. Prior to her move, Jean spent 10 years on the staff of Ghost Ranch, a national conference center of the Presbyterian Church U.S.A. located in New Mexico. A Presbyterian minister, she has worked in a variety of professional capacities in retreat settings for the past 18 years. A national facilitator of the Center for Courage & Renewal, she has led over 30 Courage and Renewal programs. Earlier in her career, Jean served as a community organizer, urban pastor, consultant and adjunct faculty member with San Francisco Theological Seminary.

Stepping Forward into Hope: Reconnecting Soul and Role

By Marcie Ellerbe

Whenever you take a step forward, you are bound to disturb something.

---Gandhi

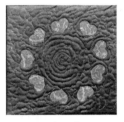 The way the wind blew through the screened-in porch of our lake house was magical. The porch was the perfect place for my little-girl self to play school. I could take my school papers, place them against the screen, and they would stay perfectly attentive as I taught class.

Back in my bedroom, I had the smartest collection of stuffed animals you could imagine. They hung on every word I read, each one sitting upright against my bedroom wall, eager to respond to any question I asked. My playtime was filled with one thing: teaching. From a very early age, there was never any doubt about what I wanted to do when I grew up.

I remember my first day of teaching in my own classroom as if it were yesterday. I was twenty-one years old and feeling as if I had achieved my life goal. I stood at the door on the Tiger Hall and greeted each of my sixth-grade students with a smile, knowing that a lifetime of imaginative play was now a reality. But as the tardy bell rang and I closed the door and stepped forward to the front of the classroom, I remember my insides beginning to panic. I had my plans for the day and the week written neatly in the boxes in my lesson plan book. I knew the long-term grade level standards and the expectations for the end-of-the-year test. On paper, I looked like I knew what I was doing, but I realized that the faces that looked back at me had been students for over 1,000 days, and I was now just a few minutes into day one of teaching-on-my-own. The students were so much more experienced than I. I may have had some smart teddy bears, but now I wondered what I really knew about how to help these children become better readers and writers.

GOOD AT TEACHING

Turns out, I was good at teaching. My students performed well and seemed to enjoy our class. I was honored as Teacher of the Year at every school in which I taught. Yes, I was good at teaching, but that did not stop me from continually questioning the system and myself. I was always the one asking questions like, "Why should we have our students do this?"; "Is there a more efficient way of accomplishing our goals?"; and "How can we help each student feel successful?" Questioning authority can create tension, but I was blessed to have principals, colleagues, and mentors who recognized my constant inquiry as a sign of someone who wanted to better understand her work. My family, friends, colleagues, and mentors never stopped encouraging my questions; they continually nudged me to step forward and seek opportunities to learn and grow, regardless of where this led. Because I knew strong people were standing behind me, stepping forward was never difficult.

After eight years of classroom teaching (four as a middle-school special-education teacher and four in a regular fourth grade), I stepped forward into the position of curriculum specialist in an elementary school. I loved this expanded opportunity to support the work of my colleagues as a site-based professional development provider. I served as a curriculum specialist for three years before accepting work as a teacher-on-loan from my school district to provide consulting for schools across South Carolina. Then, after twelve years in the safety of my school and district, I stepped forward again to begin full-time work on my doctoral degree in literacy education at the University of

South Carolina. I was thirty-three and felt like I had entered a new chapter of my life.

For the next six years, I lived a hurried life with more to do in each day and week than seemed possible. I was commuting halfway across the state while teaching courses for the university, continuing to provide independent consulting, and taking classes. Life was busy during this time, with a never-ending stream of books to read, papers to write, classes to plan, papers to grade, schools to contact, presentations to prepare, research to do, classes to attend, miles to drive, and family gatherings to miss. But I settled into the busyness of it because achieving the degree meant fulfilling the goal.

Amid the franticness of life, my husband frequently asked, "What are you going to do when you finish your degree?" My response remained steady for those six years: "Whatever I want to do." I always mustered my most-confident-of-voices when I said this, but in reality, his repeated nudging brought forth the same panicked feeling I had on that first day of teaching. The realization hit me that I had stepped forward with absolutely no idea of where I would land. The end of my doctoral journey jolted me into looking within, both personally and professionally. It was a time of intense and somewhat unexpected emotional reflection. Facing the challenge of **what** I would do next had me questioning **who** I had become. The possibilities this milestone brought were inspiring, challenging, and frightening. I had been in the field of education for nineteen years, and for the first time in my career, I was unsure of my path. I worked so hard to get "here," only to realize that I was not sure where I was.

NOTHING NEXT ON MY LIST

I felt like a runaway returning home. I had been away from my school district for a long time, and even though I had returned home to work fulltime on writing my dissertation, I was lonely and isolated from any colleagues. I was scared that I would not be able to find my place within my local professional community again. Uneasy about my future, I opened up to some of my closest friends and explained that I was in a career-void. One by one, my friends told me that I needed to give it time and trust that what I needed would come. That was not a comfortable thought to embrace for this goal-oriented person whose entire life had been driven by living a plan: set a goal, work toward the goal, and check it off the list. Suddenly, there was nothing next on my list, and I wondered what I had done.

I panicked as the sudden halt to my forward momentum brought forth an unwelcome disturbance – the time to stop and look around. Stepping forward was comfortable and familiar, but looking around was something I did not know how to do. Then, as if a higher power had answered my prayers, a convergence of opportunities presented themselves, and once again, I stepped forward. A position was offered at a local university, and I accepted and began a new chapter in my teaching career, in the world of higher education. My advisor cautioned me that teaching full-time while completing my dissertation would be difficult, but not being one to back down from impossible feats, I was confident I could fulfill all my responsibilities. I knew life would once again be busy, but busy was something I knew. Not to mention, I was finally able to give a firm answer to the question of "What next?"!

The academic year started, and I quickly settled into an all-too-familiar routine: plan, teach, grade, write. Just when I felt things were a little Energizer-bunny-esque, a colleague informed me that applications were being invited for a South Carolina TeacherLeader Circle of Trust. The opportunity to be involved in The Courage to Teach work had been a career-long dream, and I immediately submitted my application. A few weeks later, I was accepted into this year-long retreat series, and was immediately grateful for the chance to become a member of a professional community as I continued to learn how to be a full-time instructor and dissertation writer. I was thirty-nine and feeling like my life was once again on track.

LIFE INTERFERES

Two months into the school year, my mother-in-law, Mimi, was diagnosed with asymptomatic colon cancer, and unexpectedly a new item was added to my checklist – Life. My husband and I had begun dating when I was eighteen, so Mimi had been a huge part of my life for twenty-one years. I had grown up with her. Sometimes I just went to spend the night with her in the same way I did with my girlfriends when I was in elementary school. She and I would send Opa to bed after dinner and stay up long into the early morning, talking about life. So often we hear horror stories of "monsters-in-law," but I always felt blessed to have such a special bond with my mother-in-law. Mimi's diagnosis was delivered on a cool Tuesday evening in early October 2011. Just the weekend before, my husband and I had taken her to Charleston to celebrate our niece's 21st birthday. We had a wonderful time, eating fresh seafood and walking through the historic market. We returned home to Myrtle Beach on Sunday with no mention of Mimi feeling poorly. In fact, aside from the occasional sinus infection, Mimi had never really been sick in all the years I had known her. She raised seven children (four sons and three grandchildren), and I guess there was just no time to be sick. So when my brother-in-law called to tell us that Mimi wanted us to take her to the hospital, we knew something was wrong. The diagnosis came just a few hours later in the hospital emergency room. Cancer. Mimi never walked again. Her passing was quick. We went from diagnosis to final goodbyes in just under six short weeks. She asked her family to provide care for her final days in her home, and we did.

Similarly to welcoming a new life into the world, there is much to do when you know you are supporting someone's exit from the world. Mimi's last six weeks were busy with doctors and checklists and medication and phone calls and appointments and visitors all squeezed in between teaching and planning and grading and writing. As she and I spent our final days and hours together, I realized I had lived such a hurried life I had never made time to get to the list of things Mimi and I wanted to do together. The morning she slipped away from us, I held her hand and mentally read over our to-do list: let Mimi teach me to sew, take an art class together, go through family pictures and make albums, write a family history book together. On and on I read, slowly making my way to the bottom. The list was long, and nothing was checked off, because each item was always waiting on, "When Marcie finishes ____, we will ____."

Never before had I been faced with the harsh reality that time was so limited and precious. Weeks became months of adjusting to life without Mimi. I found myself continually comparing the items on my "When I finish ____, I will ____" list with those items on my "I've accomplished___" list, and realized I rarely checked off items on my list not related to work. It seemed Mimi's final lesson for me was that having a checklist was a good thing, but that perhaps there was a better way for me to balance what I devoted my limited life energy to and what got checked off my list.

NAMING TENSION

After Mimi's passing, I craved my time in the Circle of Trust retreats because the weekend retreats provided me the opportunity to be with myself and my thoughts. Invited to a place of inward reflection, I began to understand the ways in which I was living a divided life. I saw work and life as separate entities, and I compartmentalized a different self within each. My work-self was a domineering bully, shoving life out of the way without hesitation or thought to sharing space and time. My life-self was meek and timid, afraid to stand up to work and tell it to back off a little bit.

This realization flung me into a place of both personal and professional tension that left me questioning if I knew myself at all. How could I be so intimate with my work-self yet treat my life-self as a distant acquaintance? The coming together of beginning a new career, realizing how precious and brief our time on earth can be, and listening more deeply to my soul allowed me to hear myself and those around me more clearly.

I heard myself telling of fears about beginning a new and pressure-filled chapter of my career and wondering if I would be successful. I heard family members saying they wished I were in touch more, and that they wanted to be involved in my life and work. I heard my students saying they felt their preservice education program was so busy and crowded they questioned if they even wanted to become teachers. Repeatedly the voices spoke, until all I heard was a need for more undividedness in my life.

As I defined for myself what undividedness means, I craved space to hear what my heart was trying to tell me. In the first seventeen years of my career, I never doubted that the work in which I was engaged was what I meant to do. Now, my heart felt unsettled. I had always been passionate about teaching and learning, and started my work in higher education excited about the opportunity to influence education by working with preservice teachers. However, the demands of higher education left me more out of balance than ever. I heard myself constantly telling my students that participation in life was essential to learning, but I had no time to practice this same advice.

My heart was telling me I needed to be present in life, reminding me there was more to life than just work. Yet week after week, I rarely even accomplished the demands of work, let alone found time to partake in the invitations of life. Attention to living a less-divided life led me to a crossroads where I was forced to stop and re-envision my identity. I wanted to be more intentional as I named what it meant for me to be a professor, a researcher, a wife, a daughter, a sister, an aunt. I wanted to reconnect soul and role.

At first, I wanted to believe that just working fewer hours in a day would help me feel more balanced. After all, eight hours of work per day, plus eight hours of life per day, plus eight hours of sleep per day equals a balanced twenty-four hour day. I tried this for a while as if I were welcoming life, work, and sleep into my world like new friends. I tried lining them up against my bedroom wall like my old teddy bears and "playing" with each one when I wanted. I made plans with my new friends and wrote these plans in detail in the boxes in my planner. But, in reality, my plans never worked like they looked on paper. For one reason or another, I never seemed to be fully in control of my plans. I tried negotiating with my new friends by borrowing hours from sleep to give to work, and promising life I would make up our lost three hours next Saturday when it was supposed to rain. I spent so much time trying to force a literal balance of time into my day and week that I found myself growing angry with work, life, and sleep.

I was angry at work for being new and challenging and too time-consuming. I was angry at life because it liked to sit in the corner and taunt me, saying things like, "You're crazy for working as much as you do. What do you think the purpose of all that work is? One day, I'll be gone and you'll never be able to get me back." I was angry at sleep because it was never around enough.

Suddenly, I had to add time in my plan for revising my plans! I was working so hard to achieve balance that I could feel a state of discontent enveloping me. Like watching a storm front roll in, I could see discontent encroaching from every vantage point, and discontent did not foster creativity or productivity. Discontent simply made me want to quit. I knew I had to rethink my plan for seeking balance by reframing my relationship with my three "friends." Rather than finding balance, perhaps I needed to consider how my work-self and my life-self could inform one another. Where did life and work overlap? Why did they separate? I needed to name and notice which aspects of life and work gave me energy and were life-affirming, and which aspects of each evoked that cloud of discontent. I needed to give voice to these noticings by naming them and sharing them with those around me. I needed to nurture the parts of life and work that I named as most significant and to find ways to hold these most significant elements gently as I sought to embrace them in a way that was both/and, not either/or.

NEW DETERMINATION

Noticing, naming, and nurturing required conversations with myself and with others. I found that journaling gave me a quiet outlet to listen to my heart. My journal was nonjudgmental and welcomed all celebrations, hopes, and fears with care. Rereading my journal gave me the chance to hear myself into deeper understanding and appreciate the space that silence offered for listening to my inner voice.

> I want to create silence with and for others...
> This takes courage, but I believe courage
> thrives and exists in action. Therefore, it is
> not enough for me to sit back and wait on
> the world to change. I must accept my place
> in this community...a place of pondering,
> of listening, of wondering. What are we
> doing together that is for our children *and*
> ourselves? What does it mean to me, for me,
> to be an agent for change?
>
> --- Ellerbe, personal journal

Growing more familiar with myself, I sought conversations with friends and colleagues who could support the unsettledness of seeking balance... Friends who sought not to provide me with answers to that which was causing disturbance in my life, but who understood the power of listening and questioning... Friends who knew answers were likely not attainable and maybe not even desirable, who knew the power to name what was meaningful for my work-self and my life-self could only come from within.

133

Shifting my perspective on how I interacted with my work-self and my life-self created room for each self to breathe and space to name what I wanted. I realized I could not change the pressure and the demands of time that come with a tenure track position, but I could change how I responded, how I accepted the challenges. When I reframed my viewpoint from seeing work demands as life-zapping towards seeing those demands as opportunities to give back, I began to see the young people who entered my classroom as more than just students. I saw myself in them. I saw them as the future of teaching, as my hope for educational reform. And with my hope so-named came a determination to create meaningful work.

LIVING INTO HOPE

I see the art of teaching not as a pursuit to impart knowledge to students, but as a journey of sharing my true self with students in ways that create space for them to come to understand learning as a process of constructing and reconstructing understandings. In the *Heart of Higher Education,* Parker Palmer reminds us that we should not remove our true selves from those with whom we interact or that which we try to accomplish. Parker's words fill me with determination to know and name more intimately this "me" who has now been named to the role of professor. In much the same way that a pair of shoes a half size too small feel uncomfortable, I have trouble with this self, this role so-named. The word *professor* carries with it a connotation that stands in contrast to how I see myself. For me, *professor* conjures images of an expert and all-knowing being, of one who tells rather than one who listens and asks questions. I see myself as a questioner, a learner, an advocate for the professionalism of teachers. As a professor, I have choices to make, and the first of these seems to be a choice in how I will integrate my professor-role with my true self.

I see my role in higher education centered on igniting a spark that reminds the educators who are my students of their significance in growing our profession. As such, I know that only a small part of my work involves sharing pedagogical content. Perhaps the most important part of my work rests in providing time and space for individuals to discover themselves as learners, to reconnect with personal belief systems, to know their passion for our profession. In the face of high pressure, high stakes accountability and decreased budgets, this work is complex at best; at worst, it sometimes seems hopeless. Yet hope is alive in me.

I am passionate about creating an educational system in this country that is socially just, student-centered, and purpose-filled. To this end, I see higher education as an opportunity for me to impact educational reform, one teacher at a time. The face and landscape of our profession has changed dramatically since I entered the field in 1994. As I work with preservice and inservice teachers, I wonder how to create space for educators to grapple with the difficult task of naming for themselves the purposes of education and then considering pedagogy that best supports those purposes. Through this lens, the questions I am living are. What Is the work of higher education in preparing preservice teachers to enter the field as activists and agents of change? How can I nurture preservice teachers into their role as professional educators? What is my role as a professor in creating professional communities of practice between preservice and inservice teachers? How does my work connect to living a full life?

At the time of this writing, I am in my second year of work as an assistant professor and still wondering where living into these questions will take me. I am forty-one and working hard to listen to my life, as Parker Palmer suggests in *Let your Life Speak*:

Before you tell your life what you intend to do with it, listen for what it intends to do with you. Before you tell your life what truths and values you have decided to live up to, let your life tell you what truths you embody, what values you represent.

My journey towards a less divided life has not yet been achieved. Perhaps it never will be. But my determination to live into these questions fills me with hope... Hope that my work will be meaningful... Hope that my life will be lived well... Hope that I can find ways to merge work as life and life as work.

I am not sure where hope will lead, but the promise of hope is life-sustaining. At the moment, hope stands in front of me as vast and mysterious as the universe. Stepping forward into that vastness is not easy because I have come to understand how intentional I want to be as I step forward into a less divided life. Mimi's death helped me understand how fleeting and precious time is; although I still believe I can do whatever I want with this life, I am now trying to create space for my life to tell me what it wants. I accept that each step forward brings with it disturbance. But now I embrace disturbance as a welcome sign that I *am* stepping forward. I am a force in motion, creating the life I want to live, letting the Beauty I love be what I do, stepping forward into hope.

 Marcie Ellerbe is an assistant professor of Literacy Education in the Spadoni College of Education at Coastal Carolina University. She is a lifelong resident of South Carolina, and a proud product of South Carolina Public Schools. Marcie lives with her husband, Bob, and their two feline furry friends, Decker and Tanner, in Myrtle Beach, SC. She can be reached at mlknox@coastal.edu.

The Light Over My Shoulder

By Anna Marie Robinson

What is essential is invisible to the eye.
--Antoine de Saint-Exupéry, *The Little Prince*

In a magnificent sacred place on Pawleys Island, South Carolina, I have found a place of worship. I have discovered the depth and strength of soul. I have always felt the presence of spirit in my life. I have always felt truly close to something greater, stronger, and divine. I am most at one, at ease, and at peace, when in nature.

At Sea View Inn on Pawleys Island, I love waking up early . . . walking beside the ocean . . . watching darkness change to light. As the sun comes up, I stretch to the sky. I reach up as far as I can feel. Perhaps this is my heart's response to a message being sent.

Raised in a family that did not attend church, I find it life-affirming to be among the community attending a Circle of Trust retreat. These retreats have now become for me a place of sanctuary, a place of faith. In the integrity of spirit-driven facilitation, inner courage may be found. For me, the retreat experience has heightened my propensity to follow the signs . . . to follow the arrows.

When I returned from my most recent retreat, my mother noticed how rested I looked. I know how rested I felt; how much at peace I was, after three intensive days of restoration, contemplation and realignment. I feel gratitude to the facilitators for the life-giving space.

In the way a surgeon cuts into a body to remove toxins, the facilitators are, to me, spiritual surgeons, who open the body and mind to self. In my case, when work drains me and too many toxins deplete energy, my potential for being my best is lessened. My trust in self evaporates; my strength to lead diminishes. However, when my spirit is restored in the soothing companionship of silence, I realize I have to be good to myself to be at my best with others. (Ask my husband!)

The gift within retreat is that time does not clamp its usual shackles upon us. Retreat-time leaves us free . . . first to *be*, then to *become*. As intended, we are led inward to wholeness in solitude and community. Each time I leave Pawleys Island, I am grounded in new intentions I set for myself. I return kinder, gentler and stronger. Time spent in retreat circles has given me the courage to share this story.

How do I live divided no more? How do I choose to let the beauty I love be what I do?
I accept the mysteries of life. I follow the signs. I have courage to trust the messages I receive.
I live in celebration of the gifts I have been given. But, I wasn't always this way, and I didn't always trust the universe, or the voice of my inner teacher. Until . . .

MY STORY BEGINS

Thirty-five years ago my life changed for the better. It changed the moment I met Mary Murray, who was then director of the University of New Brunswick (UNB) English Language Programme (ELP). ELP is a place where people from around the world choose to come to learn English. Guided by energies of the heart, ELP is a joyous and wonder-filled place. We live by the motto: *together we can do more than any one of us can do individually*. We develop both independently and collectively, by honoring a commitment to treat each other with respect, even when we disagree.

ELP has become a way of being for many of us who have spent a lifetime there. Mary's vision was that ELP become a positive place, where lives could be influenced for the better. It is she who reinforced with all of us the conviction that *a class without a laugh is an ordeal*. True also in living . . . we need to celebrate success and generate joy. It took time, but gradually, as I trusted, I learned she was right. Now, another generation of ELPers is experiencing our bonding goals. We are a place of positive energy, a place where *WOWs* reverberate and where *WOW* parties are our celebrations of incredible learning. This is our norm.

So, imagine the magnitude this place of energy was to a new graduate, young and fresh out of university, ready to begin her teaching career. I thank the angels with me then, and the spirits with me now, who have guided me forward. The day I entered the world of ELP, I had no idea that what was about to happen would turn my life around.

When Mary and I met in 1980, she talked to me about the impact ELP might have. Today, I can still remember her saying: "Anna Marie, you may learn a lot about yourself here." My response, representing my twenty-one years of wisdom was, "Mary, I think I know everything about myself there is to know." Stress on the word **everything**. Ouch! Yikes! Today, I can smile; then, I grimaced. The moment those words were released, I clearly heard a voice inside me say, *You just said the wrong words to this person*. There it was, my inner teacher. But, I was young and in a vulnerable emotional space.

In my first week of university, my younger brother was killed in a car accident. At age eighteen, I entered the darkest phase of my life. Although I survived and succeeded in my university work, three years later, grief was still corroding my core. I was teetering dangerously close to the edges of dark inner craters. Despite everything, I held onto the hope that I would become a teacher. In spite of my external bravado and presentation of cheer, internally my spirit was in desperate search for a place of optimism and joy. I needed to find a place with life and light.

Mary Murray helped me manage the negative bombardment from outer spheres. She helped me align my outer self with my spiritual interior. Baby-step by baby-step, I cautiously allowed myself to move closer to joy, towards my potential, and nearer a better, kinder, less-condemning self. I doubt I would have the *WOW* power I do now without the spiritual guidance and support. Mary and ELP pulled me back from the edge of the crater.

Mary has always seemed in touch with her inner teacher. She has passion for the ELP community she developed. (So do I!) She embraces life with soul-powered beauty, and she has helped me sustain the energies surrounding this life-enriching workplace, this home, this extraordinary place we call ELP.

In 1980, when I joined the staff, there were two names synonymous with the expansion of ELP to a year-round organization: Mary and Chuddy. Chuddy, like Mary, was a larger-than-life presence . . . once met, always remembered. He had a different aura. (In the seventies, we would have said, hubba hubba!) In the mid-1980's, Chuddy followed his dream of completing his master's degree. In January, 1989, he passed away, at age thirty-seven. Those of us who knew him well, know his spirit may be still perceived at ELP . . . he shows up when we need him.

CHUDDY'S GIFT

How do these story threads connect? Let me explain: I am connected to Mary . . . Mary is connected to Chuddy . . . Chuddy is connected to a gift. The beauty in the connections of all these life-lines will eventually come to light.

For twenty years, Mary and I shared an office space. Near her desk was a print Chuddy gave her when he went on to study. He chose the image well. Mary liked it. I didn't, but I did wonder why I did not feel a connection. Now, looking back, I understand why.

Let's fast-forward a few years to 2002, when I moved into the director's chair. The process was no simple matter. In fact, when Mary retired, I was uncertain as to whether or not I, too, would resign. I struggled, battling an inner lack of confidence that was, in part, emotional residue from my pre-ELP life. Spirits guided . . . here I remain . . . enjoying the challenges coming my way.

When I became director, I rearranged very few things in the office Mary and I had shared. I thought about putting a new picture or two on the walls. I considered repositioning the Chuddy print . . . but why would I? So, the print held its space. In reality, I did not feel any need to make the work space mine . . . it already was. A changed title did not dictate a change in decor. It was never a priority to redecorate a space that I already felt was my work-home.

Now let's fast forward ten years more. The TESOL (Teachers of English to Speakers of Other Languages) convention was in Philadelphia. That winter, my mother had been in poor health, and I decided not to travel. Our conference team made plans in January for the March event, organizing everything, as we always did, to maximize learning outcomes and to be cost-efficient.

The previous year, I had started to question my energy levels, wondering within my soul if I had enough strength to continue my commitment as director of our growing program. Life was full and my fuel tank seemed empty. Considering how low my inner resources were becoming, I thought it was right to send the team and remain home. Not only was my mother's health precarious, but I also needed to think about my life's path. Unbeknownst to me, the universe was about to change the direction of my intentions. It is a pattern I have lived before, but, this time, I did not see the learning waiting for me. The week before the team was to travel, I began feeling restless, unsettled and uncertain. One afternoon, from out of the blue, I heard a voice say: *Anna Marie, go to Philadelphia.* The message was clear; I picked up the phone and booked my flights.

The last time I sensed such a voice of clarity was more than twenty years ago, a week before my father died. On that Sunday morning, I was sitting at my breakfast table, marking student papers. All I heard was my name. Prior to that moment there had been only silence in the room. Writing this text now, here at the same table, I can still see and feel everything as it was in that moment. The sun was shining; a light snow was falling softly and quietly. The resonance and vibration of *Anna Marie* stopped time within the space surrounding me. The light shining into the dining room, through the back windows, had altered. There was a new brilliance present in the light, a density in the air. Thinking my husband might have called my name, I went down the hall to see if he were awake . . . he was not. I knew the voice was not his. Within minutes, the phone rang, and my mother told me the doctor said my father had a week to live. My father passed away six days later.

Now, hearing the voice say, *Go to Philadelphia,* I knew I had to trust the messenger and respond. When I tried to reserve additional space to be with the team, there was none available. The accommodations I finally found were at the opposite end of the city, far away from action central. I was disappointed, in part because I would not be with my staff, but also because I have no sense of direction and would inevitably get lost. (Ask my husband!) When I arrived at my hotel, however, I was thrilled . . . speechless, in fact. When I looked up the street I could see the Philadelphia Museum of Art with a gigantic sign: VAN GOGH. My first priority was the convention, but I promised myself *aloud* I would - *no matter what happened -*

see the Van Gogh exhibit before the end of the week. I LOVE Van Gogh. I LOVE sunflowers. I spent a year in Aix-en-Provence; the last time I had seen Van Gogh was in France. In my mind, I was certain, there was nothing, absolutely nothing, to prevent me from seeing the exhibit.

Mid-week, after too many presentation rooms with too few windows, I needed fresh air. My mind was full. A gremlin of self-doubt, and perhaps fatigue, re-emerged. Should I leave my work? Was I really where I should be at this time in my life? I was contemplating where and how I would find energy to continue my commitment to ELP's intense environment. Darkness was moving in. In retrospect, I needed a spiritual realignment, a connection to light.

Walking out of the building, I had no idea which door I exited. I was not attentive to direction: north, south, east or west. Where was I? Was I getting lost again? (Growing up in a village of 500 people, I still rely on Nature's signposts to be my guides. I just walk in the direction I am headed . . . or, where I am destined to go.) I walked a few blocks until a sign, written in chalk on the sidewalk, caught my attention: *Come in*. Funny, I thought, but kept walking, and turned the corner. A little further, the same message showed up again, this time on a billboard leaning against a building: *Come in*. Why not, I thought . . . and followed a series of arrows. I responded to the invitation, not realizing the mystery opening to me. I associate angels more with golden halos than with chalk arrows, but *then again* . . .

I entered the foyer; it was beautiful, with exquisite architecture. As I walked up an elaborate set of stairs, I wondered if Van Gogh might be my guiding source. To the right was a small lunch area, with seating for about a dozen people. Wow, this place is gorgeous, I thought; I loved it. There were no seats available. Those already seated appeared to be the art scene cafeteria regulars, fully engaged in conversation. As I turned to leave, an elderly gentleman, with his lunch in hand, nodded to me and offered me his seat in the center of the room. I accepted,

143

purchased a coffee and sandwich and moved towards my pre-destined place. I tried not to tip tables or disturb others as I juggled food tray, thoughts, and my belongings into what appeared to be the smallest of all seating places. Suddenly, from out of nowhere, a man pulled up a chair to my table and asked if he could join me for lunch. Where did he come from? I hadn't noticed him earlier. My instinct, honed as a child working in my father's general store, was to trust the familiar and the unfamiliar, and within seconds, I learned this man's wife was attending the TESOL convention. He was an architect from Chicago. Overhearing our conversation, a woman from another table maneuvered her way towards us and pulled up her chair to join us. We learned she was an artist. Was this a *mere* coincidence . . . a party of three at a table for one . . . the architect, the artist and the teacher?

THE ART OF TANNER

The architect and the artist quickly connected on topics of mutual interest. Limited in my knowledge of an art world they knew intimately, I was fascinated with their conversation. I felt as if I had just enrolled in my first day of art school as the artist asked the architect if he were familiar with the art of H. O. Tanner. Amazingly, the architect had just been to the Tanner exhibit next door, but admitted he was ambivalent about Tanner's work. The artist reacted to his indifference: her response to Tanner's work was solidly at the other end of the spectrum. She then talked about her favorite Tanner work, the power and presence of light, and why he, the architect, should revisit the gallery to take a second look with more care.

Until then, I had had no knowledge of Tanner and had not even heard his name. It was a joy to experience the energy fields generated by the conversation. I loved being able to listen to the debate from a neutral and unbiased state of mind, with no reference point from which to offer an opinion. I wondered who Tanner was and made a mental note to look into his work later. After all, I had already made my commitment, aloud, to attend the Van Gogh exhibit. I would think about Tanner when I returned home. I felt deeply grateful to the artist and the architect for the art lesson I had experienced this day.

We found a myriad of life-line connections in our two-hour conversation. We shared bits and pieces of our life-paths, as strangers do, until we realized the cafeteria doors were closing. Leaving, I asked the artist which direction to take to find the Tanner exhibit, deciding because the exhibit was so close, to see the painting of a boat that had caused such disagreement between my lunchtime friends.

I hurried through the exhibit. I felt nothing, and left . . . wondering why.

On the last day of TESOL conventions, our ELP tradition is to have an afternoon of personal choice, so on that Saturday, each of us headed off toward separate adventures. The time had come for my pilgrimage to Van Gogh! Five days of intention . . . I was on my way.

Van Gogh was to the left. Tanner was to the right. The debate between the architect and the artist overtook me. I replayed it in my head. What had they been talking about? What was I missing? I decided to revisit Tanner's work. What did Tanner have to show me? For a soul-deepening reason, I knew I was meant to return; I knew I had to go there. The minute I walked in the door of the gallery, a tiny woman, dressed in a bright red sweater and wearing beautiful silver jewelry asked, "Who else is here as part of the pre-arranged tour?"

THE PRESENCE OF LIGHT

"I am!" I said. In truth, I heard the words come out of me, but, there is *no way*, under normal circumstances, I would do this. I joined a group of professionally dressed individuals. Looking at the docent, this petite lady, this strong presence, I became mesmerized by a light surrounding her as she spoke.

She talked about the symbolism of light in Tanner's paintings. Her energy and passion were brilliant. Painting by painting, I began to understand more and more about the energy and colors in the images. Only days ago I had given them cursive, superficial attention, during my rapid walk-by. Amazing, what I had missed.

My appreciation of Tanner's work was growing. I began to be completely absorbed by the spirituality. I understood the magnetic field my artist-friend had described; I was feeling an invisible field of energy as well. Painting after painting, my connection with Tanner's work grew; waves of light were increasing for me. In front of these works of beauty, my soul was present, my fatigue was disappearing. A weight was being lifted, and my heart responded.

Painting after painting, the docent's stories opened my eyes. Her knowledge and insight were invitations to visit the inner meanings these paintings held. She invited us to let our interpretations connect to the light in Tanner's work. I recall her saying, "*Some people see the light and some people do not: the interpretation of Tanner is yours. . .*"

Light was present in every painting I saw.

When we were nearing the end of the tour, the docent explained that the curator, quite unfortunately, had been unable to procure one of Tanner's most famous paintings. She pointed out the spot on one wall where this work was to have been placed. All through the exhibit, alongside each original was a tiny replica with accompanying information. But, in this location, there was a mismatch as the miniature was a replica of the intended painting, not the one on the wall. Standing at the back of the group, I looked at the three-by-three square. In this small space was the miniature of the print given to Mary by Chuddy.

Chuddy's gift to Mary had been a print of H. O. Tanner's *The*

Banjo Lesson . . . it had been over my shoulder all along. My entire body froze; I could not move. I could not speak, and tears came to my eyes. The group moved on; I could not. The message became clear . . . *this* is what drew me to Philadelphia. Inside, I realized I *was* where I was meant to be. Therein, the beauty.

When I returned to my office, I looked closely at the print for a signature. There it was. I felt as if the universe were sharing the message Dorothy received in the Wizard of Oz. All along, through the struggles, through the self-doubt, the light had been near me . . . *but invisible to me* . . . the whole time.

Since Philadelphia, I have encountered Tanner's *The Banjo Lesson* twice.

In the fall of 2013, my husband and I were in Acadia National Park, Maine, to celebrate our anniversary. Every anniversary, we spend time in nature. Where better to experience beauty and be closest to our souls than near the ocean, within the mountains, surrounded by the sounds of the forest? One day, en route to Bar Harbor to walk about the town, we saw a sign for Echo Lake. Why not, we thought? The sun was shining, the weather was beautiful, we had all the time in the world to explore. Even though we were dressed more appropriately for shopping than hiking, we felt drawn towards a particular mountain top. We carefully wound our way up. At each turn, we moved higher, surprised at how our energy was rising with our climb. We were absorbing the beauty with every step. When we reached the first ledge, we rested and looked out towards the lake. From our vantage point, the October light, from every angle, was mesmerizing; we both felt as if we were looking at a painting. We were breathing in the day and locking the moment into our memories as our camera was in the car. We peacefully, silently, absorbed the mountain's presence and the sun's radiance.

The silence was broken by the voices of another couple

climbing up the hill towards us. We nodded acknowledgment as they approached. Then, instead of heading downward as planned, we moved steadily upward. When we arrived at the next plateau, we were faced with the prospect of climbing up an iron ladder, drilled into a ledge, positioned solidly at a precarious angle. My husband moved onward and upward; I stayed at the base of the precipice, receiving my husband's promise that he would return within the hour. I had the ideal vantage point to watch the light around me change . . . the fall colors of the mountain were spectacular. The couple we had acknowledged earlier arrived. While he chose to climb, she stayed; we chatted.

Our conversation began with a normal exchange. We were from the east coast; they were from the west coast. We were celebrating an anniversary; they were visiting the area. But, then coincidence began. She and I were both language teachers. She had retired ten years ago; I had ten years of work still ahead of me. I asked how she now filled her days; she said she was an amateur artist. They were on their way to Boston to see the work of the American artist, John Singer Sargent. She asked if I knew his work, and I said I did not. I then told her that I recently had a new affinity for the American artist H. O. Tanner. What a coincidence . . . her mother had given her a Tanner print, years before. The print was one she had had in her office, and, later moved to her home. It was *The Banjo Lesson*.

Again, on a mountain in Maine, Tanner . . . on a day when the world was a painting . . . in a place where the light was exquisite.

What is essential is invisible to the eye, the Little Prince tells us. Only those who understand this, understand this. The invisible thread connecting us all is present if we listen, and if we engage ourselves in the dialogue.

Three weeks after our anniversary celebration in Maine, I was attending a Circle of Trust retreat on Pawleys Island. I had a premonition Tanner would appear. On the second day, I decided to cast my net at the dinner table. I wanted affirmation that I was meant to be there. I shared the incredible experiences I had had in Maine and in Philadelphia. Sitting beside me was the one retreat participant with whom I had not yet connected. When I told my story, she looked at me and said, "I have that painting in my home."

Of course she does, I thought. Why would I doubt? I told her that, in the beginning, I had not felt affinity with the image, but I also felt I couldn't move it. When I asked her thoughts about why I hadn't moved the print, she spoke with conviction, "You couldn't move it because it wouldn't let you."

There it was: the third presence and present from the universe. She and I have since exchanged e-mail images of where the Tanner print lives with us. Hers is in the entrance to her home; mine has never moved from its original place. Chuddy's gift to Mary is where it has always been . . . and I *now* see the light over my shoulder.

How do I live divided no more? How do I choose to let the beauty I love be what I do?

I accept the mysteries of life. I follow the signs. I have courage to trust the messages I receive. I live in celebration of the gifts I have been given. But, I wasn't always this way, and I didn't always trust the universe, or the voice of my inner teacher. Until . . .

Anna Marie Robinson is Director of the University of New Brunswick English Language Programme, located in Fredericton, New Brunswick, Canada. She and her husband live just outside the city of Fredericton in a house surrounded by trees. They share their home with Anna Marie's mother, who lives in an attached granny suite. Two four-legged family members, Scooter-boy and Saligal, meander between the two homes, enriching family life. Anna Marie can be reached at amr@unb.ca .

Offering All We Have

By Morgan Lee

The word comes in, dribbling at first, from phone calls, from kids riding back to the school, from people near the scene and finally from a first responder who is a school district employee and a parent. Chris has been in an accident and it is not good. We meet in hallways, in offices; phone calls are made. I make my way to the local hospital 15 miles away. This is not my gift right now; I don't know what to say. Yet, they will expect the principal of the high school to be there. To support family and friends; to be with the students who flock to the hospital; to represent the school and the school district. He dies sometime later; more phone calls are made, plans are put into place, discussions are had, and prayers are offered. He was a senior and scheduled to graduate in a couple of weeks. It will not happen.

The school is eerily quiet. It has never been this way. Well, maybe on Sunday afternoons and holidays when I work with no people in the building. Never, ever during a school day. Students pass in the hallways, they cry, teachers weep in private. Even the strongest of us cannot hold out without a break. We make it through the day. That is all we can do. Make it through the day.

Almost a year and a half later, in the same small school, word comes around that there has been some type of accident. It is a few days into the new year, right after winter break, and teachers are working but the students have yet to return. A secretary reports news from the community. Finally, a call comes to me, the principal, that a student has been killed by another student. A hunting accident of some kind. The news people call. An interview takes place on a local news station. The principal of the school is reporting the sad news to people across the local area. They don't know this young man. It is a sad story. They don't know that this small, rural high school will go through the pain of losing another student in a tragic accident. Tim is dead. He was a good friend to Chris who died a year and a half before. They were brothers in a sense, teammates on baseball and football teams, they played together in the sand lots, in the streets and fields of Orangeburg County, South Carolina. One black. One white.

We cry again. We stand strong. We offer all we have.

We are only a school, not really a family as we profess to be; yet we are stronger than a family in so many ways. We live together, we eat breakfast and lunch together, we fight, we love, we play, we learn, we are all that a family may be. People, who don't know us, judge us by our old, proud building. They look at our test scores. They try to figure us out. How to fix us. How to copy our successes. How to grade us. How to explain us to others.

We are on a mission. It is work, yet it is so much more than work. We are all teachers. We are all learners. All in a school; all teaching and learning together. The principal, the curriculum folks, the classroom teachers, the coaches, the food service workers, the custodians, the bus drivers, the parents and guardians. All of us are teachers. As the principal, I am to be the teacher of teachers, the master teacher, the leader, the instructional guru, the great manager, the head honcho, the pastor, the rabbi, the priest, the disciplinarian, the parent of parents, the fixer, the guide. I struggle with what is important. I long to have discussions with faculty members about the great works of the world, about dreams we have of what our school can be, of how we can help ourselves by helping ourselves.

I want to make the time to teach lessons to students and to have the joy of having them teach me in return. I want to hold the hand of the parent who is struggling with so very much while rearing this child. I want to open the eyes of the district office boss who has forgotten what it is like to work in a school each day. How can I be what I was called to be? How can I help others to be what they were called to be?

Years later, I am in my dream job, where I am paid to help others as they grow and develop as school leaders. It is professional development at its best. It is a way for me to work for the state while also being allowed to espouse some of my most passionate thoughts about public education and school leadership. I am working with all of the new principals in the state each year. I am working with teacher leaders as they find themselves on their road to continued leadership development. I want to support those who are living into their roles as school leaders. The pressure comes to teach the stuff of leadership. The stuff of school. The stuff of policies, law, rules and regulations. "But, you don't understand," I seem to continuously say. I say this to the bosses, to the supervisor-types, to the superintendent-types, and even to my colleagues. You don't understand that leading in schools is not about regulations and test scores and policies and wasteful lesson plans and rote memorization, and grades, and laws, and evaluations, and assessments, and instructional practices. Leading in schools is about loving and caring and advocating and, yes, it is even about dealing with life and death. It is so much more than what we learn in teacher and principal preparation programs. It is about who we are, what we bring with us, and the spirit in which we help one another to learn and to grow. How do we teach that? How do we help others to look inside themselves and know that they teach who they are?

JOINING THE CIRCLE

I kind of invited myself into this new (for me) Circle. I do not belong, but yet I do. I had read some of Parker Palmer's work.

I had seen him in person at an event a few years earlier. I was especially excited after reading *A Hidden Wholeness.* The "third thing" Parker spoke of in the work really hit home with me. The discernment in community and the ways of being, the touchstones, were fresh to me. It was what I had always done with my adolescent students, but also what I was struggling with when facilitating the sessions with adults. I asked Sally if I could join the group, already in progress. Sally and Sandie, the facilitators, asked the group if I could be included. It was a group of school leaders: principals and district office leaders who had begun this Circle together back in the summer. It was a Circle where they were working individually while in community on the process of reclaiming the reality and power of their inner lives. Parker, in his work, spoke of the inner teacher, the inner light. This idea made sense to me. I had one of those; I had an inner teacher that taught me so much. I just never knew what to call it. I had never been in community with people where the process became listening to my inner teacher while also being present with others. And, present with other educators who knew, understood, and lived in my world. Lived sometimes a divided life between who we really are and who we are forced to be to make it in the institutional part of public education.

They had been together as a community and as a group for a while. I was new. I was from "the state." I was someone they really did not know. Yet, they were all open to me. Welcoming. Gracious. Loving. I sat with them, learned with them, cried with them and opened my eyes to what could be. How I could be with people. Yes, the process, the ways all of these things are in the books. Parker's work can be read and seen online. It can be experienced and even practiced that way. Yet, sitting in this Circle, with these people, alive and well, was powerful; even, primal. This is professional development. This is the way we can be with people! Connecting soul and role? You bet!

Courage work changed me. It changed who I am. It changed my approach to the work I do in my life and the life I have in my work. I speak differently. I write differently. I am at peace because of the work.

I learn to listen. I learn to question differently. I learn to create space. I learn to hold space. I learn to be there. I learn to have presence and to be present. I learn touchstones, not just for the Circle work, but for my life. I learn courage. I learn to take the work into the world.

People have always asked me to listen to them. I have always tried. Now, I know how.

A teacher leader is invited back to a private conference room. She talks. I listen. I am with her as she cries and pleads to have someone understand, to know the pain of being asked to do things that have nothing to do with helping her young students, to understand that she no longer enjoys her work because of the pressure of working for a principal and for others who lack knowledge of who she is and what she is about. I've learned to ask questions; the questions that allow her to hear herself. "What do you know about why you teach?" "Who do your students say you are?" "Who are your teachers?" She begins to see things, hear things. She leaves after some time, and I realize how much I have helped just by being with her. Not fixing her. Not offering advice. Not giving her options. Just being there.

He needs someone to talk to. He is a new principal and is already ready to move to a new place. He wants my advice. He wants me to help him make a decision. In the past I would have agreed. I would have worried about what I could tell him, how I could help him. How to help him make the decision that would affect his career and, indeed, his life. Instead, I listen. I allow for silence in the space where, before, I may have made up words. He asks questions. I listen. He answers his own questions. We are alone, together, in this small room. He is talking and listening to himself. He startles himself by saying, "I know what to do." We shake hands, hug a moment, and he leaves. It dawns on me after a couple of minutes of being by myself after our meeting. All he needed was someone to be with him, to listen to him. He brought his own questions. I don't remember asking him any questions at all. He had the answers within him. He needed my presence to help him to know himself.

Another principal shows up to a mandated meeting. Afterwards, instead of being in a small-group session, he wants to talk with me. After our brief conversation, I encourage him to take time for himself rather than coming to tomorrow's session for new principals. "Be with yourself," I say, "Get back with me whenever you are ready." He comes a few weeks later. Humble. Looking a bit downtrodden. "I don't think I can do this anymore." As with so many of the people I see in this new job of theirs, they really did not know how much time comes with the job. How they have to borrow time from family and friends. I feel I need to just be present with him and to ask honest, open questions to help him to live into the answers. "What is your knowing about family?" "How are you with your family?" "What gives you joy?" He is a courageous one. He will do what is right for him and for his family, not right for his career and his ambition or even his ego. He leaves the job. I name him Courage. I speak about him with honor in the talks I give and in the lessons I try to teach others. His story comes to me, because I learned to be with him.

THE CALL TO CONTINUE

During my time of discernment as a possible facilitator of Courage work, I attended a retreat sponsored by the Center for Courage & Renewal on Bainbridge Island, near Seattle. I had been through several Circles of Trust and felt the call to continue on my journey. The Circle on the island was made up of about twenty of us who were in the "process of possibility," as I like to call it. We met together. We spent time together and alone. We planted seeds and we discussed our seed growth with one another. This time I really began to understand the way I could do inner work in community.

On the way back to the ferry to take me off the island, I caught a ride with Rick, one of our leaders. We were riding along in his little blue car; I was in the shotgun seat. Rick and I talked a bit and he asked me what I thought about the retreat and about becoming a facilitator of the work. I said that I loved what the work had done for me, but that I was not sure that I could ever learn the language that I heard so many Courage people use. Things like creating space and holding safe space and stuff like that were a bit foreign to my ears and, even more so, foreign to my tongue. He said something that has been with me since. He made a simple, yet profound statement that resonated with me while riding along those back-island roads and continues to be with me today. He said, "You don't have to learn the language, you are living the language."

Yep. I'm living the language. I am not perfect and the language is a bit thick and hazy sometimes. Of course, when I am too lost, I simply call up Sally or Sandie, those first people of Courage I met. Those two who have mentored and listened to me. Those two who have encouraged and been patient with me. And, we have a mini-clearness committee on the telephone! I am not sure that the technique we use is in any manual or any handbook. It is, though, that we trust and love one another. It is that we give courage and hope to one another. It is about the work and the people behind the work. It is who we are.

I am still learning the language. I am trying to live the language each day.

Morgan Lee is a teacher and learner who lives in Columbia, South Carolina, with his wife, Lena, and his son, Chapman. Professionally, he works at the SC Department of Education, where he facilitates learning for all of the new principals in SC through the South Carolina Principal Induction Program, and facilitates learning of SC teacher leaders, who are the soul of their schools, through the Foundations in School Leadership program. Morgan has facilitated Courage groups with school leaders, school faculties, school leadership teams, and with groups of public-school educators. He has facilitated numerous groups in Cultural Responsive Education in public-school districts, with school faculties, in higher education and with community groups. Morgan also has experience in spiritual formation in formal and informal settings, and has facilitated congregational groups. He is especially excited about his new journey into the art and profession of spiritual direction. He may be contacted at LEENHS@yahoo.com .

What is Courage Work?
What is this Work we call a Circle of Trust?

The **Circle of Trust® approach**, described by Parker J. Palmer in *A Hidden Wholeness,* is offered by facilitators prepared by the Center for Courage & Renewal (**www.couragerenewal.org**) to encourage each participant to connect the inner life of mind and spirit with the outer life of work and service, to re-connect soul and role, to let the Beauty s/he loves be her/his work in the world. With the divisiveness on our planet and Parker's new writing about what he calls the "politics of the brokenhearted," facilitators have become even more intentional in including the role of citizen as they create the space for reconnecting soul and role, for the journey to the undivided life.

The Courage to Teach, The Courage to Lead, and **Circle of Trust** are some of the names for the programs grounded in the principle that, without denying or abandoning the outer world, we must reclaim the reality and power of our inner lives. Many of the participants in those various programs affectionately call the work "Courage Work"! **The Courage to Teach** was initially created to sustain and inspire public school teachers, but people in other professions soon expressed their needs for this work. Participants now include people in education, healthcare, ministry, business, government, philanthropy, nonprofits and others who wish to work and live more wholeheartedly. Beginning with the individual, the Circle of Trust approach has the potential to weave together soul, role, institution and social transformation.

157

Key principles of this work include:

- **Everyone has an inner teacher**: Every person has access to an inner source of truth, named in various wisdom traditions as identity, true self, heart, spirit or soul. The inner teacher is a source of guidance and strength that helps us find our way through life's complexities and challenges. Circles of Trust give people a chance to listen to this source, learn from it and discover its imperatives for their work and their lives.

- **Inner work requires solitude and community**: In Circles of Trust we make space for the solitude that allows us to learn from within, while supporting that solitude with the resources of community. Participants take an inner journey in community where we learn how to evoke and challenge each other without being judgmental, directive or invasive.

- **Inner work must be invitational**: Circles of Trust are never "share or die" events, but times and places where people have the freedom within a purposeful process to learn and grow in their own way, on their own schedule and at their own level of need. From start to finish, this approach invites participation rather than insisting upon it, because the inner teacher speaks by choice, not on command.

- **Our lives move in cycles like the seasons**: By using metaphors drawn from the seasons to frame our exploration of the inner life, we create a hospitable space that allows people of diverse backgrounds and perspectives to engage in a respectful dialogue. These metaphors represent cycles of life—such as the alternation of darkness and light, death and new life—

shared by everyone in a secular, pluralistic society, regardless of philosophical, religious or spiritual differences

- **An appreciation of paradox enriches our lives and helps us hold greater complexity**: The journey we take in a Circle of Trust teaches us to approach the many polarities that come with being human as "both–ands" rather than "either–ors," holding them in ways that open us to new insights and possibilities. We listen to the inner teacher and to the voices in the Circle, letting our own insights and the wisdom that can emerge in conversation check and balance each other. We trust both our intellects and the knowledge that comes through our bodies, intuitions and emotions.

- **We live with greater integrity when we see ourselves whole**: Integrity means integrating all that we are into our sense of self, embracing our shadows and limitations as well as our light and our gifts. As we deepen the congruence between our inner and outer lives, we show up more fully in the key relationships and events of our lives, increasing our capacity to be authentic and courageous in life and work.

- **A "hidden wholeness" underlies our lives**: Whatever brokenness we experience in ourselves and in the world, a "hidden wholeness" can be found just beneath the surface. The capacity to stand and act with integrity in the gap between what is and what could be or should be—resisting both the corrosive cynicism that comes from seeing only what is broken and the irrelevant idealism that comes from seeing only what is not—has been key to every life-giving movement and is among the fruits of the Circle of Trust approach.

Fill As You Pour

By Marian R. David

Life can only be understood backwards;
but it must be lived forwards.

---Soren Kierkegaard

Perhaps I am in a divine tryst with the ocean. Walking beside it is a natural source of comfort. The gentle sound of the waves soothes me, easing tension and stress. I am in awe of how the ocean forms a unique shoreline by natural design. I find inspiration and learn many lessons as I stroll along the shores. I completely open myself, allowing the 10,000-petal flower of my soul to unfold, therein awakening possibilities and answers to my innermost questions.

One day, walking on the beach and deeply contemplating how best to reunify my divine calling, professional work, and personal life, a wave came raging up to me, breaking the natural shoreline along with my silence. It startled me because, prior to this moment, I had been respectfully admiring how the ocean seemed to honor its natural boundaries. The water engulfed my feet and caused me to shift my thoughts to the wave and the ocean and the fact that it was not exactly the constant I thought it to be. Though it mostly stayed within its boundaries along the shores, it can and had run awry of its imaginary borders and came towering in on people and buildings and whatever was in its path.

What a paradox! This gentle, loving, warm ocean that soothed me to sleep and rocked me like a baby, could also roar ferociously and become violent. How could something so calming and peaceful become such a force with which to be reckoned? How could it be that something that brought such joy and delight also be the source of pain and grief?

On first thought, it seemed simple; it was out of balance. Though that was the easy answer, more careful consideration revealed that it was within the nature of the ocean to follow its own path and to overrun what I might think was its natural border. The ocean was not one-dimensional as I was depicting it in my mind; it was multi-dimensional. Like anything and everything else in life, the ocean had many facets, which I had to understand to fully appreciate its wonders.

Continuing my walk, I began to juxtapose the ocean and my life. I started to reflect in particular on my relationship to the work that calls to my heart. On one hand, it is a source of joy. However, this same work has been the source of stress and burnout. Like the ocean, that which brings joy can potentially bring pain and everything along the spectrum. It is not even that one is good and the other bad because I have no need to vility one. Rather, it is about my accepting all aspects of whatever it is in life. To fully embrace the work that calls to me is to accept the fact that, inherent in the work of giving of self and supporting others, whether that is teaching, ministering, being a caregiver, or whatever, is the need to take care of oneself. The question for me is how to do this in the midst of my busy life.

My awareness of the need to take care of the whole person has manifested itself in the work that I do now, *Sustaining the Soul that Serves*; however, that is later. Herein I share the journey to that work, which I have come to discover was within me all along. The words of 19th century philosopher and theologian, Soren Kierkegaard, echo my journey into my work and back anew, "Life can only be understood backwards; but it must be lived forwards."

MY JOURNEY AS EDUCATOR

I considered myself the consummate educator. From my earliest childhood memories, I wanted to be a teacher and follow in the footsteps of my adored and respected aunts. I have fond memories of playing school with my cousins under the huge shade oak tree in the front yard of our grandparents' home. At that time, everyone wanted to be the teacher to get to boss the other children and be the one that everyone had to look up to. Even as children, we had great respect for the teacher in charge. Sure enough, I, and almost all of my cousins, followed our childhood dream to become teachers. That was our way to save the world!

I was on top of the world at age 20 when I graduated from college and became a certified teacher with my very own classroom! I began my teaching career bright-eyed and bushy-tailed, ready to embrace every child and ultimately save the world! I had all of the excitement of a mountain climber who had finally reached the summit after having dreamed and planned the climb for years. I loved every minute of teaching and had the illusion that all the other teachers at the school equally enjoyed their experiences. I loved working with the children. I enjoyed sharing stories of the children with their parents. I was living my dream.

Over time, when I finally allowed myself to come out of the clouds and look around, I began to notice that there was a marked difference in teachers. Some had a sparkle in their eyes and saw beauty in their students, while others had more complaints than successes and no teacher-glow. Some teachers had become jaded and no longer believed in what they were doing. They didn't believe they could make a difference in the lives of the children and, consequently, had very low expectations of them. There are any number of things that could have contributed to teaching without sparkle: one new program after another to implement, overcrowded classrooms, lack of classroom management and discipline, or uncooperative and irate parents. Whatever the reason, clearly the thrill and excitement were not intrinsic for every teacher.

I went from teaching to counseling and continued to enjoy my work until... I didn't. I began to take on too much. Clearly it was not just *those* teachers; I, too, began to feel something wane within myself. I remember a moment, after dealing with a harrowing sexual abuse case that had to go to court. The child had clearly been molested, but due to legal maneuvering, the criminal got off. I felt myself a failure and could no longer support the child emotionally, fight the case and balance my workload at school and my personal life. It was not just me. The county's young social worker, with whom I had worked very closely on the case and who had put her entire heart and soul into this case, obviously felt it, too. I saw the sparkle leave her eyes that day in court. She left without a word and never looked back. She simply walked away from the job and we never spoke again.

Drained, burned out, empty, I was on my way to work very early the following morning In the cold rain. I was going to fulfill my duties as a counselor and help other people with their problems, but I was dying inside. I was empty. I did not understand that you have to fill as you pour. I was like a desert, dry and hard and sunburned. But still, I was on my way to work, to counsel others. All of a sudden, in the midst of my tears, mixed in with the rain, I heard these words, sung softly directly to me (I later learned the singer was Larnell Harris):

> *I miss my time with you*
> *Those moments together*
> *I need to be with you each day*
> *And it hurts me when you say*
> *You're too busy, busy trying to serve me*
> *But how can you serve me*
> *When your spirit's empty?*

I stopped the car. I turned around in the road, called work, and went home to bed. I stayed out of work for a solid week and spent most of that time under the covers. I was finally admitting to myself that I was empty.

The *old people* used to talk about going to the well to fill up. Where was that proverbial well anyway? I remember hearing about it, but I could not recall how to get there. I needed help. The counselor needed help. I had seen this in some other teachers, counselors, and social workers. There was something signaling that the fire was flickering, something brilliant had been there but it was waning; it was as if it were contagious, especially amongst the ones who cared the most. Here, now, I had caught it. I walked away from my beloved position as a counselor. I was overwhelmed and out of balance. I had not understood what I later learned from the ocean; you have to embrace all aspects of anything in life. To work and give, you have to refill. You have to fill as you pour.

MY JOURNEY AS SERVANT LEADER

Contemplating my next steps, Marian Wright Edelman, the founder of the Children's Defense Fund (CDF), invited me to one of her speaking engagements. She wanted to meet with me afterwards about spearheading the Education and Leadership Development Program in our hometown of Bennettsville, in Marlboro County, South Carolina. It was an opportunity to work with college students, teachers, children, and their parents. I excitedly accepted and was again bright-eyed and bushy tailed, ready to save the world. The goal was to provide education enrichment for school-aged children, and eventually led my position as the National Director of the CDF Freedom Schools Program, in which college students from across the country came together for training, then went into selected cities and rural counties throughout the USA to work with children.

The college students served the children well, and the program was a huge success. Like me, the students had aspirations of making great changes in the communities where they found themselves; most importantly, they wanted to make a difference in the lives of the children. Of course, the needs were varied in communities across the country, but college students noticed some common threads, including many children reading below grade level; dire conditions in schools; parents and community people facing challenges due to drugs, unemployment, and social ills; and some communities unable to coalesce in support of the children.

The college students became increasingly aware of their responsibility for the next generation. Addressing the demands of the children, families, and the community, coupled with making sense of their own lives, and in many cases figuring out how to finance their college education, many became overwhelmed trying to balance everything. I began to see that sparkle diminish and a familiar weariness creep into their eyes. Rather than feeling renewed and energized to serve more, many of these young people were on a fast track to burnout. This time I accepted responsibility because I was designing the training and I was in the leadership position. Looking at students trying to balance life with work and studies and juggling financial burdens was reminiscent of Howard Thurman's experience as Dean of Rankin Chapel at Howard University, when he found that many students there were working up to three jobs and showing signs of breaking under the pressure of trying to balance it all. Thurman addressed, in his *Meditations of the Heart,* the need for an "Island of Peace within one's own soul," speaking to the need for each person to find an inner place of refuge within their own souls—to commune, pray, meditate, just be, and honor their authentic selves:

> *The only hope for surcease, the only possibility of stability for the person, is to establish an Island of Peace within one's own soul. Here one brings for review the purposes and dreams to which one's life is tied. This is the place where there is no pretense, no dishonesty, no adulteration. What passes over the*

threshold is simon-pure. What one really thinks and feels about one's own life stands revealed; what one really thinks and feels about other people far and near is seen with every nuance honestly labeled: love is love, hate is hate, fear is fear. Well within the island is the Temple where God dwells – not the God of the creed, the church, the family, but the God of one's heart.

Not only were many of the college students losing their glow, but so was I. The paradox was that I was able to do my work from the outside quite well, while on the inside, I felt I was a failure for not doing a better job taking care of myself, let alone the college leaders. Ironically, it was quite possible to continue to give and help others while receding from within. This, too, was part of the illusion. The great program had a flaw: there was nothing to sustain the very people trained to do the work. I worried the people doing the work were on the verge of burnout by the very work that calls to their souls.

When I came across these words from Thomas Merton in an article, I felt as if I had committed a crime:

There is a pervasive form of contemporary violence to which the idealist most easily succumbs: activism and overwork. The rush and pressures of modern life are a form, perhaps the most common form, of its innate violence. To allow oneself to be carried away by a multitude of conflicting concerns, to surrender to too many demands, to commit oneself to too many projects, to want to help everyone in everything is to succumb to violence. More than that, it is cooperation in violence. The frenzy of the activist neutralizes his/ work for peace.... it kills the root of inner wisdom which makes work fruitful.

166

I was clear that my work was fundamentally counterproductive. It was the source of violence to overwork myself and to train others to do the work without teaching them how to take care of themselves.

How exactly do people find that Island of Peace? In my work, I had been feeling a chasm between my inner and outer life. The outside kept moving forward and getting the work done, while the inside was falling farther and farther behind. In fact, it seemed like the more productive I was in forging through and getting the work done, the more disconnected I felt. Though I had the illusion of success on one level of meeting the needs of others and directing programs, the emptiness inside could not be denied. It called me to come into the quietness, to seek solitude, and to take a reprieve from the busyness of work and life. I feared that it would be discovered that I was empty inside and something in me was dying. I no longer felt alive, bright-eyed, and ready to make my mark in the world. The excitement I used to awaken with each day was long forgotten. It was as if my head were functioning without my heart. One of my challenges was finding how my head and my heart could remain connected, especially during the most challenging times.

I had yet to receive the message from the ocean to take into consideration all aspects of the work. So I did what I do so well when I become overwhelmed after giving my heart and soul -- I left. I simply walked away from the work of my heart. Taking Howard Thurman, the legacy of my fore-parents, the college students, and the children, I set out to find that elusive Island of Peace. I knew if I found it for myself, I could share it with others. Accepting Howard Thurman's invitation to take "a reprieve from the busyness of life," I went on a journey that ended up taking me full-circle—into a fellowship program at Massachusetts Institute of Technology (MIT) to research, to California to study at theology school, to a monastery to spend time in quiet listening, and back to my work in serving.

MY JOURNEY AS RESEARCHER

I took a sabbatical from my work with CDF to accept a fellowship in the Community Fellows Program at MIT under the leadership of Mel King. I knew that this program would provide the opportunity for me to design my studies and research, while having the privilege to coalesce with change agents from across the country. I wanted to understand how people stayed true to their authentic selves and sustained themselves under horrific circumstances and dire situations. I studied the Slave Narratives and the life of Dr. Martin Luther King, Jr. I read about Mrs. Rosa Parks, South African President Nelson Mandela, and others. I retraced and gleaned from the stories of people from my childhood whom I witnessed working tirelessly, wherein giving up was never an option. They found strength from a source deep inside. They had a strong spiritual connection that grounded and sustained them, and I came to fully understand that the church was as much a social justice institution as it was a place of spiritual formation. It was the stronghold for Dr. King, the leaders of the Civil Rights Movement, and people in my childhood as well.

While I did not initially feel that my research provided the answers for which I was searching, it did help me to define my questions more clearly. My interviews and gatherings with seasoned and emerging leaders confirmed that the missing ingredient for which I had been searching perhaps didn't exist yet in familiar form. In 1996, with support from the Fetzer Institute, Kellogg Foundation, and the George Family Foundation, I conducted focus groups, interviews, and gatherings across the country in diverse communities from South Carolina to Second Mesa, from Tennessee to the Navaho Nations, from California to the Pueblos, and from Washington State to Washington, D.C. Together we shared, explored, designed, piloted, and developed training and programs to support all who serve. Out of this I developed *Sustaining the Soul that Serves*, a program which honors the whole person, acknowledges the many dimensions of service, and addresses the need for renewal. My new program invited all who serve to explore an array of contemplative practices to renew and sustain themselves so that they can remain true to the work of their hearts.

MY JOURNEY INTO MINISTRY

Searching to ground myself more spiritually and to deepen the Sustaining the Soul work, I went to seminary. Even before this, I had been feeling a tug in this direction for some time to ponder my innermost call and to serve more deeply. I recalled many happy memories from my childhood when church and spiritual nurturing were part of what made me who I am. There were no dividing lines between church, school, home, family and friends. All was one quilt that wrapped around me seamlessly and encircled me completely. I recalled the many hot and hard days of everyone's working in the cotton fields and at the tobacco barn; together, everyone endured. Despite many challenges and injustices, love was the pervasive energy. During that time, the very laws that should have protected us discriminated against us; yet we felt a peace that ran as deep as still waters and as solid as stone, and we held nothing and no one in contempt. Though we were in bondage by the law, we were free souls, not held captive by hatred.

I went to seminary and recognized that was not the answer. This was a far stretch from the life of love and forgiveness that I had lived in childhood and read about from the Civil Rights Movement. Maybe I was nostalgic when I arrived, but I soon had a wake-up call. If I had seen the plague amongst college students and teachers, and counselors, then what I saw amongst many students at theology school was a severe epidemic, 100 times worse. Too many ministers were burned out; in fact, research showed that heart attack and stroke rates were much higher amongst ministers than the general population, making insurance companies reluctant to cover ministers.

This heightened my concern for people serving other people. It was not just teachers, counselors, and the college students in service learning programs; it was, in general, people serving others. What was it about people caring about and working on behalf of others that made them ill? There had to be a way to balance heart and service, because I did not want to catch the disease I saw there.

I came to accept that the answers for which I was searching were not to be found in a theological box. In fact, I saw an amazing vision of a banquet table that was beautifully spread out in an open natural area and many people, of all nationalities, sizes, styles, were coming to partake as they chose. No one decided for anyone else, but all tried what they wanted and if they did not like what they tried, they tried something else. They let their souls become satisfied. Still not yet having the lesson from the ocean, I did what I do best: I left. I simply walked away.

MY JOURNEY AS SOJOURNER

I found myself staying in a cold dark monastery in the middle of nowhere, surrounded by nothing but green fields and mountains. Though I do not recall many details about my travels there, what is most prominent in my mind is the silence like I had never experienced before. It was frightfully loud and I felt as if it were taunting me. There was the lurking of silence down every long dark hallway. I was afraid to turn the corner in fear of the silence it would bring. Around one corner, by chance I saw a monk. In that one split second, my heart leaped, thinking that this human encounter might bring meaning to the silence. I thought perhaps I would get a message from his silence, but just as quickly as the thought came, he passed by. The only thing I noticed was his silent stare through me, which was more haunting than the silence around the next corner. I was invisible.

The first two days, I thought I would run away; that is just how uncomfortable I was with the still quietness of the place. Inside, my mind was racing and conjuring up images and sounds that filled me with fear. We were told that speaking was allowed for 30 minutes a day, but that only meant a monk sat in front of the seven of us guests at dinner while we ate and asked if we had any questions. Yes, that is what talking for 30 minutes a day meant: if you had a question, you could speak it to the monk and he would respond. If you had no question, you must remain silent. "Questions?" he asked. My first was, "Why am I here?" Of course, that was within, not for the monk. Finally, about the third day, I began to tire of fighting myself. Maybe if I didn't fight against it, time would go by faster and my designated time there would be over. Then I could get back into my life and meet some of the demands that were jostling for a place of prominence in my head. In this monastery I thought I would hear my answers, but the more I tried to listen, the noisier it became.

It was around that time when I lost my will to fight against being there. The old adage is true, that struggle creates struggle. Somewhere between the noisy silence and my tiredness, I surrendered. I slowly let go and became present in the moment. I began to go with the silence, and the more I went along with it, the noises started to subside in my head; I finally let go of everything that was jostling for first place in my mind.

When I really came to accept all aspects of the quiet, when I really focused, what I needed powerfully presented itself. Beyond doubt, I came to a place of knowing. With this knowing, it was time to explore within myself what it takes to be true to self while serving others. If this were indeed my calling in life, fulfilling this very calling should not burn me out. It should renew and reenergize me. It had to be simple. The *old people* had it. What did they do? They drew from their faith, they sang, they danced. They laughed out loud, they pulled together, they celebrated, they ate healthy food, they moved their bodies, and they communed in nature. These are the things that I recall from my childhood, and they were still **my** *things*.

MY JOURNEY TO SELF

I went on a journey into the wildness, into the dark night of the soul. I turned over stones, only to find what I was looking for was here all along. The answers for which I was searching all over and out there, were in here, inside of me. I had to discover them anew and allow them to unfold. That was the simple message from the ocean: inherent in the work is the potential for joy and pain and everything on that spectrum. Sustaining self is a part of the work.

I understand life much better from this vantage point, now that I have lived a little and served more. As I reflect on my journey thus far, I see mine as a classic story of perhaps running from life in search of something that is already there. Dorothy, in the Wizard of Oz, was running from the challenges she faced, while looking for something that she already had. Dorothy and her companions went down that infamous yellow brick road where they encountered all kinds of challenges, which led them to recognize that which was inside them all along. The challenges helped them to recognize it, perhaps even to fully develop what was there. Not unlike my journey, through research, theology school, and monastery life, it all led me back to me. The journey was about recognizing and unleashing my power within. I had to sit with me and go inside to discover anew that I have what I need.

Once I opened my heart, I heard answers everywhere, especially in the safety message on airplanes given just prior to takeoff, "If you are traveling with a child or an older adult, in the unlikely event of an emergency, be sure to secure your own mask before helping others." This seems counterintuitive, because most people want to take care of children or vulnerable adults first. But the essence of this message is that, if those providing assistance fail to put on their masks first, they may run out of oxygen and become unable to help themselves **or** others. The message offers a crucial metaphor for the many educators, parents, and community leaders who currently work on behalf of others, trying to effect change in **their** lives, without taking adequate care of themselves, so that they are able to remain connected to their heart's work. Over time, this leads to burnout, workplace stress, and what some are calling compassion fatigue. This essentially reduces productivity, increases absenteeism, and leads to stress-related illnesses. In addition to the possible disconnection to the work, stress in the workplace can subsequently cause unhealthy relationships at work and home.

Multidimensional training can prevent work fatigue. Thomas M. Skovholt, professor of educational psychology at the University of Minnesota, approaches this when he asks:

> How does the opera singer care for the voice?
> The baseball player, the arm?
> The photographer, the eyes?
> The ballerina, the legs?
> The counselor, teacher, (helping professional), the self?

Again, the message is clear: just as professional dancers and athletes have to prepare their bodies, minds, and all of themselves to do their work, so do counselors, teachers, and those in the helping professions. It is equally important, if not more so, for those who serve others to take care of themselves; this was what I already knew, even as a child. The flowers, the trees, the music, the dance, prayer, love, all are there to support and uplift. It is the Sustaining the Soul work.

MY JOURNEY FROM SELF TO ALLNESS

A characteristic of the work of teaching and counseling and serving is that the end product is not always seen. When a farmer plants a crop, in a season she will go from planting the seed to seeing the full crop and reaping the benefits thereof. It is rewarding to see the full cycle of growth and the benefits of your labor. Service work is rarely like that. Often the difficult child or case, whatever it may be, is not seen from beginning to the happy ending. There are not numerous occasions to

173

celebrate huge successes. Many times a teacher does not see the most challenging child make a full turn in her classroom, or even see mountain-sized changes in behavior. Yet teachers continue to plant the seeds. This can lead us to feel as if our efforts are in vain, that what we do does not matter.

My journey has brought me to my work, *Sustaining the Soul that Serves®*, which emboldens those who serve to find that which sustains them, to find their truth, regardless of whether they see the fruits of their labor or get recognition for what they do. It provides the space and opportunities for people to listen, to awaken to that innermost voice of knowing that Island of Peace, as Howard Thurman called it; to embrace all dimensions of the work of their hearts. My work invites serving professionals, educators, program directors, administrators, and others to explore the questions:

How do I prepare myself to embrace all aspects of my work?
How can I care for and sustain myself as I do this work?
How do I maintain my connection and compassion?
What can I do to avoid burnout and too much stress?

In pondering these questions, participants are invited through meditation, journaling, prayer, dance and other creative expressions to explore what calls to their hearts to sustain themselves.

I offered the program in many different formats, including retreat settings, workshops, trainings, and conferences. It grew faster and larger than even I anticipated, and ironically, I found myself burning out and becoming over-stressed in the very work that I designed for renewal and balance. I left when it became more than a program and grew quickly into an organization, wherein staff and payroll and the overall business became larger than the work. Again, I ran away.

Finally after a few years away, I am back with the courage to embrace what has been calling to my heart all along. Knowing my propensity to run, a dear friend has lovingly reassured me of what I know better now. I have all the support that I need on this journey and I am not alone. Writing these words has brought to mind the South African word **ubuntu**, which loosely translates into English as "I am because you are and you are because I am." The word represents an African worldview of a spirit of kinship, which Archbishop Emeritus Desmond Tutu best explains: "Ubuntu is to say: My humanity is caught up, is inextricably bound up, in what is yours..."

This work is larger than my small notions, and it is tied to all who serve. I see it interconnected with other programs sharing the same goals, forming a network to support people who dedicate themselves to serve and care. Subsequently, I see it expand into holistic compassionate work, into a physical space for leadership development, healing, and renewal. I see it as welcoming all who serve to gather in retreats, workshops, trainings, and sabbaticals; common ground where participants share their journeys and explore various means to renew and sustain themselves to fulfill their life's purpose/heart's calling. Ultimately, I see an Island of Peace that brings forth healing of the mind, body, spirit, and all that ails.

Yes, I am in a divine tryst with the ocean. I continue to enjoy walking along the ocean, allowing that 10,000-petal flower to unfold with offerings and opportunities. The waves still soothe me, easing tension and stress; and the glistening sunrays, sparkling like diamonds, keep me in awesome wonder. The ocean is my constant reminder that life is a journey and it continues, that I must fill as I pour, that life can only be understood backwards, **and** I must continue to live forward.

Marian R. David, a native of Bennettsville, SC, is founding director of Sustaining the Soul that Serves (www.sustainingthesoulthatserves.org). She enjoys facilitating professional development, spiritual renewal workshops, retreats, and training. She invites others to join her in the circle of creating space/a Center to house this common work. She can be reached at uarepeace@aol.com.

Not There Yet: The Journey to the Undivided Life

By Patricia T. Mulroy

I looked in the mirror as I was talking to my sister on the phone. I told her that I was heading to a concert at a place where I thought I could be myself, a gay woman, and maybe even meet someone. She asked if I could try, just one more time, to meet a guy. I remember laughing, and with a resounding NO, I recounted my failures when I had tried to please others. I smiled as I walked out the door. I had spoken my truth.

Looking back, I guess what happened was what I now would call an inner knowing. I never imagined that a Carrie Newcomer concert, at Kirkridge Retreat and Study Center, on a cold November night, would be such a significant entrance to my journey toward an undivided life. The night before, I had been sitting at the computer in my living room, alone again on a Friday night, reading and re-reading the invitation from the director of Kirkridge to hear Carrie Newcomer. I had never heard of Carrie, so I downloaded an album from iTunes. Not bad, I thought.

A few months before, the director of Kirkridge had come to my office to welcome me to my new position as superintendent of schools. Jean Richardson gave me a copy of Parker Palmer's *The Courage to Teach* and invited me to experience the Circle of Trust retreats at Kirkridge, grounded in Parker's writing. I was intrigued, and the book sat at the corner of my desk for months.

I would glance at the cover as I thought about doing the work of my heart, leading a school district where my challenge was to raise expectations and create schools where excellence was an expectation for everyone. By that night in November, I felt like I was tripping and falling with every step on the road. My call to raise expectations was met with consternation and bitterness by the very people who claimed they wanted excellence and welcomed me to the seat.

I shared my fears and doubts about the path I was traveling as I walked with Jean in the night under a starry sky. For so many years, I had hidden the voice I heard when I sat alone in the chapel of my high school in the 1970's. Naming who you are can be a daunting proposition. Yet, naming yourself is vital, not just important, to becoming whole. I thought that if I worked harder, did more, compromised, no one would notice my "flaw." I went through my young adulthood working very hard to be successful; I was smart, athletic, and musical. I read and I practiced. I enjoyed life and had a lot of friends. But something was always missing.

In the days and months following the concert, I listened to Carrie's music and finally picked up the book that Jean had given me the previous August. Like a harbinger of things to come, *The Courage to Teach* sat, right there, on the corner of my desk. I could see it from every vantage point in my office. Maybe I thought if I picked it up, it might explode; more likely, I knew deep within that I might explode. For all those months, I didn't answer any of Jean's e-mails – as she wondered if I had read the book yet. I was riddled with guilt when each new e-mail arrived, brimming with Jean's excited questions about whether I liked the book. Questions were percolating inside me that I didn't really want to answer.

COURAGE COMES FROM HEART

Looking back now, I realized that I instinctively knew once I picked up that book, things would never, ever be the same! So

177

here I was, with this book that had sat all those months on the corner of my desk; I could no longer quiet the voice whispering from a distant place that sounded like home. I cracked the cover and I read. Day by day, I sat in silence, hearing a familiar call, a voice of someone I knew. I felt fear and trepidation as I remembered this call from years ago, sitting in the chapel of my high school, early in the morning, before throngs of young women filled the halls. Maybe, just maybe, I knew this voice, this call that had been buried deep, away from the crowds of people I thought I was supposed to please. As I read I became more convinced that I needed to raise expectations for every child. I had ideas and I was moving fast... maybe too fast.

That cold, dark and starry night at Kirkridge let me know I was not alone. I finished reading Parker's *Courage to Teach* and signed up for a Courage retreat, facilitated by Jean and Sally Z. Hare. When I timidly showed up at Kirkridge that February in the middle of a blizzard, my heart and soul mirrored the cold, snowy winter weather of Pennsylvania's Pocono Mountains. Called to the circle of strangers, I listened to Sally explain that the root of the word *courage* is the Latin *cor*, meaning heart.

Could it be that who I am lies at the center of **my** *cor*? I set myself on a path to figure out what this strange and determined pull was that tugged at my heart and occupied my thinking. The work that I had loved so dearly now felt tiresome and sad. Did I have the courage to help the children who were struggling? Could I persuade others that each child should leave our school ready for the world? As a leader I wanted the best for everyone, but as I pushed for equal opportunities for children, I feared I would meet resistance and that my "flaw" would be found out. Then what??

I sat at that Circle of Trust retreat in the February snow in silence and knew it was true. I was naming the missing piece of the puzzle. Just like in the chapel in high school, away from the crowd, I could hear a voice deep inside me explaining what I feared, what no one wanted to talk about. In the 70's, being

178

gay was labeled as a psychological dysfunction, a religious abomination, and a social deviation. I heard popular performer Anita Bryant on the TV and radio, making statements like, "If gays are granted rights, next we'll have to give rights to prostitutes and to people who sleep with St. Bernards...." and I realized that most people were afraid. Even the people who loved me were afraid. I was afraid. If I were gay, then people were going to be afraid of **me**. But I knew I wasn't any of those things: I wasn't sick or an abomination or deviant. I was athletic and strong, I sang and played my guitar each week in church, and I certainly followed all the rules (well, maybe). People liked me. I was a young leader. The shadow of fear and doubt haunted me, and I hid behind my success and my smile – in high school, in college, and in the world.

During that cold February blizzard I was broken open in the company of strangers. I pondered the blizzard of my life in metaphor and story. Where was my rope that would help me find home in this blizzard; how would I find my way? Early in my teaching career, when I had followed in the footsteps of a mentor and tried on his methods for a while, I failed miserably at connecting to the students. They saw right through me. Masquerading as someone else didn't work. Now, here I stood, feeling that same struggle between hearing my own voice or trying to please others. The facilitators spoke of the Mobius strip, the seamlessness of the inner and outer journey. I left the retreat with more questions than answers. Remembering my early failure when I mimicked a style that was not my own, I knew the choice I would have to make – but what would the consequences be? Would I have the courage to stand in my own truth? Could I, would I, claim my identity in the blizzard of who I am, who I was, and who I would be in the world?

The words "someone they trusted" tumbled into my head. Despite the call to slow down, to quell the millions of ideas, I knew I couldn't slow down or stop believing that there was a better way to meet children where they were. I needed to listen, I did. But to whom should I listen? Should I follow along with legislation and politics, or hear parents and teachers and children? I was short-tempered with people who wanted me to slow down. How could I slow down? For some children and families we were the only chance they had to create something better. I cringed when I heard a teacher claim a fourth-grade child would never amount to anything! How could we write off a nine-year-old?

I had come to my work believing that each of us wants our children to succeed. Somewhere along this road I found that to be a truth that could be elusive, with many different definitions. Somewhere along the way I realized that not everyone believed or cared that all children can learn. Could I restore that hope for teachers and leaders? Did I still believe we can make a difference? Pitted against each other, educators and taxpayers and politicians, we were all leaving the children behind. What could I do?

I returned to a circle of strangers again in July, this time in New Hampshire with different facilitators, hopeful that the Courage work could help heal my own broken heart and give me the resilience to stay in a job that I truly believed was my calling. Shrouded in a failed attempt to create a school budget that included the voices of *all*, one that satisfied my own heart, I figured I had nothing to lose. My courage was waning as I drove into the White Mountains of New Hampshire. Winter's blizzards and darkness had subsided, but spring brought rain, with mud and murkiness. Would the promised abundance come in the summer? Sitting again in the silence, I realized that I liked the challenge more than the job. I sat with the question, am I doing my heart's work? I was feeling brokenhearted **and** I was feeling alive.

LISTENING TO MY OWN HEART

The importance of identity and integrity bubbled to the surface for me as I listened to my own heart and soul in several Circles of Trust over the next year. The voice that had been quiet and subdued for so long was becoming stronger. I could hear a call to authenticity in the words of poets and prophets, mystics and songwriters. I found the same sense of safety in the Circle that I had in the chapel of my youth and in the songs of the Indigo Girls and Carrie Newcomer. I shook with fear most days as I climbed into my car and headed to work. I turned up the volume to the songs that spoke of courage and sang along. The music gave me courage to face myself as I climbed the steps to an office that felt like a foreign land. Would my ability to accept myself give me the ability to value the other? Could I become present for those to whom no one was listening? How could I sustain the courage to keep showing up?

So much has happened since that cold November night when I first showed up at Kirkridge. I said to a friend recently that I felt I was finished -- and she said that perhaps I was finished, but not there yet. That somehow resonates; finished with so much, but not there yet. As I let go of thoughts I have been holding so tightly, I feel lighter...

and
Nothing is truly mine....

I hold my thoughts only briefly
and they are gone.
I scratch them out on a piece of paper.
At times they fly so fast
that they don't get down
into the lead
and onto the pressed paper.
Out into the universe.
I think of all those thoughts floating freely.

One time I was reading,
I think from *Chaos Theory*,
of those ideas and images
out in the universe,
beyond our ideas and thoughts.
No original ideas.

181

Right here in this moment
someone else is scheming up
the same plan for a necklace, a school,
a prayer bead, a book;
a phrase drops out,
a marvelous creation,
or chicken soup.

Not ours - yours and mine to keep
but to share for a moment.
Savoring the taste of your mouth,
the sweetness of your skin,
it is neither yours nor mine.
But we share in the dreaminess
of the moment,
the connection, the bliss.

And it is gone.

---Patricia Mulroy

I have traveled through many seasons on this journey to living undivided. Much is finished, but I am not there yet. Not long ago, I stood at the top of the mountain that is Kirkridge and said my marriage vows. Yes, naming is vital to wholeness: marriage matters, and Jean is my wife.

I no longer climb the stairs to an office. I left my job as the superintendent. I have explored my heart from fall into winter, then into spring. I have sat with poets and priests, visited schools and churches, searching for the heart and soul of what I can bring to education. Today, I am one step closer to opening a school, one that is welcoming, a school grounded in democracy at Kirkridge. I am not there yet: it is not a public school, and I will have to raise funds to make it affordable and accessible. I never dreamed of walking away from the public education I value; I never dreamed that I would be on this path.

I am thankful for the people I have met along the way, people who spoke their own truth. I met people who did not set limits on possibility, who opened my eyes, who spoke of schools that honored creativity and spirit; schools where adults trust that children will learn. I listened carefully as they shared about their schools, rooted in the belief that children can be trusted with their own learning. As they spoke, I found myself wondering, could I do this? My answer was yes, and I will. Summer, in its abundance, has blessed me. I have experienced darkness, abundance and light. With great hope and anticipation I walk on a path to wholeness and integrity every day.

When I wake each morning, I center down in my own personal circle of trust with my wife, before I bustle to my station to create and dream of spaces that help students learn in their time, not mine. I now work with Blended Schools Network, someone else's dream of creating learning spaces that empower students and teachers. We deliver world languages to schools that can't afford to offer critical languages like Russian, Japanese, Chinese and Arabic. I show up whole as I talk to teachers in Egypt and Taiwan, Washington and Pennsylvania, who teach students all across the US. We meet on common ground and people learn about language and culture! Opportunities that would not exist without a lot of creativity and the internet. No, I do not walk the steps of an institution that binds me to put all children in one classroom or learn at someone else's pace.

I am finding my way home these days. I am finished with a lot. But I am not there yet, as I continue this journey to the undivided life.

 Dr. Patricia T. Mulroy, Learning Institute Coordinator at Blended Schools Network and Consultant. She has been a public school administrator and teacher in East Stroudsburg and Bangor, PA. She lives in Bangor, PA with her wife, Jean Richardson and their children, Daro, Kera, Alek and Peter and two crazy Labrador retrievers, Tootsie and Babe. More of Pat's work can be found at patmulroy.blogspot.com and you can contact her by email: mulroy.pat@gmail.com

My Inner Journey with the Circle of Trust

By Sue E. Small

Writing is an exploration. You start from nothing and learn as you go.

> --- E.L. Doctorow

$\mathbf{M}$y journey began years ago in my heart.

As a little girl growing up in the 1940's and 50's, I was trying to make sense of the meaning of life as I experienced and could "see" it. There was a lot going on: World War II, the Holocaust, the Servicemen's Readjustment Act (the G.I. Bill of Rights), the death of Franklin Delano Roosevelt, the Supreme Court Decision *Brown v. Board of Education*, and the Civil Rights Movement, to mention a few.

As these significant events were occurring, we were also seeing some major changes in the structure of the American family. Although women worked in the factories for war-related production for much of the 1940's, many were sent home when the returning GI's needed the jobs; however, more women than ever before continued to join the workforce. The birth rate went up from the decline during the Great Depression, as the post-World War II business cycle brought nearly full employment. By 1950, the stereotyped ideal for an American family was seen as a working father, stay-at-home mother, and one child, maybe two.

My family was like that: father, mother, and child living in the Heartland of the United States of America. As a privileged only child, who didn't really want a new little brother, I was challenged by the dilemma that an addition to our family created. So when I was five and my brother was born with a genetic disorder, Down syndrome, I thought it was my fault. I had not really "wanted" a new brother, and when he was found to have an intellectual disability with serious medical problems, I felt responsible. I prayed and prayed every night, "Please God, let him get well and come home." That was not possible and the situation was life-changing for me.

I could not forgive myself. So my journey started long ago in my heart when, as a young and only child, I was unable to understand the circumstances of life, and I lost the capacity to trust God or myself.

Yet years later, when I reviewed the most significant events of my life, I found family and siblings to be the first and probably the most important steps in my journey of learning to trust. This dilemma of my childhood is just one of several paradoxes that are part of my story of how I discovered the Circle of Trust to be the trustworthy companion I needed for my journey. Guided by the principles, practices, and touchstones conceptualized by Parker J. Palmer and the Center for Courage & Renewal and the Courage facilitators who hold the safe space for the participants to do our individual work, Circles of Trust become exactly what each of us needs them to be.

For me, it has been a journey of faith. I didn't realize it at the beginning, but now it is becoming clearer. My journey has taken me into the unknown, the deepest parts of my Self, still a mystery to me and still in the process of developing. While my little-girl Self didn't understand, I could only see God then as punishing and remote, unless I saw through the eyes of His Son, probably because of my relationship with two aspects of the Three-Person God in my religious roots. Only much later, as an adult in the Circles of Trust, could I comprehend the idea of a Holy Spirit or Inner Teacher within me. I have come to know that this third side of God, in the Three-Person God of my childhood, is within to guide me into Truth, especially about myself and my hidden wholeness. It was, and still is, to me as fragile as a delicate flower; it must be tended and nurtured. The Circle of Trust sustains me with that loving care.

FIRST CIRCLE OF TRUST CHANGED HOW I SEE

Looking back at my life and my long career in education, I see a significant change when I applied for and attended my first Circle of Trust retreat. I had decided to give myself the gift of this retreat for a significant birthday milestone. At this time I was 65 years old and had spent 46 years in education. This gift to myself began my journey with Circles of Trust (COT), and I began to "see" things differently.

Although, prior to this time, I had been engaged in several religious and spiritual practices, my reflective writings were from my heart, too impatient to wait for my soul to show up. I did not trust others or myself until I came to the COT retreat. There I learned to speak from my soul in a community where I was "heard into speech," as I remember Nelle Morton's words, after taking the time to write from my heart and hear **myself** into speech. For the first time, I began to see my life as a journey, a process of movement in a spiritual sense, of advancing from one state to another with my own internal compass, rather than a trip with success as the destination and the need for someone else's map. This was quite a different experience from any I had had in other practices, perhaps because I was not ready before. I had come to a new intersection of my traditional Christian upbringing and COT.

Sustaining Identity and Integrity in Professional Life was that first retreat, in November, 2005, in Chapel Hill, North Carolina. I wondered "what's next" with little idea of what to expect, even though I had read Parker's description in *A Hidden Wholeness* that a "circle of trust" is the kind of community "that knows how to welcome the soul and help us to hear its voice." During that retreat, I was invited to recount the Stepping Stones in my life; there, within that space, I was able to write about the turning points in my life as beginning with the "birth of

186

siblings." As I wrote and then told my story to another person, this time I heard it with new meaning and purpose.

I wrote that "my brother was born with Down syndrome; it changed our lives." AND I added, "Later, when my sister and another brother were born, they enriched our lives and gave us something and someone else to live for. By that time I was a third parent or part of the team holding the family together." I was able to see a new truth about responsibility and forgiveness. That turning point, reached in that first Circle of Trust, moved me forward after many years of keeping the secret inside my heart, first as a child and later as an adult. It was within the Circle of Trust that I was able to see more clearly the illusion of hiding within my heart or running away from that which was real. So the journey of beginning within, or from inside out, at the intersection of my perceptions of formal religious beliefs and formation of spiritual direction, was sustained within a Circle of Trust.

In the closing circle we were invited to speak into to the circle, without any need for dialogue or discussion. My evidence that all of me could show up, including my soul, surprised me when I stood and sang and danced around the circle, inviting the Circle of Trust to be my companion on this new journey. My song? "May I have this dance for the rest of my life? Will you be my partner every night? When we're together, it feels so right. May I have this dance for the rest of my life?" Believe it or not, a woman named Sandy got up and danced around the circle with me! My heart was opening. I was with like-minded people. I had begun to reclaim my identity and act with integrity in what I could "see" as a safe, trusted environment.

During that first retreat, I "saw" the Circle of Trust itself as my companion on the journey toward the "hidden wholeness" I was seeking. Seeing my life in terms beyond success and my career, I uncovered some of those parts that had been carefully hidden in what Peggy McIntosh calls the "invisible knapsack of white privilege." The touchstones based on the guiding principles and practices of Courage work, poems and other third things, silence and solitude, and the community of others who were in attendance became new aspects of a community where I could find myself. With the gentle invitation to identify "Stepping Stones" that were turning points in my life, I noticed and named those people, events, and experiences which, upon reflection today, still are embedded in my life and career, though with new meaning and purpose.

LIVING THE QUESTIONS

By the time I applied for my third retreat the next year, this time in San Rafael, CA, I began my application with the words, "Is it well? Is it well with my soul?" In voicing that question, I could see a shift, a movement toward more clarity, as I let go of my illusion that success is of utmost importance, and moved towards knowing that my hidden wholeness is more important. This question was the one I carried with me from my second Circle of Trust retreat in Pawleys Island, South Carolina, where we explored the poet Rilke's idea of living the questions, as he suggested in his letter to a young poet:

> *...have patience with everything unresolved in your heart and try to love the questions themselves as if they were locked rooms or books written in a very foreign language. Don't search for the answers, which could not be given to you now because you would not be able to live them. And, the point is to live everything.*
> *Live the questions now.*
> *Perhaps then, someday far in the future, you will gradually, without even noticing it, live your way into the answer.*

I understood that if I am to continue this work toward wholeness, I must begin within, in my heart where my journey had begun.

In that third COT retreat, in response to the Wendell Berry's

188

Manifesto: The Mad Farmer Liberation Front, I wrote my own Manifesto, declaring that I would live with my new companion and according to a principle that was new to me, *trust*.

Trust
So, friends, every day we will do something.
Anything.
Whatever we do will be enough.

Smile and laugh at ourselves for doing...
whatever it was.
While it may have been noble and good,
it probably was not necessary.

Whatever and whoever we are is
enough for that day.
Sleep. Dream. Wake up.

Begin a new day—
again.

Trust.

There, with a Circle of Trust as my reliable companion, In addition to singing and dancing, I had begun to write poetry!

COT's are now my reliable escorts into the unknown, guides that sustain my search for meaning and purpose in the journey of my life. As I have journeyed to retreats in all parts of the country, I have embraced the knowing that I must continue with these steadfast companions until the journey's end. When I began the journey, I thought I was living undivided, as I had been unable to separate my life and career; my career actually dictated my life. What I treasured was my work in teaching and learning. Although I now understand that my career may have been undivided, I name and claim that my life is more than my work and so am I!

DISCOVERING MY HIDDEN SELVES

I attended a recent COT, *Writing Along the Mobius Strip: A*

189

Practice to Set Your Heart at Rest, with my sister (one of the siblings I am so grateful to have). We were encouraged to identify the hidden parts of ourselves and to get to know all the parts of ourselves that contribute to healing and wholeness in our lives, as well as all the parts that are carrying the burdens of deforming experiences. During my time in that retreat, I was able to identify Martha Sue who likes to tell me (and others) what to do, as well as Jenny Ann who likes to make fun her plan, and Mary Grace who wants to see God face to face. This revelation did not take place immediately.

After that retreat, my sister and I spent every Friday morning talking about our hidden selves and how we wanted the best ones to show up for each of the situations we faced in our very different lives. Circles of Trust had become companions on our journey as a family to knowing what child we had left behind, and to enabling us, now as adults, to finally call our best Selves to the front of the room for each specific time and life situation. We were able to talk about and say to ourselves, "When I am partnering with my very best Self, what does it look like and feel like I am doing?" In addition we asked, "When I am partnering and it's hard, what does it look like, feel like, and what am I doing?"

Since that COT experience we have been able to continue the process of identifying those hidden parts of ourselves and to get to know all the parts of ourselves that contribute to healing and wholeness. Now we feel we are empowered to meet our hidden selves more often!

Each COT is grounded in the same principles and practices, but each has a different theme, a different way of inviting the soul. In the fall of 2013, I attended another retreat in Pawleys Island with the theme of *Seeking: The Journey to An Undivided Life.* There I understood the process of seeking in a deeper way, and realized that, while it may be a prolonged journey over my lifetime, I finally identified what I have been and, perhaps still am, seeking... to know and accept myself, just as I am.

After more than twenty COT retreats over the past eight years, I know that I am still seeking **MY** Story, listening for what my life wants to do with me instead of what I want to do with my life. I am celebrating the life I have and have had. When I returned from the Seeking retreat and read the letter I had written to myself, I was able to hear myself say, *I love my life* and mean it, the dark sides as well as the light. I am still *living the questions* that came in early Circles of Trust. At the same time I continue to live into new questions as I seek ways to go deeper.

With the Circle of Trust as my companion, I am beginning to SEE what I do (and have done) with "soft eyes," letting that which I have DONE and LEFT UNDONE actually BE the beauty I love... without criticizing, just accepting that I am who I am, with forgiveness and gratitude for the life I have lived. Yet as I reread my journals, my letters to myself, and notes from Clearness Committees, I find patterns and themes that reoccur: issues of identity, trust, conflict, privilege.

In preparation for a retreat last spring at Kirkridge Retreat and Study Center in Pennsylvania, I painted a picture of myself in the midst of a great storm, holding fast to a tree. I named it, "Painting the Picture of My Life: Holding On." I shared this experience with a COT friend, and later received a note with the Havelock Ellis quote: "The art of living lies in a fine mingling of letting go and holding on." So then after the retreat, I painted another picture, of a procession of faculty and students at graduation; I was in it. I named this one, "Graduation Day: Letting Go, Living the Dream." Once more, with the Circle of Trust as my companion, I found that I can express myself, see, and hear my voice, this time through the artist's way.

My journey began long ago in my heart – and as I have continued to journey within Circles of Trust, I have changed the way I see. My paradigm has shifted from trying to understand how I might contribute to the reform of education, especially teacher education, and participate in a movement for non-violence, to one of spiritual formation, one I had never recognized in my religious practices. I have found my Inner Teacher and with that, gathering of the Three-Persons of God and the selves I have discovered within. Those selves, born as I wrestled with God and supported by my Circle of Trust, are merging into a new hidden Self, and I name her Hope.

I can acknowledge that I am who I am and, at the same time, I can change. I will be what I will be. Now, as I am preparing to leave my long career as a teacher and college professor, I am again facing the lifelong challenge of learning to trust and to live undivided, with my not-so-hidden wholeness. I am at another intersection on the journey. I need companions. I want to know My Story and find the courage to share my story. I want to teach what I most need to learn, to let go.

That understanding has been continuing to develop even as I am part of **this** Writers Circle of Trust. Through this experience I am seeing the words of E.L. Doctorow come to life: **"Writing is an exploration. You start from nothing and learn as you go."** I am beginning to let what I do be the beauty that I see... and to let the beauty that I see be what I do. Looking back with soft eyes at the divided ambitious young woman driven by a culture that insisted I should reach the American Dream through hard work and the invisible benefits of White Privilege to where I am now, reconnecting soul and role as an elder who is learning to take the time to get to know and trust herself through the Circles of Trust, my hope is to finish well.

Dr. Sue E. Small is Clinical Associate Professor of Education at University of Maryland Baltimore County (UMBC) and partner in the Human Resource Group (HRG). She lives in Lutherville-Timonium, Maryland, with her friend, LeRoy R. Johnson, where she reads and watches the deer, the trees, the foxes, the birds, and the sun come up in the morning. She can be **contacted through e-mail at** sue17small@verizon.net **or** small@umbc.edu

From the Margins to the Center

By Veta Goler

For years, I described myself as existing on the margin of the margins. That was how I expressed my experience of being different from mainstream society—and from countercultural elements, too—in almost every measurable way.

I am an African American woman, self-described free spirit, and a practitioner of an Eastern spiritual path with a guru. I am an artist (a dancer—and modern dance, at that) and a nature-lover, and I have been in a committed, loving relationship with a most wonderful woman for over 20 years. All of this definitely placed me on the outer edges—even of those seen as "other."

Twenty-six years ago, I joined the dance faculty at Spelman College, the preeminent liberal arts college for black women. I feel honored to be there. Spelman is highly regarded for producing talented, capable and visionary young women who go on to make major positive changes in the world. Although there are several ways that I am "other" to members of the Spelman community, I have found a comfortable work home there. Without having to worry about sexism or racism, and with the presence of some forward-thinking faculty, presidents, provosts and other administrators, I have found a safe space to be myself, a place where I can follow my heart.

I didn't always feel this way. There were years when my sense of being "other" at Spelman was overwhelming and disheartening.

DANCE DEJECTION

I came to Spelman as a modern dance choreographer, performer and teacher. Yet, few students had heard of modern dance; they knew only the ballet and jazz they had seen on television or on Broadway, or the African dance forms they had experienced at cultural centers. Many seemed resistant to the dance I had to offer. One painful example was my choreographic work, Tattoo, the dance I created based on Toni Morrison's novel, *Sula*. Students refused to perform some of the movements I had created that expressed the deep friendship between Sula and Nell and rejected some of my costuming choices. In addition, some of my faculty colleagues seemed to view the arts with skepticism, as if we artists didn't belong at a liberal arts college. We were fine as entertainment, but our disciplines were not to be taken seriously as academic courses of study. I remember feeling dejected after college-wide faculty meetings because I felt so out of place, so unseen and unappreciated.

A bright spot during this time was the development of my relationship with my life partner. When we met in early 1992, despite her inner knowing that I would be important to her and the fact that we had much in common—and fantastic conversations—I resisted pursing a romantic relationship. I had made the decision to be "normal." For two years we shared lots of meals, went to arts events regularly and talked and talked—often about Spelman. Finally, I realized that she had all the qualities I was looking for in a life partner; my issue was what society would think. Fortunately, I had the strength to follow my heart, and the friendship we had developed over the two years provided a wonderful base for a loving, fulfilling partnership.

After I earned my doctorate, began serving on college-wide committees, moved from dance performance to dance history, and gained tenure, things began to change at Spelman. I had acquired a degree of legitimacy. Eventually, I chaired my department and led the faculty as president of Spelman's faculty senate.

However, as I was becoming more a part of campus life, I started to feel a different kind of distress. I was aware of an emptiness inside. In some ways, this didn't make sense. The pieces of my life were all good. I did the noble work of educating young black women, I spent lots of quality time with my partner and other members of my wonderful circle of family and friends, and I was in good health. But something was missing.

THE MISSING WHOLE

What was missing was a spiritual focus for my life, a commitment to living a contemplative life that would allow me to live in wholeness rather than divided parts. Yes, the pieces were all good. But they were pieces... Separate fragments.

In retrospect, I realize that my inner self had a particular vision for my life and that, before I consciously knew what that was, I was already taking steps in that direction. I was doing things that I later saw were connected by a contemplative thread. These things, these steps, actually created a path for my life. Later, when the path was clear and I moved on it more intentionally, it didn't feel like a path, it felt like my true life... My undivided life.

It all began in 1996, when I discovered my spiritual path and began regular practices of meditation, silence, chanting, journaling and going on spiritual retreats. In the late 1990's, I read Parker Palmer's book, *The Courage to Teach,* and began organizing discussions and other activities inspired by the book with different faculty groups at Spelman.

In August, 2003, I had been on spiritual retreat for seven weeks at an ashram near Mumbai, India, and was preparing to return home. As I was meditating one morning, I received the message to spiritualize my work life. Spiritualize my work life? On one hand, this seemed a very odd message, as work and spirituality are usually separate in U.S. academic institutions. On the other hand, it seemed right. I no longer wanted to compartmentalize my life by balancing career, emotional, spiritual, and other aspects of life as if they were separate, though related, entities.

I knew instinctively that everything is spiritual—not religious, but spiritual. I had come to believe that we are spiritual beings having human experiences, and if we each connect with and follow our inner voice, the decisions we make and actions we take will help us to fulfill our dreams and achieve our goals.

Once I committed myself to spiritualizing my work life, opportunities to do so flourished.

For example, a serendipitous work trip led me to the website of the Center for Courage & Renewal and to Parker Palmer's book, *A Hidden Wholeness.* I then registered for a retreat based on the book, which was being held in Pawleys Island, South Carolina, at the end of November, 2003. This retreat changed my life. I felt that I was at a spiritual retreat, but it was in the context of my work life. I felt free, willing to risk revealing my true self, and supported by complete strangers. I felt like I had come home. This retreat led to a two-year Courage to Teach retreat series and many other Circle of Trust retreats. I cherish these retreats. Stepping out of my daily rounds and devoting my time and energy to listening to my inner self profoundly refreshes me. My soul resonates with these experiences, and as I fulfill my soul, I realize more of my potential.

THE COURAGE TO FACILITATE

I knew very early in the Courage to Teach series that I wanted to become a Courage facilitator, and I completed the facilitator preparation program in 2007. Since then, I have been able to bring together my contemplative practices, my commitment to helping others explore contemplative endeavors, my creativity, my love of nature, and my love of being on retreat—all in a work context—through retreat facilitation. When I am facilitating Courage retreats, I know I am using my birthright gifts, and I am making important positive contributions to the world.

Soon after my first Courage retreat, I discovered another organization important in my efforts to spiritualize my work life. The Association for Contemplative Mind in Higher Education (ACMHE), which exists under the auspices of the Center for Contemplative Mind in Society, offers contemplative pedagogy seminars and webinars, contemplative retreats for academics; a resource rich website with articles and syllabi on contemplative research and courses, and a network of like-minded people.

My intention to spiritualize my work life also led me to add to the things I was already doing. I continued to have a few moments of "centering silence" at the start of my dance history classes—one of the contemplative practices I used to help students connect with and hear their own inner voices. I talked with the Dean of the Chapel about adding a meditation room to her renovation plans for the building that would house her offices. When renovations were complete, I began holding weekly meditation sessions for students, faculty and staff. These sessions continue today, but in a larger space because of demand.

Later, I developed a course, Contemplative Practices and the Arts, in which students learn about and engage in different contemplative practices, study artists who create contemplatively, explore art works with spiritual themes, and try their own hand at making art contemplatively. Another conversation with the Dean of the Chapel has led to the construction of a labyrinth on campus. I have offered "Instant Sabbaticals" workshops and similar lunch-and-learn sessions for faculty and staff. I have created a faculty group that comes together for contemplative practices and to discuss contemplative pedagogy, and I have led two day-long Courage retreats for Spelman faculty and staff.

I have also created space for other Spelman faculty to feel safe enough to be themselves more fully. For three years, President Beverly Daniel Tatum and I co-hosted a series of faculty dinners at her campus home. We took a contemplative approach to our dialogues, assigning readings for each session, but not discussing them in the typical academic way. Instead, we used the readings as jumping-off points for reflective activities. I was always profoundly moved by the depth with which people shared and am proud that fifty faculty members were able to experience a different way of being on campus, a way in which others got to know them beyond their disciplines, as themselves. And I am delighted that contemplative efforts were at the heart of these dialogues.

THE CONSCIENCE OF SPELMAN

In fact, I have become the contemplative "go-to" person at Spelman and am often invited to lead meditation sessions for different campus groups. Most recently, I gave a presentation on The Contemplative Leader at a retreat for Spelman's student leadership group. As I was preparing to talk and lead the students in a meditation practice, the program director introduced me as one of a few people she considers to be "the conscience of Spelman College." She and I have had several good conversations about the power of contemplative practices, but I hadn't realized how much she values what I offer.

The conscience of Spelman. That is a long way from being on the periphery of the institution. What changed? I believe that my constant little steps over time—coupled with greater openness in society and in the Spelman community—have led people to see me less as "other."

At the same time, my own personal practices and willingness to follow my inner voice have resulted in my redefining what center is—and placing myself there. This change in how I see myself is important, not just for myself, but also for Spelman students. I recently received a thank-you note from a student in one of my Contemplative Practices and the Arts classes after I recommended her for graduate school. She wrote, "Thank you for your unyielding gentleness and support of my academic goals and personal joys. I am grateful for your patience, your willingness to think outside of the box and your embodiment of spirit. Your equanimity is a gift and I am often looking to my experience of you as I grow into a more measured, self-valuing adult. So thank you for being so steadily yourself."

I was moved to tears by this beautiful note. I felt that my efforts to be myself have paid off. This student clearly saw and valued me for who and what and how I am. I stopped referring to myself as being on the margins of the margin a few years ago. I know now that I am solidly centered in my own eyes, most importantly, but also in the eyes of at least a few others.

Veta Goler, PhD, is Arts and Humanities Division Chair and Associate Professor of Dance at Spelman College. A dance historian and former modern dance artist, she has been a national Circle of Trust® facilitator since 2007 and can be reached at vetagoler@gmail.com.

You've Gotta Do Your Homework

By Carolyn Ellis

I asked, when old enough to think to ask,
And young enough to expect an answer,
"When will I know? Is it Chance, or God,
Or Choice – My Choice – that makes my life?
The kind eyes and the kind words of my Baptist
Sunday school teacher gave this gift:
"You will probably never know."

Jacob wrestled with God face to face, engaged
In a fight that left him limping and renamed, not
"Led by God," not "Guided by God," but now
Israel, "The One Who Strives With God."

Clay asked, my son wanted to know, "Why does
God not just give us all we need to know?"
His eight year old soul was wondering
About wrestling with multiplication and spelling.

He did not want to do his homework.

--Carolyn Ellis

I wrote this poem in 2009. I was
remembering a time when I was about
thirteen and asked my Sunday school teacher when I would
know the truth, when I would have all the answers. I do not
recall the particular issue I was struggling with at the time,
but the feeling still haunted me. Perhaps it was integration
or some other social issue of the 1960's. Perhaps it was
a question of the correct time and form for baptism or

200

some other theological or ecclesiastical issue related to the Southern Baptist Church I attended. Maybe I was trying to imagine what I would do with my life or what I would be when I grew up.

LOOKING FOR A FILE FULL OF ANSWERS

I often wondered what God was calling me to do. I had a lot of questions in those days. What I really wanted was a filing cabinet containing all the answers so that all I would have to do was identify the problem or dilemma, flip through the files, and have the solution or resolution—the answer.

Fortunately for me, my teacher's answer was, "Probably never." I do not remember being disappointed with his reply, even though I'd hoped for more. I found it unsettling to not have a filing cabinet of answers, an infallible pope, and an inerrant holy book. I wanted the Truth.

My teacher could have answered my query, "When will I have the Truth?" with something like, "We have given you the Truth. You must accept Jesus as your Savior." And if I had been someone other than who I am, I might have accepted his answer. Instead, for a the past fifty years I have found myself invigorated by the freedom that Sunday school teacher's evaluation of the nature of life gave me.

I have listened to voices questioning authority and have enjoyed honest and vigorous debate that rocks the boat of the status quo. I like being part of conversations that lead to new and healthy understandings of issues. I like not having all the answers.

Apparently my Sunday school teacher was not as happy with his answer as I was. Some fifteen years later I was visiting my hometown and I ran into him at the local tire store. When we ended up waiting together for our repairs to be completed, he hesitantly asked me if I remembered the incident and he wanted to apologize. I wondered if he'd come to realize he'd granted me too much leeway. Maybe he felt cynical or lax in his religious duties. He had worried for all those years about telling me I would probably never have all the answers. I tried to assure him that his handling of my question had not warped me in any way, that, in fact, I'd been enlivened by his response. I told him he had done me an enormous favor, and I still feel that way today.

When our son was about eight, he asked a question similar to mine. He wanted to know why God didn't just zap him with everything he needed to know. I launched into an explanation about humans and their need to learn. I told him about instinct, the innate, genetic inborn-knowing of lower animals. My answer was infinitely more involved than, "Probably never." I am sure Clay did not listen to or appreciate my explanation because what he really wanted to avoid was the pain and effort of doing his homework.

While I don't consider myself a scholar, I have always enjoyed doing my homework. Researching and expanding my knowledge are exciting pursuits. I remain grateful to my Sunday school teacher for leaving the door open to learning more about the universe outside myself. I am thankful for eventually coming to what I call soul work, homework of the deepest sort. I would never have found the depth and mystery I experience inside a file cabinet full of answers.

Looking back, it seems obvious that my existential plight could not be addressed by anything short of searching my own soul, but home and my religious traditions directed the search for God, Truth, and Meaning outside of my Self. When I asked my Sunday school teacher for answers, I fully expected that they would and could come to me from an outside source. I thought that Truth could be given to me. I had no idea I could look for it on my own, much less within myself. I was taught I might have glimpses, but I would always be lacking. In fact, when I look at it more closely, what I was taught was to diminish my Self

202

in order to find God/Meaning/Truth. The message was clear: "Do not trust your own heart, mind, or soul to find the Truth."

FIRST STEPS

My initial departure from what I'd been taught about original sin, atonement, and a patriarchal and theistic God, began with reading. I read Paul Tillich, Marcus Borg, John Shelby Spong, and Karen Armstrong, just to name a few. Their words began to loosen the control of the voices that taught me what to believe as a child. I felt confused and challenged as my previous thinking began to give way to new ideas.

I had difficulty liberating myself from the image of God as an old white man who lived in the upper tier of a three-tiered hierarchal universe. For a long time I had functioned with the understanding that God is in Heaven and my job was to appeal to his masculine being. Now I was beginning to question and even to reject this concept. I was grateful to Paul Tillich and others for helping and continuing to help me turn the ocean liner of my perception of God to the significant insight that God is not a being, but is Being Itself or the Ground of All Being.

This shift in my perspective was painful and laborious, but as time passed, it also became more important. I loved and was enlivened by the academic exploration of new and intellectually compatible ideas of Truth. My mind and my heart were opening as I took my first steps toward finding my own Truth. The insights and gifts of those who walked before me provided much strength for my soul. These writers served as reliable guides as I worked to find my way toward the undivided life I want to live. I was beginning to know I would never have the answers I once sought. This knowledge was freeing and somewhat daunting as I surrendered wanting answers and moved into knowing that the dance toward Truth is full of questions and is never ending.

There is a significant difference between discussing the inner journey and actually taking the necessary steps on it. The next step on my journey toward Truth took place serendipitously when I attended my first Circle of Trust, led by Sally Z. Hare and grounded in Parker Palmer's *Politics of the Brokenhearted*. Fortunately for me, this is where my most effective soul work began. I was introduced to the idea that breaking my heart could open my heart to new possibilities. Parker describes a way of being that "begins 'in here' as we work on reconciling whatever divides us from ourselves."

I have attended three other Circles of Trust as a way of a giving myself effective homework/soul work. It is always difficult for me to put into words what happens to my soul and my being at these retreats, but something does happen and the results are life-changing. Being invited into this Writers Circle of Trust has challenged me to take stock and try to convey what I am learning on this journey toward Truth and my Self.

THIRD THINGS

One of the practices employed in Circles of Trust is the use of a third thing, which may be a poem, story, piece of music, or anything really that, when presented into the circle, invites individuals to go more deeply inside to hear themselves; they then are invited to share within the safe community. That's important; the process is always one of invitation; it's never share or die! There are no right and wrong answers, and the space within the circle is safely held. I have found greater insight and learned from myself through this invitational use of third things. A particularly significant teacher for me has been John O'Donohue's "For Presence" from *To Bless the Space Between Us*. After reading it, I so wanted the blessing to be a part of me that I decided to memorize it so I could use it as a meditation.

Some interesting things happened as I was working to memorize the piece. One line, "Respond to the call of your gift and the courage to follow its path," took me awhile to master. I kept saying, "Respond to the gift of your call," rather than "the call of your gift." There were other lines where my brain resisted the poem and insisted upon changing the words, giving me insights into myself. Was I still, fifty years later, waiting to be zapped with the outside call from beyond? Was I still looking for the filing cabinet full of answers? As I sat with those questions in the midst of meditation, I caught my breath and my spirit in the realization that it is not egocentric to trust my inner voice. It is essential.

Another breath and spirit-catching aspect of our retreats is suggested in the first line of O'Donohue's blessing: "Awaken to the mystery of being here." Again I found that I stumbled as I tried to memorize and make this blessing a part of me. I wanted the word in the poem to be blessing, not mystery. Still hoping to find concrete answers, I reminded myself that my Sunday school teacher's answer had freed me from the impoverishment of thinking I had then. And I still hear in my heart Paul Tillich's words from *Dynamics of Faith,* "Man's ultimate concern must be expressed symbolically, because symbolic language alone is able to express the ultimate."

Another third thing from our retreats that speaks to me is from Emily Dickinson. "Tell all the truth but tell it slant.../The truth must dazzle gradually/Or every man be blind." Jacob's story that I allude to in my opening poem is just one of the surprising evidences in holy stories that the human experience is deep and ultimate truth is best communicated aslant, symbolically, metaphorically, or mythically. Moses' view of the backside of God, Job's prostration before the mysteries of God's ways, and Elijah's experience of God in a whisper, not the thunder, are all stories that are best translated into words on a slant.

Rather than struggle against the reality that words are inadequate to recreate the experience of Truth, I have come to celebrate that paradox enriches our lives and helps us hold greater complexity. Nineteenth century Romantic poet, John

Keats, would have loved sitting in front of the fire at Sea View Inn on Pawleys Island in a Circle of Trust and sharing his thoughts about "Negative Capability"—that living the questions and celebrating the mysterious are more productive than answers and certitude in grasping Truth and Beauty. He, too, uses a third thing, a Grecian Urn, to draw us into the excitement of the tension between question and answer as he concludes:

Beauty is truth, truth beauty,—that is all
Ye know on earth, and all ye need to know.

THE CALL OF MY GIFT

Another of the significant and non-fungible wordings in O'Donohue's blessing is the completion of "Respond to the call of your gift" with "and the courage to follow its path." As an English teacher, I was sure that the writer had suffered either a typographical error or a serious failure to make sense. I was sure that he should have said something like, "Respond to the call of your gift and have the courage to follow its path." But true to my other experiences with this blessing, I discovered that O'Donohue had said exactly the right and accurate thing about the experience of presence and its effects. Once I awakened to the mystery of my own presence, I almost inevitably responded to the call of my gift and certainly to the resulting courage to follow its path. Once I entered the "quiet immensity of my own presence," grammatically, rhetorically, and emotionally, the object of the preposition *to* is both call of your gift and courage. Similarly, the previous line urges the reception of "encouragement when (not if) new horizons beckon."

Some people might guess that the experience of mystery would result in inaction or lack of enthusiasm for a work. Actually for me the opposite is true. Today I am a teacher with a classroom that includes the Grand Strand and the entire state of South Carolina. As I have paid attention to my dream that not only I, but all people AND especially all children, will have the opportunity to reach their full potential, the doors have opened and the horizons have beckoned to me to teach in a very natural but empowered way to policy makers and policy influencers. I am not teaching nouns and verbs and Hamlet to high school or junior college students; instead, I am explaining the economic and social benefits of quality early childcare and education to funders and senators.

Out of the experience of listening to my inner voice and being present to mystery comes the courage to follow the call of my gift. I am able, as Parker Palmer describes, to move "out with healing power into a world of many divides, drawing light out of darkness, community out of chaos, and life out of death." As I walk the beaches of Murrells Inlet, South Carolina, correctly reciting "For Presence," I gradually realize that the blessing I was pronouncing on myself is really addressed to an "other." I have begun naming the others: my grandchildren, my children, my husband, my friends, the early learners of Georgetown County and those who care for them—all the people for whom I am an advocate.

I may never bump into my Sunday school teacher again. We may never discuss his impact on my life or the questions I still have. I probably will never share with him the Truth I have glimpsed. But I can be the one who continues to do my own homework, who encourages awakening to the inner voice, living the questions, rejoicing in mystery, and moving with healing power into the world. This, I believe, is letting the beauty I love be what I do.

 Carolyn Ellis's education and experience are in English education. Her recent passion has become early education and childcare. She currently serves as co-chair of the Early Learning Council of Georgetown County and works with similar efforts in Horry County. She serves on the boards of directors for Freedom Readers in Horry County, for First Steps of Georgetown County, and for the Institute for Child Success of South Carolina; and on the Board of Visitors for the Spadoni College of Education at Coastal Carolina University. She and her husband Cliff have three adult children, two sons-in-law, and the most perfect grandchildren in the world. She can be reached by email at crellis@mindspring.com.

Reaching In to Reach Out to Others

By Kay Stewart

Neither the hair shirt or the soft birth will do. The place where God calls you to is the place where your deep gladness and the world's deep hunger meet.

--- Frederick Buechner

Central to the beauty I love is fully listening to that place where my deep gladness and the world's hunger meet, what theologian Frederick Buechner names as the place where God calls us, the place we discover our vocational call. I know this call to be an invitation to experience the beauty we love. For me, it is also an invitation to know the place where my deep hunger and the world's gladness meet. One flows seamlessly into the other as I listen to that still small voice within.

I love teaching and learning, and my call to teach cannot be separated from who I am. For more than twenty years, I taught physical fitness to undergraduate students at Emory. While I fully embrace the health benefits of physical activity, I now understand that physical exercise alone is inadequate. I have come to see a pressing need for healing and wholeness that comes through a contemplative approach. To connect with our wholeness, we must counter the pull of cultural influences that direct our attention outward to material things. At this time in my life, I find myself turning my attention inward to cultivate the healing and life-giving potential of wholeness that derives from integrating mind, body, and spirit.

Living life whole **IS** the beauty I love – and that has led me to take a late-in-life journey to graduate school to study Mindfulness and Contemplative Education. I chose this academic journey to expand my work and capacity to let the beauty I love be what I do, encouraged by the truths evoked in me by words from the poet Mark Nepo: "Each person is born with an unencumbered spot – free of expectation and regret, free of ambition and embarrassment, free of fear and worry – an umbilical spot of grace where we were each first touched by God. It is this spot of grace that issues peace. . . to know this spot of inwardness is to know who we are. . ."

I am living into two truths: (1) that there is a spot of grace within me. . . given freely as a gift from God, and (2) I am open to receive God's grace when I tap into this spot of inwardness with my whole heart. I made the decision to tap into this spot of inwardness, to know who I am, and to re-discover my vocational gladness; to do that, I decided to return to graduate school for a master's degree in Education.

I already knew, from my fitness classes at Emory and from existing research, that we needed to name and claim an integrative approach to health, along with a new paradigm for the word "fit." For me, this new paradigm had to include the mind as well as the body *and* be big enough to tap into the resilience of the human spirit. Words I heard years ago from Dr. Pamela Peeke during a wellness conference stuck with me: "We have an amazing capacity to heal and live well, and it all begins with the mind."

The dictionary defines the word *fit* as being "adapted to a purpose" and tapping into purpose points toward fitness through the lens of wholeness. In traditional educational settings, the word "fit" is often de-formed or misconstrued as all about the physical. That was my reason for developing a course at Emory in 2007, *Wellness: An Inside/Out Approach.* Grounded in self-reflection and self-discovery, my students were invited to observe habits of mind and heart in an effort to shift unhealthy perspectives and consider how they were being "adapted to a purpose." Turning attention inward to explore mental maps or perspectives helped the students see that they could respond rather than react as they made choices about their health. A few comments from my students illuminated what is possible through simply slowing down, making a friend of silence, and reflecting on meaning and purpose:

> **. . . Our reflecting period was very helpful in establishing what guides me and what the purpose of my doings and being are.**

> **. . . This experience was incredible . . . I truly believe it touched every person in this room and opened our eyes to a new perception of our lives and the mysteries of life.**

Once I observed that paying attention with intention in the class offered the students a source of healing and wholeness, I realized it was possible to enhance the inner lives of not only students, but also adults, by approaching learning, growth, and the concept of health as wholeness from within. So I turned to graduate study in Mindfulness and Contemplative Education to stretch myself and to hopefully increase my competency and my credibility as I designed a program that would allow me to teach who I am, to share the beauty I love.

For several years, I had explored a number of different approaches and practices to balance my doing with my being by living a more contemplative life, a life of integrity. The two programs that had resonated most with me in recent years are Jon Kabat-Zinn's Mindfulness-Based Stress Reduction (MBSR) and Parker Palmer's Circle of Trust (COT), and I wanted to find a way to draw from both MBSR and COT to create a program that invites a self-reflective, mindfulness-based approach to health that would be widely accessible. MBSR was designed to build stress resilience through cultivation of our innate human capacity of mindfulness. COT was designed to reveal what Parker Palmer described as *a hidden wholeness*, a phrase inspired by Thomas Merton, a Catholic monk and spiritual teacher who says that in all things there is a wholeness that often becomes obscured from view as we lose touch with our interconnectedness within mind, body, heart, and soul.

Now I have completed that graduate program, with that new program as my thesis. I love that my new work is congruent with my long standing *inside/out* approach to well-being, reflecting my strong knowing that *wellness* is a word that must be large enough to hold mind, body, heart, and spirit in an integrated and healthy wholeness. That kind of wellness represents a paradox in that it begins within each individual, but it is that very individual wholeness that then allows the person to be a whole member of a community, so I chose the name *Reaching In to Reach Out to Others*.

SOLITUDE AND COMMUNITY

The bold words of Dietrich Bonhoeffer speak to me: *Let the person who cannot be alone beware of community. Let the person who Is not in community beware of being alone.* I believe we need both solitude and community, and both are essential in *Reaching In to Reach Out to Others*. While I tend to be one who finds energy in community and have long described myself as an extrovert, I now know that I need time in solitude to cultivate inner resources that fuel resilient health and meaningful relationships. I am learning to experience a silence that is life-giving and trustworthy rather than a silence that encumbers or constrains.

In our increasingly fast-paced, technologically-connected world, the demands of life seem endless. Chronic stress is pervasive and is taking its toll on mental and physical health, relationships, and overall well-being. As the pace of life increases, endless information and distractions contribute to increasing levels of stress and anxiety. Drowning in "to-do" lists, we have lost our capacity to ride the waves of awareness that can carry us to calmer seas of clarity and connection. Alarming levels of chronic stress point to a need to cultivate inner capacities, including mindfulness, courage, and resilience. In our noisy, urgency-addicted world, I am clear about the need to find wholeness through contemplative practice. It takes practice to remember that we are, after all, *human beings*, NOT *human doings*. We begin by renewing the mind; in order to find our balance, renew, and live life whole, we must slow down to the rhythm of life.

The shift I am living into is the paradox of *going in* as a pathway to connect more deeply with myself and with others, thus opening me to *reach out* in a more grace-filled way. For me, it is the seamless flow of reaching in and reaching out that allows the beauty I love to be what I do. Clearly, my *doing* becomes stale and stagnant without a regular rhythm of renewal and reflection. This being human is a practice of returning again and again to the wellspring of grace that makes us whole and opens us to love.

So I practice solitude in order to know God and myself more clearly and to better prepare myself to offer the work of *Reaching In to Reach Out to Others*. I find that without my time alone, I become encumbered by expectation, regret, fear, and worry. My thinking mind piles on layers of outward "stuff," crowding out my heart. Buried in the heaviness of fear and worry, I am nothing but a bundle of negative energy, moving through community like a noisy gong or clanging symbol. If I am to be an instrument of renewal and wholeness, I must return to that spot of grace that issues peace and allows me to teach who I am.

I'm inspired by the words of theologian Howard Thurman: *"Don't ask yourself what the world needs. Ask yourself what makes you come alive and then go do that. Because what the world needs is people who have come alive."* So in my yearning to contribute something of value to our world, I must know this spot of inwardness in order to know what makes me come alive. How does this inform my work in the world? While I have long been called to teach habits of health and renewal, I'm now hearing the call to invite others to slow down and listen deeply for that place of grace inside where sustainable health and wholeness spring forth. This healing place opens me to the place where life-giving questions are born. What makes me come alive? What does it mean to live life fully and well? What opens me to see and feel the beauty that I love? It is in living the questions and listening deeply, from the *inside out*, that we may breathe into the answers that sustain us, heart and soul.

Author Parker Palmer has become one of my greatest teachers on the contemplative path, and his reminder about solitude and community resonates as I live into the beauty and promise of paradox: *"We have much to learn from within, but it's easy to get lost in the labyrinth of inner life. We have much to learn from others, but it's easy to get lost in the confusion of the crowd. So we need solitude and community simultaneously. What we learn in one mode can check and balance what we learn in the other. Together they can make us whole, like breathing in and breathing out. . ."*

SERVICE AND CELEBRATION

I feel alive at the thought of taking my new work into the world by inviting others to discover the life-giving benefits of mind renewal through mindfulness and self-reflective practice. In both service and celebration, I seek to live into what my Presbyterian faith tradition names as the chief aim in life — *to glorify God and enjoy Him forever*! And integrity for me comes as I listen to my new work in the context of my faith tradition, and as I listen to the teachings of my faith tradition in the context of my new work. I need my faith community to keep me grounded, to allow me to listen to what is beneath and beyond words and beliefs. As I slow down to the rhythm of life, I breathe in service and breathe out celebration, and I breathe in celebration and breathe out service. A seamless flow of serving and celebrating life with enthusiasm allows me to fully be the teacher and learner I want to be. Day by day, moment by moment, my intention is to have fresh eyes, wide open to the grace and goodness that surround me. In order to allow the beauty I love to be what I do, in teaching and in life, I must be deeply rooted in what is life-giving. A faithful way of life begins by cultivating the roots that enable me to grow the fruits of my uniqueness, always living into who God created me to be. By renewing my mind, I go deeply inside, and I see more clearly that I am also inextricably linked to others, to the created world, and to God. The flow of reaching in and reaching out offers glimpses of grace in every glance. By connecting to that unencumbered spot of grace within, I am able to see life through the lens of genuine love and wholeness. Awareness and attention to wholeness cultivates the roots of resilience and the courage to acknowledge both strengths and vulnerabilities.

As I write now to share this new program with you, I realize a sense of integrity and authenticity in knowing that *Reaching In to Reach Out to Others* represents my own long journey, beginning in my early work with Emory undergraduates, that motivated me to embrace interdisciplinary graduate study in Mindfulness and Contemplative Education. Continuing to reflect on that journey, I feel alive in knowing that my work in mindfulness and self-reflection is grounded in my faith and in the qualities of gratitude, generosity, gentleness, and grace. I am tempted to describe this as *heart work,* and yet that seems too small, so I must name another paradox: it **is** heart, which comes from the Latin *cor* and is the root of the word *courage* – **but** it is heart in its original meaning rather than today's sentimental one. This heart work is at the core of mind-body-spirit, and it invites a faithful way of life through healthy mind renewal as a pathway to wholeness, integrity, and meaning.

My newly-created program offers a fresh, scientifically sound approach to renewing the mind by combining essential elements and practices from both Circles of Trust (COT) and Mindfulness-Based Stress Reduction (MBSR). *Reaching In to*

214

Reach Out to Others represents a tangible way to allow *the beauty I love be what I do*. It reclaims the root of the word educate (from the Latin *educare* – to call forth), by calling forth the wholeness within as the tap root of living life fully and well. As the poet Rumi says, "You already have within you the precious mixture that will make you well. Use it!"

REACHING IN TO REACH OUT TO OTHERS

I designed *Reaching in to Reach Out to Others* as an invitation that embraces body, mind, **and** soul. It intentionally invites spiritual health and encourages spiritual renewal by nurturing the hidden wholeness in each of us. Encouraging an exploration of mindfulness practice and self-reflection invites wholeness and connection rather than compartmentalization. We must not exclude all things spiritual, and we can do this in a way that honors all faith traditions and spiritual paths. It is possible to nourish the soul of well-being using language and metaphors intentionally selected to foster understanding and receptivity within my cultural context, and specifically within the Christian community that is so important to me. My intention is to dispel fear stemming from misunderstandings about what mindfulness meditation practice is and what it isn't. Though mindfulness is *not* religious, it has deepened my own spiritual practice and strengthened my faith, and this inspires me to invite others to explore these rich and life-giving experiences of growth.

My desire is to widen the circle of compassion and connection through practices that, while secular, are also interconnected with what is sacred and spiritual. I am intentional with the language I use in my work from the first moment, introducing mind renewal using the biblical phrase, "Be ye transformed by the renewing of your mind" (Romans 12:2). Mind renewal is about slowing down, and I want to invite a faithful, healthy way of life by inviting participants to listen deeply. "Be still and know that I am God" (Psalm 46:10).

Kabat-Zinn's MBSR and Palmer's COT have meant so much to me and are foundational in my new work. What I name as mindfulness practices and self-reflective courage invitations are offered in an experience designed to strengthen both our human capacity for intentional awareness and our yearning for connection, meaning, and purpose. Mindfulness feeds self-reflection and self-reflection feeds mindfulness. The interplay of mindfulness practice and self-reflection are woven throughout the SLOW process in order to settle the mind, listen to the body, open the heart, and wait for the soul.

THE CONTINUOUS CYCLE OF SEEING, BEING, DOING

My model offers a way into the complex interconnections around seeing, being, and doing as a useful reminder of the importance of practices that inform both our doing and our being. The doing drives the being and the being drives the doing, with both springing out of our *seeing,* out of how we view the world. Mindfulness and self-reflection offer clear seeing and discernment, as they offer a way to examine our paradigms and deeply ingrained patterns of reacting. MBSR and COT inform the practices that emerge from the process of SLOW, allowing us to see the world with both the fresh eyes of wonder and the soft eyes of compassion.

I use the acronym SLOW to describe what I offer in my new program, and I see it almost as a "Food Guide" Pyramid for Healthy Minds. The analogy of slow food is useful here, as the slow food movement encourages eating locally grown, organic foods; foods that are as close as possible to their natural existence. Building on the SLOW metaphor, *Reaching In to Reach Out to Others* is about nourishing the soul with natural locally grown, organic food. This metaphoric *soul food* allows us to imagine a healthy platter of contemplative practices for the mind.

The SLOW frame is grounded in the attitudinal qualities of patience, acceptance, trust, non-striving, non-judgment, and

216

letting go or letting be. The dynamic interplay of this non-linear SLOW process informs the weaving and rhythm of the following themes for each component:

Settle the Mind.

In our fast-paced world it is important to notice, name, and nurture the intention to slow down. Simply slowing down the pace of life helps us to tap into our innate capacity for mindfulness. The theme of slowing down is inherent to the entire *Reaching In to Reach Out to Others* experience. Settling the mind is the base of my pyramid. Participants are invited to *pay attention with intention* relative to the overall workshop experience, as well as each practice. *Courage invitations* in the form of poetry and reflection are used to practice *paying attention with intention*. Brief meditation practices are introduced with a focus on the theme *Be Still and Know.*

Listen to the Body.

In order to tap into the wisdom of the body, participants are guided in practices involving mindful movement, including gentle yoga and walking meditation. Listening to the body forms the second level of my pyramid. A brief body scan practice grounds participants in body awareness. The debrief of practices illuminates foundational qualities, including the soft eyes of non-judgment and the fresh eyes of curiosity. Bodywork also invites exploration of how it is possible to hold tension and paradox in a life-giving way.

Open the Heart.

A variety of courage invitations open the heart to self-reflection around the theme of connecting with seeds of self and sources of meaning and purpose, forming the third level of my pyramid. Exploration of self includes paying attention to birthright gifts, so self-reflective practices build on this theme. This is heart work, so loving kindness practice offers a meditation that speaks directly to the cultivation of kindness and compassion.

217

Waiting for the Soul.

Waiting for the soul illustrates the theme of befriending silence, the top level of the pyramid. Participants are carefully prepared for an experience of extended silence as an opportunity to listen deeply for whispers of the soul. This offers spaciousness and the deeply felt connection of being alone together. Experiencing silence in community is powerful, and a careful debrief is central to weaving together the interwoven strands of settling the mind, listening to the body, opening the heart, and waiting for the soul.

The core values foundational to *Reaching In to Reach Out to Others* are gratitude, generosity, gentleness, and grace. These core values undergird my guiding beliefs:

*Wholeness involves a complex interplay of mind, body, heart, soul, and relationships.

*Wholeness and vitality come through an integrative approach to life and well-being.

*Wholeness and integrity are grounded in our capacity to hold tension in life-giving ways, which begins mind renewal and is nurtured in both solitude and community.

*An integrative approach to vibrant living intentionally includes spiritual health sustained by inner resources of mind, body, heart, and soul.

*Balance and health require holding tension with both focus and receptive awareness.

*Intention + Attention = Healthy Tension

*Life is filled with infinite possibilities . . . Renewal illuminates pathways to wholeness.

SLOW offers the overall frame for my programs, and the

acronym that names the model also becomes my reminder to support participants in bringing mindfulness and self-reflection into their daily lives. In a sense I am inviting a journey down the *slow road,* less traveled. *Reaching in to Reach to Reach Out to Others* is about practice, reflection, and lived experience.

FAIR, KIND, AND HUMBLE

SLOWing down allows us to BE FAIR, BE KIND, BE HUMBLE (Micah 6:8). The multidimensional process of SLOW involves a two-fold process of first accepting the overall invitation to mind-renewal and then choosing to accept courage invitations as portals to the mind, body, heart, and soul. The process allows the mind to settle, creating inner space that is flexible, aware, intentional, and responsive, as shown with the acronym FAIR. The settled mind is also kind, and it is humble.

A settled mind is FAIR. *FAIR stands for:*

- **Flexible** – A settled mind is an open, flexible mind, able to hold paradox, to embrace both/and rather than either/or.

- **Aware** – A settled mind opens and allows us to pay attention to present moment experience with curiosity and a sense of wonder.

- **Intentional** – A settled mind touches intention through the eyes of the heart, thus creating space to respond based on our deepest values and longings.

- **Responsive** – A settled mind is a responsive mind. We can respond rather than revert to habitual patterns by creating the space to call upon our capacities of awareness, imagination, conscience, and will. The settled mind has the capacity to choose our response in any situation. We become response-able.

A settled mind is KIND.
Kindheartedness is unconditional goodwill. When our minds are settled we can choose to respond with kindness and love, and we naturally feel better when we do. Kindness opens a well of life-giving emotions including contentment, joy, compassion, and a sense of peace.

A settled mind is HUMBLE.
A settled mind is humble and grounded. It is deeply connected to the wisdom of the body, thus tapping into the integrative wisdom of the mind, body, and spirit. Humility embraces both our shadows and our light, and it literally grounds us. When we are grounded, we are stable and balanced. We are aware of both our gifts and our limitations. We are aware of our hidden hunger for healing silence and our deep need to listen. We sense our hunger for connectedness and our need to listen in both solitude and community.

Theologian Paul Tillich reminds us, "The first act of love is to listen." Cultivating the skill of listening requires the humility and reverence to see and acknowledge our perceptual limitations. We listen with the eyes of the heart through mindfulness and self-reflection.

WELCOME TO THE PARTY

I know that many paths lead to that spot of grace that issues peace. Buechner tells us: *"The grace of God means something like: Here is your life. You might never have been, but you are because the party wouldn't have been complete without you. Here is the world. Beautiful and terrible things will happen. Don't be afraid. I am with you. Nothing can ever separate us. It's for you I created the universe. I love you. There's only one catch. Like any other gift, the gift of grace can be yours only if you'll reach out and take it. Maybe being able to reach out and take it is a gift too."*

220

So the beauty I love is in reaching in and reaching out. Beauty begins in both accepting the invitation to the party *and* in opening to receive the gift. There are hundreds of ways to celebrate the party and receive God's gift of grace. When I listen for God in silence and in quiet moments of meditation, reflection, and worship, I hear that still small voice within and see infinite possibilities through the eyes of grace. Both solitude and community ground me and open me to God's grace in my work *and* my life, my being and my doing. Service and celebration and a soul-deep connection all point toward who I am and the beauty that I love. As a teacher and a child of God, I claim my knowing that the party wouldn't be complete without me.

My prayer is that, together, we accept the invitation to renewal and receive the gift of grace. In so doing, we have the best chance of connecting with the beauty that we love. May we all discover what makes us come alive in both reaching in and reaching out, because the party isn't complete without ALL of us!

 Kay Stewart, M.Ed., is founder of Stillwaters Mindfulness Training (www.stillwatersmindfulness.com). Kay facilitates retreats at the intersection of mindfulness and self-reflective spiritual renewal. She offers Mindfulness-Based Stress Reduction (MBSR) programs through Shallowford Family Counseling Center, housed within her home church. Kay is also an active community volunteer and is currently sharing the Mindful Schools curriculum with her daughter's first-grade classroom! Kay loves celebrating life with her husband of 34 years, their young adult children, and the most amazing friends and faith community in the world!

Poetry's Call: An Exploration of Let and Letting

By John Fox, CPT

Today, like every other day, we wake up empty
and frightened. Don't open the door to the study
and begin reading. Take down a musical instrument.
Let the beauty we love be what we do.
There are hundreds of ways to kneel and kiss the ground.

---Rumi, translated by Coleman Barks

Love, beauty and the declaration to let the beauty I love be what I do – all of that feels true and real for what matters in my life, true to the point of leaving illusion behind and entering into a holy place, a place of sacrament.

I will share my thoughts with you in four parts. First: elements of my life that turned me towards doing what I love. Second: an exploration of the connection between *letting* and *calling*. Third: a consideration of what the words *let* and *letting* mean. Fourth: an experience of me doing what I love.

PART ONE

As a child and teenager I played the cello. Those bow sounds, particularly a down bow on the C or D string, moved me. I stopped playing the cello at seventeen but those sounds still move me like nothing else. Playing that instrument gave me a felt sense that art is connected to the human body and heart. This was amplified when I heard a recording of the great Spanish cellist, Pablo Casals.

The first vinyl record I owned (at the age of nine) was a live performance by Senor Casals at the Kennedy White House in November 1961. As he played, Casals sighed. I heard him sighing!

More than my physical heart, my heart of feeling was made forever active. The cello helped me make that heart. From that place it would be an easy joy to take down a musical instrument (metaphorically now!) and write about the beauty of what I love doing. Then again, I could write to you about feeling empty and frightened. That may show you and me something more about the kind of letting Rumi urges. There have been times in my life when emptiness and fright have riven me to my core. In their thrall, I've felt outside the help of anything, especially the help of God. Nothing could touch my desolation.

This happened with ferocity during my freshman year at Boston University. Faced with making the decision to have my right leg amputated below the knee, I felt as if I were wrestling with the Devil. Since the age of four, everything was involved – nerve, bone, circulatory system – all impacted, all gone askew. As I turned seventeen, it was quite painful and deteriorating swiftly. But I could not give up on it.

Actually, regarding my wrestling, there was no "as if." Darkness was more real than I can describe to you. Fright and Emptiness weren't only the faces of grief I *anticipated*, but in their company, my worth as a human being was shattering. *Was I cursed?*

I made the decision and went through that surgery in late May. And I have to say here that things were not always entirely dark. I remember blessings. Moments before I was anesthetized, a nurse smiled at me in the operating room. Her smile was much more than a professional nicety. The anesthesiologist (who was not a happy man that morning or perhaps any morning) was unable to find a vein in my arm so he kept sticking me with a needle. I remember turning my head left, towards his grim, rotund face and looking away.

Then, I looked up, towards this nurse standing at the foot of the operating table. She looked down the length of that hard table into my eyes. I was aware of a joy flowing from this nurse and through her beaming smile, bearing witness with me. Time stopped. It is likely I will remember her smile when I die. (Later, I learned this nurse's name was Mary Kleitz. I learned Mary wasn't even involved in my surgery that morning. She said she'd heard an inner voice that said to follow me into that operating room. She let that voice guide her.) Her glance was but moments in duration before I dissolved into drug-induced sleep. Yet like a revelation, her smile and face live in an inviolate place more vivid than memory.

That powerful bright moment, however, would not and could not prevent subsequent storms. I returned to B.U. ready to act as if very little had happened. A nice but flimsy plan because a contusion erupting on my stump soon put me face-to-face with not being able to wear my newly fitted prosthesis. How could I be seen on crutches without my leg? The image of that happening threw me into a maelstrom of shame and terror.

For some days, I holed up in my dorm room, 22C, at Myles Standish Hall. How long would my strategy of denial last? I needed help. I had an excellent counselor, John Lambdin. While knowing I was in great pain, he didn't flinch. He helped me face it. What's the worst that could happen? A poem came to me and it helped, too:

Even To This

What my thoughts have troubled about
all through the night after night!

It's so very scary
>   sometimes
>   I feel
>   would rather
what's the worst that could happen?

because it just hurts too much
or having had enough of my own self-hatred

against myself, lonely is
nowhere else to go --

time to stop feeling sorry
for myself,

time to open my heart
even to this

and call to God.

>   ---**John Fox**

I never would tell someone else that self-pity was the problem they needed to get over, but this poem allowed me, in a very condensed way, to say *everything.* I could say that about my own self-pity. I could write the life-changing line *nowhere else to go in italics.*

Even in my struggle, in my call for help, not too far from my fright and emptiness, I felt my heart cello long for a connection to beauty. Even in the raging storm, that deep longing helped me make a *commitment* to live for beauty.

>   Not to make loss beautiful,
>   But to make loss the place
>   Where beauty starts. Where
>   the heart understands
>   For the first time
>   The nature of its journey.

>   --- **Gregory Orr**

I have felt this longing for beauty for a very long time. Mary's smile reflected it to me and I was open to it. Let me share with you more about those places of opening.

When I was twelve, thirteen, and fourteen, three formational events critical for my character development and essential for setting a direction in life, happened.

I was watching a girl skate at Thornton Park in Shaker Heights, OH. I was twelve. She was the only one on the ice. Gliding and turning! As she spun, I think she turned her face toward the ceiling. She wore a short chocolate-brown skating outfit.

Me? I stood outside the rink, holding an open notebook and pen. I was writing a poem. It is the first poem I ever wrote. I felt I must capture something! I wanted words to skate on the page. You can say I am making this up, that I am trying to impress you, putting it this way now, saying I wanted my words to skate, but I knew then it was so. I am sure of that.

The second story relates to the first. I don't honestly recall this event, but my mother told me it happened. I was with her and a group of her friends. Mom said to those friends, "When Charles grows up, he's going to be a poet." She told me I looked over at her and said, **"I am a poet."** I can't tell you my tone of voice but it might have been cool or maybe the tone was just matter of fact. For Mom, who, in retrospect, was only trying to affirm and support me, I imagine this was a type of resistance she was familiar with.

Poet was, apparently, something I already claimed. I didn't need to become one. Saying it out loud for myself and to others was an important moment in my life. I would give myself too much credit to say I knew this at the time, knew this kind of wisdom, but I can't help but think of this now, especially in the context of Parker Palmer's connection to writers in this book:

I was letting my life speak.

The third and last story is about waking up to murderous brutality and heartlessness. This, even more than claiming my identity as a poet, and acting upon that, may say more about why letting the beauty I love be what I do matters to me. In this story, I let the courage to stand up for what I believe is right and just *be* what I do and who I am. Why? So there will be beauty beyond me. So there will be beauty at all. If others are denied the blessings of beauty, doing what I love isn't enough for me.

One of the most beautiful forms of human expression is speaking out when courage is required -- for progress, justice and peace, and, as John Lewis implores people, not to just use words, but to "find a way to get in the way."

On Monday, May 4, 1970, I was 14 and sitting on the sunny window bench in the living room of my best friend's home. News had just come over the radio -- four students, protesting the invasion of Cambodia by Richard Nixon's administration, had been shot and killed by the Ohio National Guard at Kent State University. Nine students were shot and injured. One of those students was paralyzed for life.

I remember sitting there for a long time, dazed. I felt sad, suddenly aware my country was killing Her own citizens -- and just down the road from where I lived in Cleveland, Ohio. Young people shot and killed when expressing their dissent for Nixon's death-dealing policies and acts of war.

I learned one of the students shot dead, Allison Krause, had, the previous summer, acted as a counselor at a camp for children and teens with Down syndrome and other developmental disabilities. YES Camp was founded by my parents, Jim and Eleanor Fox, along with other parents who had children with special needs. This was unusual activism by parents in the early and mid sixties. Allison Krause's niece, Shelley, attended that camp. Shelley was the sweetest child! Allison Krause's Uncle Jack and Aunt Lynn worked alongside my parents. I knew them! They were such good people. My sister Holly was a camper at YES, too.

Newspapers reported that a few days before she was killed, Allison said: "Flowers are better than bullets." That personal connection mattered -- but even if that personal connection had not been there, I was sick at heart and angry.

The killings happened on Monday. On Tuesday, I wore a black armband to Woodbury Junior High. In ninth-grade science class, wearing her white clinician's lab coat and severely pulled-back hair, Mrs. V said to our class, "They should have shot more of them." I stood up and walked out. There was nothing else to do. I was not willing to let heartlessness and injustice stand unopposed in order to not make waves; I had to make use of the gift of courage and the requirements of my conscience.

Mrs. V, unfortunately, got her wish. Ten days later in Mississippi, at Jackson State College, in another protest against the Vietnam War, through the windows of a woman's dormitory, two students were shot and killed by state troopers. Twelve people were injured.

Poetic Medicine, written in 1997, includes a chapter called "Poems of Witness: Living with Heart in a Conflicted World." I saw the poetry of witness within the context of community as a profound necessity for my healing. These days, with hypocrisy, lies, racism and ignorance rife in what used to be called conservatism, the need is great to bear witness to the vulnerable, to nurture beauty, protect the Earth we live on. Using poetry and healing, I am called to steadfast action.

PART TWO

The river is everywhere.
--Hermann Hesse from *Siddhartha*

Over the past thirty years I've lived a life where the beauty I love -- poetry as healer – is what I do. There are so many blessings to count. I am glad to be poor at math because I can't keep up with the blessings; I have lost count.

That is not to say there aren't doubts, because there are plenty. *What about saving for retirement?* That's not to say there are not steep challenges showing up every day. *How can the Institute for Poetic Medicine survive without more funding?* That's not to say that because I am doing what I love, sadness stays away from me. It does not.

In fact, it could be the backlight of "doing what I love" that illuminates my melancholy and limitations. Sometimes a voice of mine says: *This work is like contributing a drop in the bucket to ease suffering. What's more, my own bucket has a hole in it!* These difficulties are present with me. It helps to admit it. I don't even need you to understand! What helps me is your witness. I ask for that "staying with" in this poem:

WHAT UNDERSTANDING WON'T HELP

> Does the dusk light
> that rests for moments
> upon the leaves of
> a Japanese Maple
> awaken your
> heart, like it does
> mine? And by "awaken"
> I might mean this:
> if loneliness was at least
> willing to not give in
> to despair, because
> loss felt like a sure thing.
> Could you stand there
> at that edge with me
> aware of & holding

these small realities of
our day, like a great treasure
that will not last or give
us everything we want —
but still deserve our attention,
like the leaf that catches
last light is lifted up to our sight
by a shadow
that silently cares for it,
and everything underneath
that can't be said?

---John Fox

This poem speaks to me about the closeness beauty keeps with the aching heart. There is something in the poem regarding the importance of paying attention to life and the necessities of shadow. Poetry offers this miracle: there is a place deeper than paradox where disparities are held together.

I feel the paradox and yet I am part of wholeness.

Here is where I feel something beyond what I know. That something is different than my capacity to let — something meets me in the act of letting and welcomes my willingness. Like the invisible current in a river, poetry as healer has a pull larger than myself. I feel this work comes as a calling, and that call is far beyond my doing. That current and that call only ask this of me: that I pay attention.

We must begin thinking like a river if we are to leave a legacy
of beauty and life for future generations.

--- David Brower, Founder, Sierra Club

I've introduced an important word here – call.

Poetry's call was at work within me long before I began to hear it at the level I do now. I could ignore it or remain unaware of it, but the call did not go away. This inability to escape my calling, like a river's current, something I have no control over, is also true for what I have to go through in my life, especially the travails. I could not escape my life.

The words call and calling introduced me to the words let and letting. Or perhaps (like my earlier personification of Fright and Emptiness), as happens during those times in life when there is a real emergency, there are no introductions, no small talk and pleasantries. Call and Let get thrown together. They must respond to something critical.

They have to come up with a life-saving plan.

As Whitman wrote, "Oh me! Oh life! of the questions of these recurring...That the powerful play goes on, and you may contribute a verse." What will give meaning to life? How do I make meaning out of my life? What will my verse be?

I am drawn to "let" and "call" because I feel edges and connections with those words and what they mean for me. By edge I mean that there is something to confront, something to engage with, grapple with, something that could, by letting it in, strip me down so I might actually let go and hear/feel what calls me. By connection I mean the river current I am speaking of, feeling that current, that flow between the unknown and myself. In my relationship to the world, to life on the planet I need to learn how and where and why and the ways my letting responds to that call.

PART THREE

This little light of mine, I'm going to let it shine
This little light of mine, I'm going to let it shine
This little light of mine, I'm going to let it shine
Let it shine, Let it shine, Let it shine.

--- Harry Dixon Loes

Odetta (1930 – 2008), considered by many to be the voice of the Civil Rights Movement, performed *This Little Light of Mine* with the Boys' Choir of Harlem on The Late Show with David

Letterman on September 17, 2001. This was the first Letterman show following the tragic events of September 11, 2001. This gospel song puts a dynamic focus on the word let. I invite you to first listen to this. (Type Odetta, Letterman, Harlem Boys' Choir into your browser -- or go to https://www.youtube.com/watch?v=7yrB7ePz5CM)

Notice how Odetta and the Boys' Choir of Harlem practice and express the word "let." There is both a swinging into the word as the choir sings with everyone's arms in easy rhythmic motion, with brightness on their faces and then there is a dedicated and rooted intention as Odetta strides back and forth in front of the choir and in front of the audience. She is a healing priestess on national TV at a time of great trauma. She names, in a bodily and spiritual way, all that is ancient, breathing and resilient.

When you watch Odetta call forth from deep within herself the word "let," do you see it in her posture? Do you sense it in her bearing? Can you get a felt sense for it as she steps surely and deliberately? She is sobered by what has happened and holds grief for us all, but she is also letting, especially towards children. She lets those children capture our attention. We are witness to the radiant smiles of the Harlem Boys' Choir singing. They too are letting. These young men *let it shine.*

Much more than a concept, letting is an action.

At the song's conclusion, Odetta slows everything way down. She raises her hand, open-palmed, and exclaims **"LET IT."** She evokes the choir's refrain. Here, we feel and experience how the words let it **makes space** for a response.

Let and letting create space.

This is significant. It is the core of what we are looking for in our practice of letting. Making space! As much as one is letting beauty happen, we are mostly letting go of what holds us back.

232

We let go of self-judgment and doubts and criticisms of others. We are doing our part to clear out a lifetime of evaluation by ourselves and someone else. We make space for something true and real to happen through our daily life.

LET, LET·TING, LETS These are not complicated intellectual words. They are straightforward. They suggest the simplest kind of action. The Free Online Dictionary offers these definitions for let, letting and lets:

> let *v.* let, let·ting, lets *v.tr.*
> 1. To give permission or opportunity; to allow
> 2. To cause; to make
> 4. To permit to enter, proceed, or depart
> 5. To release from or as if from confinement

I'm thrilled by the first definition: to give permission or opportunity, to allow. What could be more perfect to describe what can help us -- giving ourselves permission! We make room for ourselves and for doing what we love. But there is something even more exciting possible as reflected in the second definition: to cause, to make.

It is not only permission. When we truly practice "letting" there is something In this "making" that empowers and gives joy. This making is very close to the roots, the origins, of the word "poetry." The Greek word for poetry is "poesis" and it means literally "to make."

And even more specifically, it is connected to the Greek word *poiein*, or creation. Poeisis, like the word *let*, is the act of making. I'm walking an etymological trail here with the word "let" that leads to the words cause or make, which then leads us to the words poesis and creation. Consider again the way Odetta strode and declaimed, "let it." She reminds me that this word "let" may have happened very, very early on. I wonder if "let" is not the first word spoken by that Unnameable Mystery? Let there be light: and there was light.

*In the process and act of making things, within creation,
letting is an integral part of the field of creating.*

Then it is so amazing to consider the fourth and fifth
definitions:

4. To permit to enter, proceed, or depart

When I interned with Joy Shieman at El Camino Hospital on "1
South," the mental health wing, we were one of many programs
for patients. The difference in our poetry therapy session
was this: while every other program required mandatory
attendance, Joy insisted that her poetry therapy session be
optional. People could choose. Our twice-weekly gatherings
were not only optional, but people could come and go as they
pleased. People could enter and depart as they wished.

So what would it be like if we let go, if we could simply practice
letting? That is, allow ourselves, permit ourselves to enter,
proceed and depart? What if we gave ourselves permission
for that? These words indicate a way of being, a kind of flexible
and flowing consciousness to cultivate – allow, permit, enter,
release – all resonant with letting. This may seem obvious, after
all, to let, let go. Yet the moment I say the word "obvious," I am
very close to the words "taken for granted." I believe it is only
by a daily practice of letting that beauty can blossom and help
us to feel the way it calls out freshness. And then, last, and
certainly not least, is this about *letting:*

5. To release from or as if from confinement

What are our confinements? Confined by not seeking the
beauty you love. Confined from not speaking up when injustice
and ignorance cause suffering. Confined by not letting sorrow
and joy speak. Poem-making and sharing our poems can bring
about release from confinement.

The very fact that a thing — anything — can be fitted into a
meaning built up of words, small black words, that can be

written with one hand and the stub of a pencil, means it is not big enough to be overwhelming. It is the vast, formless, unknown and unknowable things we fear. Anything which can be brought to a common point — a focus within our understanding — can be dealt with.

--- **Lara Jefferson**

Poetry is indeed a force, an act of human
magic, that alters the way we see our lives
and so changes us.

--- **Morris R. Morrison**

Let us, when swimming with the stream,
become the stream...
Let us, when moving with the music,
become the music...
Let us, when rocking the wounded,
become the suffering...

--**Mark Nepo,** *Mother of the Universe*

We are here to witness the creation and to abet it. . .
We are here to bring to consciousness
the beauty and power that are around us and to praise
the people who are here with us.

---**Annie Dillard**

Sometimes, before we can let something in, we need to allow for our release from confinement; which often means we need to let out the beauty we love.

PART FOUR

One afternoon during a four-day workshop at John F. Kennedy University in the Graduate School of Psychology, students wrote poems related to their grief experiences. These grief poems came about naturally; I hadn't offered writing prompts for them. The opportunity presented itself for us to free and reveal raw feelings usually kept under pleasant wraps. Within the safety of the circle, fine and heartbreaking poems of loss spilled out, and somehow, perhaps because of the healing nature of poetry, hearts opened. What drew these poems and this experience forward was not probing analysis but a keen open-hearted listening attention – as if we were all listening to rain. This time it was a *letting in.*

A man read his poem, and as he did, Jodie cried. He came close to sobbing. Others cried with him. Someone approached him with a box of Kleenex, but Jodie motioned with his hand saying a gentle and silent "no" to Kleenex. The box of tissue was set aside. After we had gone on, Jodie began to write. I did not interrupt him. About a half-hour later, he raised his hand and asked if he could read something that expressed why he did not want the Kleenex.

Do Not Wipe Your Tears Away

Do not wipe your tears away.
Let them flow down your cheek.
Let them create a stream on your face
to allow the healing waters to flow.
Let the waters cleanse your skin
and wash your face with silk.
Let them caress you lightly
and reveal to you, your heart.
Let the water fall to the earth,
and a tree will grow from it.
Let your tears flow from their depths
and they will release the seeds of your soul.
Do not be careful
Do not be contained
or proper or polite.
Do not wipe your tears away.
Taste them on your lips
and know that you have graced yourself, today.

--Jodie Senkyrik

Jodie's poem employs repetition woven through with a richness of changing image and vivid sensing. A rhythmic and steady flow of the word let is made even stronger by the contrasting staccato of saying what can confine us:

> Do not be careful
> Do not be contained
> or proper or polite.

Jodie says letting brings a deep personal experience that can

> heal and cleanse
> caress and reveal
> flow and release

His "let" is full of images. Letting is an act of abundant creation and extravagant grace:

> stream, silk, skin...
> seed, earth, tree...
> taste, lips, yourself.

Poetry is a way to practice letting! It encourages flow. To encourage this in others gives a gift of deep satisfaction. To see others carry on with it, in their own way, is why I continue.

I learned to allow this letting to be met by a calling. Surely that skater ignited a calling, she first showed me the power and beauty of letting, and the joining of both to live my truth. They dance together in my life.

> I am certain of nothing but the holiness of the heart's affections and the truth of the imagination — what the imagination seizes as beauty must be truth — whether it existed before or not.

> **---John Keats in a letter to Benjamin Bailey**

My first poem about the skater is long lost, but about 12 years ago a skater appeared again.

Poetry

She skates boldly onto
the page, tips one vulnerable foot
back and forth slowly, till finally
the edge of a toe
cuts a simple, sharp line
through the world's cold resistance
and with that plain courage,
a statement of intention begins;
and you can't turn back any longer
from the weight of feeling and letting go
into the flow that follows.
Poetry is a choice to feel it all,
not all at once but gradually to sink down
within ourselves, to give what fear
we hold behind our knees
to gravity and grace,
to discover what makes
our whole world turn;
the place our necessary weight
lifts to lightened joy.

---John Fox

John Fox, CPT is a poet and poetry therapist. He has been doing this work since 1981. He is the author of Poetic Medicine and Finding What You Didn't Lose. His work appears in the PBS documentary Healing Words: Poetry and Medicine. He is the President and Founder of The Institute for Poetic Medicine, a nonprofit that brings poetry as healer to marginalized people; provides training in the practice of poetry as healer; is dedicated to showing helping professions how to make this healing art part of their vocation. You can contact him at john@poeticmedicine.org and through The Institute for Poetic Medicine. John lives in Mountain View, CA. He and COT facilitator Sally Z. Hare have collaborated in a number of retreats over the past five years in which they have created space at the intersection of John's work in Poetic Medicine and Sally's Courage work.

Knowing, Growing, Evolving, Becoming, Emerging to BE the Beauty I Love

By Jacqueline Miles Stanley

 Saying yes to the two-year pilot Courage to Teach program in South Carolina started my journey towards knowing and growing and evolving and becoming and emerging to **BE** the Beauty I love. Over the last 20 years I have been given wonderful gifts that have allowed me to name and claim the ground on which I stand, to know the foundation of my core being.

The gifts of sights, sounds, people, and places have been offered to support my ongoing journey. In a recent retreat, an amazing and wonderful artist, Jonathan Green, challenged me to continue to seek, to allow the mystery of spirit and nature to guide me to a place of understanding and truth. Learning to release the past, to live fully in the present and to embrace the newness of each day are lessons I continue to learn while trying to stay awake on this Mobius journey of life. Embracing the seamlessness between my inner life and outer life, making the decision to live undivided, I am learning to attach personal meaning and particular context to events and feelings.

Connecting with other human beings in The Courage to Teach has allowed my acceptance of a very clear understanding: the order of the universe is unquestionable. I have a clear knowledge in my spirit now that has grown over time. The growth has come out of deep, dark places and places of intense light... places that may not have been named or claimed without

239

the energy and nurturing of other people who connected with my spirit, loved her and encouraged her to be—spontaneous and fully present. Laughing and crying, stopping and starting, living and dying and being quiet were all essential components for evolving into wholeness.

I now fully embrace that, as a single, sixty, sassy human spirit, it is not my purpose in life to please, fix, or solely take care of others. I must take care of myself so that I have the capacity and space in my spirit to receive the love, care, and nurture of others. Evolving into the grandmother I always wanted but never had, and becoming the mother that I always longed for in my youth, are very important to me. Being a friend to someone who needs a friend allows me to give back to the universe the friends who have been sent to me during my life. My life has been informed, encouraged, and saved by the spirits of family and friends directed to me by the most High Spirit. Finding my voice and speaking my truth have allowed my spirit to connect with and embrace the light and dark places of life where beauty had been hidden from my consciousness. The growing continues as I reflect on how I became who I am right now.

The invitation for the pilot Courage to Teach program came in 1996. After a bit of discussion and a lot of reflection on the enormity of a making a two-year commitment, I recognized the possibilities for my personal and professional growth, and said yes. The participant list showed educators from all over the country, and I recognized all of the local names on the list; I could not resist. At that time, I was walking around in an unconscious state of being alive; the automaticity of existing had taken over. I had hunkered down into survival mode and I was not coming out.

My role as new principal of the middle school in the heart of Myrtle Beach, South Carolina, was a challenge in itself, and I added to the complexity by being the first black female in this role. However, what I found there, in this divided inner-city-like school located in a resort beach community, and what I took there, in my own divided self, together produced a numbness of spirit for which I had no tools.

On the home front, my husband had just taken a job that required him to be gone all week; he would be home on weekends. Our children attended the elementary, middle and high school in a different attendance area than I was serving. My mom was living with me. My doctor had just prescribed a higher level of insulin for the increasing severity of my diabetes.

I had neatly organized and housed all my concerns about work and family in carefully-constructed compartments in my head and heart... or so I thought! The glaring spotlight of media, mean-spirited racial comments, and fear of the unknown were colliding with my lack of adequate confidence and experience and support to create the perfect storm in my life. I never saw it coming. I was not prepared.

So the invitation to join the Courage retreat series was timely, to say the least. I hoped that this Courage to Teach experience, with its opportunities for sharing with other educators and being in a different environment, might give me some insight into how to do better what I was already doing. The whole business of living divided no more, part of the description of the program, was not particularly intriguing to me at first. I did embrace the time for reflection and entered into this professional learning group as I had most experiences in my past — with great anticipation that I would change some things — not that I would be changed.

MY BEGINNINGS

My life started out typical of a young woman growing up in the segregated South. Being raised in a household of women and seven younger siblings required skills for resolving conflict, providing for the needs of others, sharing, and of course, pretending that all in the family was well. Those skills were great for cleaning the houses of others, but not for what I was being set up to do. I read a lot and excelled in school, mostly to hide the sadness of not being light-skinned with long, good hair. At the same time, I bought into the battle cry of the 70's that, no matter your skin color, if you study hard you could get a good job. Someone in the family really needed a good job.

For most of my teenage years I participated in a racial exchange program as the sole Black in a community in a small town in Iowa. I lived with white families and attended the local high school. My first year of college in Missouri thrust me into the frenzy of a race riot for which I had no skills. During the week I clung to my roommate, and on the weekend, I went to Iowa State to hang out with my high school friends.

The conflict of being me inside these experiences strained my ties with family and friends. There was no safe place to be. I was not always welcome in familiar places with familiar people and very rarely welcome in new unfamiliar places. I wish that I had known then what I know now: that horrible place of dividedness offered an absolutely wonderful opportunity for growth.

I married a young man from home and dropped out of college for a while. Then I heard from within the calling to become a teacher; it just seemed natural that teaching children would be a logical place to use all of my life experiences for good. Sharing my story through building relationships with others might just alter the negative effects of prejudice and racism. Perhaps I could help in preventing others from feeling divided about their identity and their place in society. I felt that I had come to a good place and had finally achieved wholeness again. Everything was beautiful as long as deep thought and truth-telling were closely guarded and kept neatly confined in my heart and mind.

LIFE-SAVING COURAGE

The two years in The Courage to Teach and the subsequent reunions and other Circle of Trust retreats saved my life. One can never foresee eventual patterns or chance encounters; they do exist and are orchestrated to require more reflection, deeper thought and truth-telling.

I don't really know what I expected as the journey began. I remember going to that first retreat with trepidation. I was hesitant to assume welcome as we were asked to do. I found it quite unnerving to be given choices without expectations that others may have had for me. I assumed that someone would expect me to feel some kind of way or behave in a predictable manner.

I was not at all comfortable making choices for myself based solely on my personal need and desire. My guard was fully up and fortified with self-talk that would protect me from the unknown. I could not have known that I was to find a way of being with others that would cause a transformation and illuminate my spirit and allow glimpses of unfinished business from my youth. I carried within me a lot of messages: I should always be a good person. I should always treat people well and do the right thing. I should not express anger in a loud or boisterous manner. I should not make others uncomfortable. By all means I should not act like a child because more was needed and expected of me.

This very foreign experience helped me to find a path to wholeness – a place I never even knew existed. Nor did I know I needed to search for it. I had really spent my lifetime seeing myself and existing through the eyes of others, never really getting to know myself. Slowly, over the two years, I started to accept that I could trust that in the universe all is connected the way it should be (the right people, the right place, at the right time).

Two significant encounters announced to my consciousness that I was worthy and entitled to just "be" and enjoy the beauty of being alive – really alive. What a revelation that was for me to embrace. First, like a bolt of lightning: turn to wonder! Turn to wonder. What a strange reaction I felt in my heart and gut when this boundary marker was introduced. The facilitator's introductory words indicated that it was not my responsibility to assume that I should fix anything, anyone, or even that I had the wherewithal in this Circle to do anything about tension, conflict, or tears. Really?!! I should just let it be – really??! Just let whatever comes up in my heart fly into the universe (or at least into my journal) where everything has its place in the overall design?

My other major learning came from participating in the Clearness Committee. It saved me from myself. I had been very successful in my career as determined by my peers. The Clearness experience allowed me to recognize and embrace silence as a strategy for helping to give voice, show love, share love, and hold another person and myself in the light of all that is good and true and beautiful. More important, the experience allowed me to explore and name my personal lines in the sand. No longer, and in no situation, would I allow my integrity to be compromised.

HAPPINESS IS

Recently, my daughter asked me to tell her what makes me happy. I couldn't answer right away but I knew (or as Oprah would say, "what I know for sure") money can't buy it. As I have continued to reflect on my daughter's question, I know that happiness is turning to wonder when words are not enough; sitting in silence with a friend; accepting and returning a smile; feeling the gentle little pats on my back as my granddaughter's hand soothes me as she soothes herself.

The greatest happiness for me is living my life and enjoying my work in ways that embrace the newness of each day, knowing there will be beauty for me to enjoy -- the beauty of one human being touching and being touched by the life of another. In the words of my poet friend, Jim R. Rogers:

> **I love the way a new day feels.**
> **Those few moments when**
> **Yesterday's memories**
> **Are slept into a docile file for later.**
> **When rest gives birth to new eyes**
> **That see a life with energy and hope**
> **And a chance to try again.**

I have been blessed to be touched by and to touch thousands of people over the course of my nearly 40-year career in education. My current work allows me to touch novice teachers and their mentors. My greatest lesson, which has evolved from my first Courage retreat in 1996 until now, is that I really understand that each day, in life as well as in the classroom, we teach who we are at that time **and** we continue to evolve.

Knowing this in every cell of my being is the ground on which I stand – and allows me to know that whatever I want to see and whoever I want to be, I must speak it to the universe.

I must be the beauty I want to see in the work; I must be beautiful.

I am beautiful.

Jacqueline Miles Stanley is the Coordinator of Mentoring, Professional Development and Diversity for the Horry County Schools. She has four adult children and five grandchildren. She is a member of Zeta Phi Beta sorority and attends Popular AME Church. Reach Jackie through email: Jstanley@horrycountyschools.net

Story Calls to Story:
An Invitation to a Virtual Writers Circle of Trust

By Janet Files and Sara Sanders

Keep walking, though there is no place to get to.
Don't try to see through the distances.
That's not for human beings. Move within,
But don't move the way fear makes you move.

Today, like every other day, we wake up empty and
frightened.
Don't open the door to the study and begin reading.
Take down a musical instrument.
Let the beauty we love be what we do.
There are hundreds of ways to kneel and kiss the ground.

---Rumi, translated by Coleman Barks

Rumi's call to us from the thirteenth century to live the way love makes us move rather than the way fear makes us move is a tuning fork in our lives. When life hums in tune with the beauty we love, we can bring our authentic self to family, work, and the people and events that are our life. When our enthusiasm shrivels, or our soul is buried in heavy drifts of to-do lists and fatigue, we remember it is possible to tune back in to our authentic selves by taking time to listen to the beauty we know and love. Writing is a tool we use for doing just that— becoming aware of what gives us life rather than following patterns that sap our vitality. There are always ways out of the labyrinth of confusion and exhausted indifference if we take time to stop and notice.

When we were invited to contribute a story to this book, we first began to write about the beauty we love in our own lives. We quickly realized that one aspect of beauty we find most life affirming is inviting others, like you, into writing retreat spaces where you can find your own stories of the beauty you love and, through those stories, find clarity and wholeness. We decided to craft this chapter as a virtual writing retreat with a set of invitations that have helped us to name and claim more beauty and vitality in our lives. We came to this decision simultaneously with clarity and speed and felt delighted at the prospect of creating this piece. We have come to trust that story calls to story. As we share our story with you, we hope you will notice the stories it calls forth from your own experience.

OUR JOURNEYS TOWARD CLARITY AND WHOLENESS

JANET: "Today, like every other day, we wake up empty and frightened" is a line from Rumi's poem I don't live into as often as I once did. Today, however, I did wake up with just that feeling. A wound from a rift with a long-time friend had festered in the subconscious of my dreams and deflated my confidence in myself as well as creating a sense of estrangement not just from my friend but from my Self. I knew from experience that turning to writing would help me gain perspective and set my heart at rest. Writing is my way of "taking down a musical instrument" and hearing my inner voice of wisdom. I knew this even as a child, and my career path led me deeper into this experience.

My educational journey led me to the National Writing Project in 1989. I valued the authenticity of the writing process the Writing Project created for teachers based on the belief that you can't teach something you don't do. Every writer has a unique way of bringing authentic voice to the page. The Writing Project gave teachers the chance to experience the process of finding a meaningful message, an authentic voice, and an effective way of communicating with a reader in the company of a supportive community of writers. Fueled by the vitality of our experience as writers we took the process into our classrooms and saw how it helped writers of all ages use writing as a way to clarify thoughts, feelings, and messages.

I became director of the Coastal Area Writing Project and later invited Sara to collaborate with me in that work as co-director. We discovered that we thought, taught and wrote better together than alone. Our gifts complemented each other. Sara was often the steady-on balance to my "gallop fast and free into the moment" nature.

SARA: The Coastal Area Writing Project featured an intensive three-week summer institute with plenty of time for total immersion in the writing process. Janet's crafting of that time into a safe, generative space for writing and response was magic. Janet and I did everything we asked the teachers to do during the Writing Project institutes. When they wrote, we wrote. When they shared and responded to writing, we shared and responded to writing. When they "published" pieces, we published pieces. My teaching practices were transformed by the experience of authentic engagement in a learning community in the Writing Project institutes.

JANET: When our colleague and friend, Sally Z. Hare, invited us to participate in a workshop with Parker Palmer in 1994, we eagerly accepted. What remains with me from that first encounter is what draws me back to Circles of Trust over and over again. Most of all, it was Parker's authenticity and willingness to share his story as he helped us find our own in a safe but charged space outlined and protected by boundary markers. Within this space we were invited to reflect on questions related to what keeps us divided from our authentic self. We had time alone and time to be listened to by others in a way that let us hear our own inner wisdom, or inner teacher – the "still small voice within." Parker also gave me a way to name what I had already experienced but had not found words to express. I remember his words that "teaching is not filling a space but creating a space. That space is characterized by openness, hospitality and safe boundaries." This became my teaching North Star.

SARA: A few years later, in 1996, Janet and I had the life-changing (and life-saving) opportunity to participate in a pilot two-year seasonal Courage to Teach retreat series facilitated by Sally. In each of those eight retreats, we focused on moving within and listening to what our inner teacher/authentic self had to say about who we are and whose we are and what that means for our doing and being in the world.

My son was four years old when the retreat series began. I had been offered an opportunity to teach for a year in Germany on a Fulbright grant which I'd had to turn down due to a lack of support from my home institution. I started the retreat series feeling stressed, bitter, and exhausted. (Now I'm grateful that the loss of the Fulbright opportunity left me able to accept the invitation to be a participant in the Courage to Teach retreat series.) I routinely arrived breathless for the opening circle with a car full of clothes and books flowing from the top of bags, no time for proper packing of a suitcase. I was a mess. It was a paradox. My life was both wonderful and teetering on the edge of an abyss. I had a fascinating, faithful husband, a healthy son, a fulfilling career, and good friends around the world AND I felt driven and haunted by a lack of time and sleep because I continuously said yes to new projects and plans. Deadlines were a constant worry. I gained 45 pounds, didn't exercise, had recurrent bouts of strep throat, and lost my voice every fall. (I was interested to learn that the fifth chakra, located at the throat, has to do with will. In so many ways my life was not in harmony with my will.) The retreats helped me find a space to breathe and to believe that I had within all I needed to live a joyful, meaningful, authentic life. In the months between retreats, Janet and I reached out for Courage wisdom to help us meet daily challenges. Janet, Sally, and I began to meet each month at beautiful places (gardens, beaches, aquariums) to walk and talk and write together, sharing poems and books that helped us move within and find courage in our lives.

After the retreat series, Janet and I continued our inner and outer journey with Courage by becoming national facilitators through the Center for Courage & Renewal. In addition to Circle of Trust retreats, we wanted to bring the principles and practices of the Circle of Trust retreats into the work we were doing at the university, in schools across the state, and in the community. When I became chair of the English Department, I added an item to the beginning of each departmental meeting agenda: 1.0 Creating a Space. Inspired by Circles of Trust, each department meeting began with a poem or excerpt that was a "third thing" used to invite silence and inner reflection into our time together. At the end of my term as chair, the department gave me a set of wind chimes. The plate that hangs from the center and moves in the wind is inscribed "Let the Beauty You Love Be What You Do." The sound of the chimes calls me to beauty each time the breeze stirs.

JANET: At the time we went through the facilitator preparation, we were living quite full lives that were already causing our energies and psyches to show a few stretch marks if not quite burst the seams. I had four children, a devoted husband, a rich community of friends and almost two full-time jobs: one, with the South Carolina Department of Education, preparing literacy coaches, and the other, directing the Coastal Area Writing Project at Coastal Carolina University. We couldn't find a way to stretch our already challenged energies and time to organize retreat series; yet we found our Courage and Renewal work was always with us. We brought the ways of Courage into our university courses, using third things to open the way for reflection, offering the boundary markers to help us create safe space in our classes and workshops, giving our students opportunities to share stories in triads with the boundary markers to keep them safe. The principles and practices that form the touchstones of Courage and Renewal sustained us and our students. We also brought the practice into our personal lives. We might call each other and say, "I need a Clearness Committee," and we would meet in person or by phone to hold the space for listening our way into a bit more clarity.

SARA: In 2009 The Center for Courage & Renewal invited proposals for seed grants designed to help the Center think about how to assess the work being done in Circles of Trust. Janet and I proposed to write case study stories of our own Courage journey 1996-2009, with the aim of investigating the impact in our lives and work of ongoing Courage work over a span of thirteen years. As we began to collect our data and think about how to extract insights from it, we were feeling daunted by the work we'd invited ourselves to do. We were not rushing joyfully to the writing. The sheer weight of the thirteen years of artifacts left us feeling like hiding from the work rather than "taking down a musical instrument." Rather than starting with the records of what we'd experienced, we asked ourselves these questions: What travels with us from Courage? How are our lives different because of what we've experienced in Circles of Trust? What is alive in us now that is growing from our experiences with Courage work both as individuals who try to live reflective, intentional personal lives and as professionals who facilitate safe spaces in learning circles with our students and colleagues?

The story we were telling about our Courage experiences mattered, but the writing invitations we created for ourselves mattered more. They offered a way into the knowing of true self... a way retreat participants might use after the retreat, back home, to help themselves move within. As a result of the seed grant, we wrote a book (for ourselves and other facilitators). We have now facilitated five Writers Circle of Trust retreats, using the framework in the book to invite participants to discover more about who they are and what that means for living an authentic, seamless life. As we revise *Writing Along the Mobius Strip: A Practice to Set the Heart at Rest* to reach a wider audience, we are increasingly aware of the power in our own lives of the dance between the principles and practices that guide Circle of Trust retreats and writing as a way of entering inner retreat space.

JANET: Writing the book helped Sara and me name and claim the unique birthright gifts we bring to our role as facilitators of Circle of Trust retreats. We realized we had found a way to unite the beauty we loved from our experience of creating spaces for writers to find their voices with the beauty we loved from our Courage work. We were facilitators who knew the power of writing, art, and image, as well as story and story-sharing, to help others learn to see their many selves and many birthright gifts with soft eyes. Participants in our retreats have told us that their writing in response to our invitations has led to their deepest experience of self-knowing. This affirms for us the power of bringing writing and Circle of Trust principles and practices together to create safe, charged spaces that allow others to find the beauty they love.

SARA and JANET: Writing our way into clarity has helped us create a safe space for reflection that supports us in living more intentional, less divided lives as we continue our journey toward wholeness amidst the tasks and challenges of our daily lives. Writing can be a way of traveling the Mobius strip, from inner wisdom to outer practice, from inner knowing to outer living... over and over and over again.

Writing helps us pay attention to our inner knowing as we notice and name the beauty we love. In the midst of the rich busyness of our lives, writing is a tool for rest and reflection which allows us to hold time still so we can look at and really see what is in front of us and think about what it means. Each moment presents us with choices. Some are life-affirming, and some are life-sapping. Writing helps us pay attention to the patterns and options in our lives and make life affirming choices about our thinking, doing, and being. When we take time to do this inner work, we bring more vitality, harmony, and unity to the myriad roles in our lives.

A WRITING CIRCLE OF TRUST WITH ALL YOUR SELVES

Our story gives you some sense of how we came to know that creating spaces for others to use writing as a practice for setting the heart at rest is part of the beauty we love. Now we offer you suggestions for creating space for your writing and a series of invitations that can lead you to naming and claiming more beauty and vitality in your life. Consider these invitations as suggestions that you can shape in whatever ways interest and engage you. The direction you take is entirely up to you.

When you sit down to begin writing as a way of getting in touch with your inner knowing, you can be in a kind of circle of trust with your selves, all the aspects of your personality. We have given names to our selves as a playful way of noticing and welcoming all our sources of insight and exploring more objectively some of the challenges we face. Sara's Prudence and Janet's Goerthe watch the clock and keep us on track. Sara's Maggie and Janet's Francesca and Kimberly insist that we have as much fun and adventure as possible. Sara's Eliza and Janet's Cara keep the home fires burning brightly, insisting we pause during our writing dates to enjoy the restorative pumpkin soup they have made. Sara's Zoë and Janet's Lizbet remind us that Spirit knows the way home. Janet's Maya brings yoga wisdom to the conversations, and Sara's She leads us fearlessly into projects. Janet's Giselle brings art into our writing projects, and Sara's Becky over-schedules us if she makes appointments and commitments without consulting with the rest of the "gang." Sara's Abbey and Janet's Candace lean toward criticism, self-doubt, and fretful worry, but they also help us pay attention to what is happening around us and keep track of any dragons that might be approaching. One of our invitations will help you get to know your selves who can show you a more abundant approach to living the beauty you love. If you are writing with a trusted partner, the two of you and all you have within can create safe writing and responding space together.

CREATING SAFE SPACE FOR WRITING

The same Boundary Markers from our retreat circles help to create a contemplative space for writing by establishing ways of being with yourself and with others that open a safe space for listening to your inner knowing. (You'll find them as an embellishment in this book.) Revisit these Boundary Markers periodically and let them help you (and your response partner) feel more engaged, alive, and gentle with yourself in your writing toward doing the beauty you love.

WRITING RESPONSE/RESPONSE PARTNERS

Writing can show you what you already know but may not realize you know. Reading what you've written out loud to yourself or to a trusted response partner can help you hear your inner wisdom. You can "partner" yourself as you revisit what you've written; however, joining a trusted other on your writing and response journey increases your ability to listen to your inner teacher. We suggest that you find a partner who is also interested in trying the practice of writing toward inner knowing, whether via phone or computer or in the same room.

We often wondered if we had written anything of substance or value while we were writing. (The inner critic lurks!) Our responses to each other helped us see our writing anew with surprise and delight and helped us have softer eyes toward ourselves and what our inner teacher is telling us through the writing. Help yourself and your partner find deeper meaning by asking open, honest questions. The writer has authority over the process and can choose whether or not to answer the questions. Sometimes we simply write down the questions and give them to the writer to think about for a while before deciding whether to write into an answer. Mirroring is another useful response, saying back to the writer what you heard or noticed or what stood out. Affirming what we particularly like or find interesting in a piece of writing is also a helpful response. We learned to value these three forms of response—open, honest questions, mirroring, and affirmations—in Circle of Trust Clearness Committees as a way of respecting the one seeking clearness and holding the space for that person to listen to his or her own inner voice.

WRITING INVITATIONS: WRITING TO SET THE HEART AT REST

We offer you six writing invitations to help you move within and notice, name, and nurture the beauty you love. You can revise and reshape these invitations to be what you need them to be. Let your inner teacher guide you in choosing what to write about. The invitations appear in an order that helped us, but you can do them in any order you like. Sometimes an example helps start the writing process, so we include some of our responses to these invitations (which also tell more of our story). Your responses, being uniquely yours, are likely to take you in very different directions.

INVITATION #1: LET THE BEAUTY YOU LOVE BE WHAT YOU DO—QUICK WRITE

To help you outdistance your critics and go beyond any fears that you have nothing significant to say, we suggest a strategy called quick writes which are a kind of free writing. The purpose of quick writes is to get your first thoughts and feelings on paper so you can return to them later for more reflective writing.

1. Read the lines from Rumi translated by Coleman Barks from the beginning of this chapter.

2. Write for 4 minutes about anything that resonates with you from these lines. Write whatever comes to your mind. Keep writing. Don't worry about organization, coherence, grammar or eloquence. Write down whatever surfaces--thoughts, ideas, examples or stories. Feel free to make a list instead of writing sentences. Just keep putting words on the page.

3. Beauty is a powerful force. It draws you to it like a magnet. It fills you with vitality and a certain quiet joy. It might be the beauty of a child's face at rest, or the wabi-sabi beauty of your teenage son or grandchild's room that speaks of all the awkward changes in body and emotions this loved one is experiencing. Think of the small and large things that have called to you just this week. Write a list of at least 15 of these moments you loved.

From Janet's list:

- a bird rushing by me on my porch this morning so I could feel its wing-wind

- the full moon with Saturn shining so brightly next to the moon, like a "diamond in the sky" and fresh cool January air as I walked with my husband last night

- open honest conversations with the women I work with as we took time out for lunch

- listening to Billy Collin's poem "Monday" on my car radio as I sped down I-95 last night in the dark with the moon rising

- my oldest son's texting me back an answer to my latest techno-geezer request let me know he is always responsive to his "Mamma" and my technical needs

- time trimming back the winter burn on my potted blue salvia and enjoying the warmth of winter sun on my back

- teaching yoga to my beginning yoga students who are so attentive and appreciative

- this personal writing that helps me pay attention to my daily life and what brings me joy

4. Read over your list. What patterns do you notice in the moments of beauty you love? Write for 5 minutes about the patterns.

Janet writes: Being outside is always restorative for me. I love the smell of the air, full of earth and moldering leaves. I enjoy the small surprises of the animal and plant worlds. The life force that flows through the world: sustaining and ancient and eternal. I also like shaping small parts of this natural world to bring the beauty of it more to view. I love my potted gardens... small, manageable plots of soil and plant-world that I can tend and help move through their seasons to flower and thrive again. I can hardly wait to arrange the miniature daffodils, and the riot of fuchsia, coral and deep purple dianthus waiting patiently in their plastic packs on my deck into my first spring creations. I also love relationships that are harmonious and based on equality and trust. The trust allows us to nurture and heal ourselves as we talk about things that are real in our lives. We don't try to fix each other-- we just listen and hold a space for that sharing. Last, I love learning. I took time to study my own yoga poses today and the questions my body is asking when I feel out of alignment and the small adjustments I can make to bring my body back to a sense of ease and repose in the pose. Then I love sharing this knowledge with my yoga students and watching them discover new possibilities and vitality in their bodies.

INVITATION #2: TAKE DOWN A MUSICAL INSTRUMENT- DOING BEAUTY

1. Make a list of experiences, moments, actions you long for in your life but haven't allowed yourself time to do, or have not even dared to try or perhaps have left behind from an earlier time in your life. Don't edit any out—this is play!

From Janet's list:

- singing

- playing Mozart on the piano

- watercolor painting

- personal yoga practice 6 days a week rather than 3

- traveling to Paris, India, London, Italy with my husband and/or family members

- camping (in comfort) in a pristine mountain setting in the spring or fall

- horseback riding on outdoor mountain trails

2. Choose one of these that would give you the most joy if you could find a way to add it even a tiny bit or add more of it in the next 3 months to your life. Quick write for 5 minutes picturing yourself doing this—be in the experience—write as if you are there and living this fully. There are no practical holds here—just playfully imagine.

Janet writes: I hear my Zen chime alarm go off at 5:30. My mind whispers to me, "You don't have to get up." But my "other" mind whispers back, "I know, that's why I can get up and have this next hour and a half to myself." I slip into my yoga pants and t-shirt left hanging on the Shaker peg last night and slip down the stairs in my fleece-lined slippers. Coffee comes first, and I turn on my new Pandora Mozart channel as I go through my awaken-in-the-dark ritual of boiling my water, measuring out my Sumatra dark roast coffee and warming the milk to froth. Delia, my cat, appears, scratching with her soft insistent mittens at the door. She joins my early morning ritual and arches to my hand to be petted three times a day by a human before she disappears again into her mysterious outdoor-cat day. I sit and read my *Almanac for the Soul*, Mozart playing me to another plane. Then I move to my turquoise yoga mat and begin to breathe in a steady rhythm, being a friendly witness to my breath moving in and flowing out, and open my heart and mind to the wisdom yoga will bring me on this small, magic carpet of space and time.

**INVITATION # 3: EVERY DAY WE WAKE UP EMPTY AND
FRIGHTENED –
NOTICING HOW FEAR MAKES US MOVE**

We notice that as we have been moving toward living an undivided life, guided more by the beauty we love and less by fear, we have fewer days when we wake up empty and frightened. Still, the thing that crowds out the possibility of adding more beauty to our lives, even when we can clearly name what that would be, often falls into one of two categories: practical matters (such as time or money) or dragons in our psyches.

> **Step 1.** Name for yourself what some of your particular dragons are that breathe their terrible breath and frighten you away from making room for the beauty you love. If it helps you, think of one thing that you long for that dragons get in the way of your doing. You may discover an example in the list you wrote in response to Invitation #2.

Janet's dragons that keep her from that lovely yoga practice she listed in #2 above,
- not planning ahead

- feeling that the other "to-do's" of work and family are perhaps more important

- not allowing myself to believe myself to be a "serious" yogini yet

- needing the sleep and not going to bed early enough

- not envisioning it as fun and beauty but rather as a duty of sorts

- thinking I don't have time because I have not planned the time and carved it out of my morning by setting the clock earlier and preparing for the morning the night before.

Step 2. Choose one of these dragons that has the most energy for you and write yourself into a possible solution. You might consider the question: How could a little beauty allow you to dance with the fear rather than be overwhelmed by it?

Janet's dance with her dragons: Maybe I am not seeing the "carrot" of doing yoga daily, and in my mind I feel I SHOULD do yoga daily. I know that I avoid writing, but when I finally do sit down to write with Sara, I don't want to stop. I feel caught in a kind of whirlpool of demands on my time that are not entirely real. I am in a yoga-teacher training program and perhaps I have made my daily practice feel like homework rather than a joyful self-expression within my yoga practice. In my imagined perfect practice morning quick write I had Mozart music playing. If that transports me, I could play Mozart while I practiced. The gods of yoga are not so narrow-minded that this won't add to my particular practice. Coffee before any morning practice is a must for me and is just lovely. Looking at the inwardness of the morning practice is a natural extension of my morning reading and a chance to listen to my inner knowing. I can look forward to that. Interesting....

Another one of my dragons is the "fear of imperfection." If I do sit down to write, or practice yoga or plan for an upcoming professional development session, I have often made the task into something far greater than I, with all my human frailties, could even begin. The dragons of my self-doubt can be over-ruled by the knowledge that the practice itself is what is joyful. One of my favorite quotes from BKS Iyengar is "Once the light of yoga is lit it can never be extinguished. The stronger the practice the brighter the flame." Practice, practice, practice is all there ever is—not perfection, perfection, perfection. These writing invitations are intended as a practice to set the heart at rest and to create a space for listening to your inner wisdom. Kind of like the old Nike commercial, "Just DO it!"

**INVITATION #4: MOVE WITHIN, BUT DON'T MOVE THE WAY FEAR
MAKES YOU MOVE— A SLICE OF LIFE TIMELINE**

Move within. That's what writing helps us do. We move within for sanctuary, rest, courage, encouragement, and wisdom. Fear makes us move toward anger, uncertainty, doubt, anxiety, and worry. Love makes us move with peace, joy, trust, and confidence. If we learn to listen to the positive voices of those who see us with soft eyes—and learn to notice, not judge, what we are experiencing without blaming or fixing, we move the way love makes us move. Once you have named the beauty you want more of in your life and noticed the way fear makes you move, you can be more intentional about making time for life-affirming choices.

Everybody struggles with issues around time. This invitation provides a way to notice our choices about time. When we feel stressed, a close look at a slice of time can show us what is getting lost or left out in the course of our days. Being intentional about the use of time helps us create spaces for what we value most, for doing the beauty we love. A kinder, more intentional use of time can be a gift we give ourselves.

Step 1. Think about a day or two in the recent past that had challenges as well as celebrations for you. Perhaps the day or two before a project or trip or a particular day or two in the past week, maybe even yesterday or this morning. What moments stand out for you? What moments were life-giving? What moments were hard places or life-sapping? You might even think of things you meant to do, life-giving or life-sapping, that got put aside.

Make two columns on a page. Title the left column "Life-Giving Moments" and the right column "Life-Sapping Moments." Brainstorm a list of the moments that stand out for you in the "slice of life" you're noticing. You can note what was planned but got left off in a different color or at the bottom of each list under a dotted line (the moments that "could have been").

Read over your list and give each item a number on a scale of +5 to -5 with +5 being the most life-giving and -5 being the most life-sapping. Don't over-effort this. You just want a sense of which things make you feel alive and which things drain your energy. Don't forget to code your "could have been" moments. Sara termed her moments like this "ghost moments."

Step 2. Create a chronological timeline for the period of time you've chosen.

1. Turn your paper (we like to use a larger piece of paper for this...11"x17" works well) to landscape orientation and draw a horizontal line across the middle of the page (the abscissa for math-savvy folks). This will refer to the time each event occurred. Divide the length of time into reasonable segments—perhaps morning, afternoon, and evening of each day or each hour of a 9-5 segment or before school/during school/after school, whatever segments work with the time you're considering.

2. Along the left side draw a straight vertical line and write "Life Giving" at the top left and "Life Sapping" at the bottom. Divide this into even increments and write + 1, +2, +3, +4, +5 above the horizontal line and -1, -2, -3, -4, -5 below.

3. Use colored pens or colored sticky notes to write each moment from your list in Step 2 in its place on your timeline. Consider using different colors as a code. Write each event on your timeline either above the horizontal line for life-giving moments or below the horizontal line for life-sapping moments or on the horizontal for both/and moments. Place the events on the timeline using the scale of plus or minus to show their level. For example, write the most affirming moments at the top of the chart (on the +5 line) and the most challenging moments at the bottom of the chart (on the -5 line).

4. Relax and enjoy the process of remembering and noticing.

Step 3. Write reflectively (in a journal or on your computer) about what you notice. Here are some questions to consider:

- When you look at your timeline, what's the first thing you notice? Write your reflection (a quick write).

- Look across the ups and downs on the timeline. Do you notice any patterns? Write for a moment about the patterns you notice.

- Where is the beauty you love on this timeline? Write for a moment about your answer to this question.

- What does looking at the "could have been" or "ghost" moments tell you? Is there a pattern? Write for a moment about any insights.

Step 4. Share with a partner (keeping in mind that you can partner yourself).

1. Share 1 or 2 moments from your timeline that surprise or intrigue you and tell the story. Questions that may help you reflect:

   > What patterns do you notice in the life-giving moments? What patterns do you notice in the life-sapping moments? Are there moments that were highly charged with Joy, or, conversely, that brought you a sense of panic or fear? Were there moments where you had to call upon reserves of courage or fortitude to remain present or persevere?

2. As you listen to your partner, write on a sticky note or index card two open, honest questions and one celebration or affirmation.

3. Switch roles.

4. Write about any new insights you want to hold onto or any questions you want to explore with yourself as a result of this process.

INVITATION #5: THERE ARE HUNDREDS OF WAYS TO
KNEEL— A CIRCLE OF SELVES

Among the things we carry with us from our experience in Circles of Trust is the idea of having soft eyes for ourselves and the affirmation that we have come into the world with birthright gifts. As Janet and I worked on writing invitations for *Writing Along the Mobius Strip*, we revisited a strategy we had used in the Writing Project to help teachers prepare to write short fiction as well as memoir, Julia Cameron's "Secret Selves." We noticed that our experiences with Circles of Trust led us to a new level of engagement with writing to discover more about who we are. Naming aspects of self helps us see all of who we are with softer eyes. When we name our selves, we see more clearly the gifts and strengths in our lives and embrace and understand more about the questions coming from the shadows in our lives. We bring the gifts from Circle of Trust Clearness Committees to questions for our selves about what "they" need, fear, and love. We have inner councils with our selves to get clearness about questions or decisions facing us. It has been interesting to watch our dawning awareness of selves who are hidden in plain sight. Some of the most active aspects of our selves are the ones that have taken us the longest to notice and name. As we continue to discover new selves and understand more about the gifts and challenges of each self, we become more aware of the fullness of who we are and the gifts we bring with us into the world.

Our common language reflects Walt Whitman's observation that we each "contain multitudes." We may say when making a decision or responding to a situation something like, "Part of me wants a red convertible, and part of me wants a minivan;" or "Part of me wanted to hug him and part of me wanted to send him to his room for the next fifteen years." In our journey toward conscious, authentic wholeness, we have been helped by getting to know all the parts of ourselves that contribute to healing and wholeness in our life and all the parts that are carrying burdens from deforming experiences. Some of our selves are already fully present on the stage of our life playing leading parts. Other selves have gone into hiding in the shadows due to schedule and societal pressures and/or lack of encouragement. Once we notice them, we may remember and realize anew the important contribution they make when they are invited to step out of the shadows and be more consciously present in our lives.

As we navigate life along the Mobius strip, recognizing the places where our inner wisdom and our inner insecurities meet our challenges in the world helps us live more wholly and intentionally. Rediscovering these "multitudes" of inner voices, naming them and nurturing all of them plays a part in our journey toward unity—leading a centered, balanced, focused life.

Janet writes: Goerthe is an obvious and active character on my life stage. I named her that for her Germanic inclination to take charge and demand discipline and a stiff upper lip from herself and others. She was very much with me last week when I embarked on a home detox plan which required me to give up all my comfort foods including coffee, wine and chocolate (sigh...) and replace them with raw fruits, veggies, diluted organic juices and Dr. Schultz's detox tea made with tasty bits of bark and herbs (yes, really) and a chaser of 3 shots of herbal drops that tasted like fortified dirt. "Drink it down! No whining!" Goerthe has no tolerance for "veaklings." Goerthe wears nylon parachute material hiking shorts from Mast General, a plain t-shirt, and sturdy walking shoes by Rieker. For staying on a five-day detox program, Goerthe was very helpful, and today, my whole self thanks her for my renewed health and vigor.

Francesca is another very present self who is just beginning to tentatively peek her head around the corners of my recent highly-disciplined chunk of life to see if she can come out to play again. She is my expansive, free flowing self. Francesca made herself scarce during the detox. All that denial and regimen are not her cup of tea! Francesca showed up yesterday dressed in her usual flowing scarves and dangling earrings. Sara and I were en route to our writing retreat, but stopped in Asheville, NC, to eat lunch at *Chai Pani*, a delicious Indian restaurant. After lunch Goerthe told us we had only 30 minutes to shop and had to be at the mountain retreat ready to work by 4:30. However, Francesca charmed her way in, and before you knew it we were eating an artisanal Ancient Spice Chocolate Truffle at the *Chocolate Dervish*, buying artfully-designed cards with phrases from the Buddha and Lao-Tzu at *A Far Away Place*, and then shopping for two-sided Prismacolor Premier art markers at *True Blue Art Supplies* and red moleskin notebooks at *Malaprop's Bookstore*. Asheville is Francesca's kind of town. By the time we were unpacking at the retreat it was 7pm. Goerthe got me back to work from 9:30 until midnight. No doubt she enjoyed the creative respite Francesca provided.

Sara writes: Maggie is my fun-loving self. She likes to shop, eat out, go to museums and concerts and movies, take long walks on the beach, and visit farmers' markets. She has a great time with Janet's Francesca. Maggie enjoys quiet time alone and the energy of being with others. *Mary Poppins* is one of Maggie's favorite movies. She understands that "a spoonful of sugar makes the medicine go down." Maggie drinks champagne and umbrella drinks.

Becky loves inquiry and values connection. She says yes to almost everything we're asked to do, so our schedule is packed. We get less sleep and exercise than we need, and time is always an issue for us. Becky believes that because we've been given a lot, a lot is expected from us. She works hard, cares what others think of us, and needs approval. Becky chafes at the limits imposed by clocks and calendars and pretends there will be enough time for all we want to do.

Eliza, goddess of home and hearth, understands self-care; but Becky doesn't give her much time to do it. She grew a pot of basil on the porch last summer and wants an herb garden. She does laundry in the wee hours of the morning because of Becky's schedule and is burdened by the messy, unorganized state of the house. Eliza reads cookbooks, and she makes coffee for Steve and brings in the morning paper for him.

When we were first meeting and naming our selves, Janet asked me, "Why does Becky say 'Yes' to everything?" That was, and continues to be, an important question for me to consider. When I wrote about Maggie and Eliza, Janet asked me, "Where are they?" I laughed and said that Becky had locked them in the Harry Potter closet under the stairs. "Let them OUT!!!" Janet urged. I've been trying to do just that.

INVITING YOUR SELVES TO COME OUT AND PLAY

Janet: This naming of selves is a playful idea. Our multiple selves are parts of a healthy personality. The fun is to name and know them better. It is also useful to know when they are helpful to invoke and when they are not. Francesca would have been a distraction on the strict regime of the detox program, but Goerthe was perfect. However, sometimes Goerthe shows up at the wrong time and then, as Sara's son says, she can be a real "buzz kill." If I let her in on a nice, relaxed dinner with neighbors and all of a sudden Goerthe looks at her watch, gets all anxious about the dirty dishes we have created and starts cleaning up too soon, the evening is deflated.

Step 1. List some of the personality types you see acted out by yourself over and over. Consider how they play their part within the roles you play in your life. In my role as mother, Goerthe tries to tell my grown children what they should do. Francesca just listens and supports them.

Step 2. List some of your hidden, lost, banished, or neglected selves. Take a look into the shadows for lost or neglected selves. Sometimes we have left a self behind in childhood. It may be hiding in a character you liked to use in your imaginative play.

I was often Annie Oakley in my childhood play—she was a "don't fence me in" "I can do that!" go-ahead girl. Annie had much more spunk than Dale Evans who seemed to stand in Roy's shadow. My Kimberly embodies these qualities. She is the tomboy, tree-climbing, I-can-get-it-done-and-get-dirty self.

You might uncover a missing part of you hiding under the kind of Halloween costumes you choose even now. I must admit, I always wear the most glamorous costume I can; whether I am dressed as a witch or a vamp, trust I will show up with all the over-the-top adornments in the way of bling, long gloves, and sequins. (This must be one of my ways of inviting Francesca out to play.)

You may discover a part of yourself hiding in something that used to give you great pleasure that you stopped doing for some reason. I used to draw and paint as a child. I spent hours drawing horses and exploring art with my neighbor Doug's exotic mother, Viki. Viki was a transplanted, glamorous art teacher from New York City. She was a stark contrast to my little, hard-working, home-making, garden magician, farm-daughter mother, Dottie; but they were great friends. (Think Lucy and Ethel for contrasts.) Viki didn't drive; her nails were always painted fire engine red, and in her basement makeshift art studio, she taught us how to do copper relief and how to add texture and shading to our drawings by peeling the paper off our crayons and turning them on the side to use for a richer effect. At the age of 11 my artist self took to hiding in the shadows being pushed out by the star of the show, Little Miss Academic A+ Student. Art did not get much applause in the 50's at Willard Elementary School and Burdick Junior High. I rediscovered this lost self at the age of 50 when I had the chance to take drawing lessons. I actually physically felt like part of my brain was opening up like a piece of folded crinoline springing free of a box. I have enjoyed exploring my artist self, Giselle, ever since. (She and Francesca make a great pair.)

Step 3. Choose 2 or 3 selves that are most intriguing to

you now and get to know them better.
- Name them.

We discovered along the way that Sara's version of my Goerthe is Prudence who is prudent with money and cautious about crossing streets. She follows rules and believes that work comes before play. Francesca and Sara's Maggie have a beautiful time when they get together, and they make work fun. We hope they've contributed some fun to these invitations, but it is thanks in large part to Goerthe and Prudence that we met the publishing deadline for this piece of the Writers' quilt.

- When they relax, what do they do?
- What books and magazines do they read? What movies do they watch?
- Which of your friends do they like to spend time with?
- What do they wear? Which of your clothes purchases did they influence? Which ones annoy them?
- What is their dream house? dream vacation?
- What do they need?
- What do they fear?
- What choices do they hope you'll make?
- What archetype describes them? (Ruler, Magician, Innocent, Martyr, Lover, Creator, etc.)

Step 4. Think of a role you have now that is a significant one for you. It could be interesting to explore a role where you feel you are lacking joy or a former enthusiasm. Ask yourself:

- When I am _____ing at my best which self is "on stage" or taking the lead?
- When I am _____ing and it is hardest, or most challenging, which self is taking the lead?

Think of a recent story about a challenging experience and imagine what it might have looked like with another self taking the lead. How would it have played out? Try describing the challenging situation from the perspective of several of your selves.

Step 5. Try writing a letter to yourself or to someone you love from several of the selves you've noticed and named in Step 3.

Step 6. Write about what this process of noticing and naming parts of self has illuminated for you. What insights have you gained?

Step 7. Invite your selves into a Clearness Circle about a question or situation you are facing. Write a script of their open, honest questions and responses.

Here is a snippet of Janet's script of a Clearness Circle with her selves.

Janet writes: Chai and Clearness Committee with the "Girls"
Cast of characters in order of appearance:
    Lizbet: the Wise One
    Goerthe: the Taskmaster with executive gifts
    Kate: the Perfectionist
    Francesca: the Free, Playful Spirit with Stage Presence
    Maya: the Yoga Teacher and Philosopher
    Giselle: the Artist
    Cara: the Caring Keeper of the Hearth
Lizbet: So we called this clearness committee with Kate's nudging. I think it will be helpful but wonder how it will go for all of us to be focus persons and committee members for each other.
Goerthe: As long as we follow the boundary markers of asking open and honest questions, no fixing, not demanding an answer—and at the end mirroring and affirmations—then I am comfortable.
Kate: Do you think we might do it wrong—maybe we should think on our own a little longer? I'm not sure I am ready (knitting a bit furiously on a new shawl).
Francesca: Now, you know, you actually asked us for this and we all agreed to look into how we can move away from over-efforting (to use Maya's yoga word) or working harder than we need to. I am so-o-o ready for us to have a little more "in

the moment" time—There are SOME of us who feel if we are not consciously accomplishing something we are not worthy of taking breath.(Kate blushes and rearranges her knitting. Goerthe tidies the magazines on the table.)

Lizbet: Kate—do you want to open up the recurrent sand in our oyster shell?

Kate: (Kate takes a deep breath.) Well, it seems we have all gotten very tired of this situation. Whenever we have to plan and create a presentation for work, it makes us so un-centered and almost frantic and takes us SOOO long. I know I feel overwhelmed, and all my warm and cozy emotions seem to leave me and I feel almost cold and frightened.

Francesca: Right—at least you get to be here—I am sent away entirely or locked in the bedroom with only some catalogues and travel books to entertain me.

Goerthe: You know if you only asked me to work with you in the beginning to make a plan or map of how much time we have, what kinds of things we need to do first, second, etc. Then we can get Giselle to start doing the fun creative part.

Giselle: Right—but I shrink away when you don't give me enough time—then I look like some kind of crazy person gathering up all this stuff, running from one idea to another. I need the sense of expansive time. Maybe we could even let Francesca out to add the playful part of the workshops if we had time not to run around like frightened chickens.

Lizbet: How about a question? When we were little, do you remember feeling this way?

Francesca: I remember sitting out on the roof waiting for all of you to come out and play —while you were inside copying pages and pages of boring stuff from the encyclopedia. Kate had a huge bump on her middle finger from pressing down so hard. We had to write the 40-page term paper when 10 would have done nicely.

Giselle: How old were we when that kind of thing happened? I think that was about the time I put away my paradise-colored pencils. I stopped singing for fun and had to perform at church.

Kate: it was around 6th grade. We had Mr. Ray and we all

adored him.

<The group explores a difficult experience trying to get an A on a test to please Mr. Ray ....and realize the difficulty had emerged from the struggle to compete in school that was based on an answer culture when what they needed was a question culture.>

Kate: So, it might be that trying to get an A+ all the time is not taking us to our most energizing source. Sounds like what we all love is learning and asking the questions...not getting answers.

Lizbet: It reminds me of what we were reading in Andre Agassi's memoir, *Open.* His coach helped him play a better more relaxed, more fully present, game of tennis when Agassi realized he couldn't try to hit the winning shot with each tennis swing. He just had to get it back and forth over the net. He actually started winning then and enjoying his wins and leaving his losses on the court, realizing he had played his best game at that moment.

Cara, smiling: Not "Over-efforting"—Maya will be so proud of us.

Goerthe: So, is our plan that we look at the calendar early enough to plan a REASONABLE amount of time to get the work done? AND we need to think about how many hours or days of a workshop we are planning for and plan for that, rather than facing each workshop as if it were a year-long curriculum. Each workshop doesn't have to change the world.

Giselle, quietly with a slight tease: Well, it would be nice to change the world, but we are only creating space for the participants to see something new—or maybe ask a new question.

Francesca: Right –good plan—sounds like we might even get some sleep the night before. You want me to take our workshop public—and go out there and be hospitable and extroverted, but if I have big bags under my eyes and a fog in my head, I can't put on our best front, you know.

Goerthe: Would we like to do some mirroring and affirmations?

Kate: I think we have some good insights—that maybe we are afraid we aren't enough—and won't be loved if we don't work very hard and achieve the impossible. I like thinking about just getting it back and forth over the net. That will help me not be afraid of starting.

Cara: I think we have opened a door to why we sometimes feel a little lonely. Maybe over-efforting puts us out of balance with ourselves and we don't take good care of all of us which includes taking time to be with and enjoy the ones we love.

Giselle: I think we all felt and looked more relaxed and happy when we re-read that part about a question culture. We all love the questions—we are not answer people but we have been put in that position—we need to remember that so we can keep the lightness and light in our work!

Francesca: I think we must affirm Kate's gift for trying her best—doing something toward our goal will get us there—one step at a time. Like the answer to "how do you eat an elephant?"

INVITATION #6: KISS THE GROUND—NURTURING INNER SELF WITH THE BEAUTY I LOVE

Write about what you know about beauty today and how you nurture yourself with the beauty you love.

Here are two of our personal quick writes using this invitation:

Sara writes: How do I nurture my inner self with beauty? These writing invitations create a space for noticing, naming and claiming the beauty I love. Making the choice to nurture myself with beauty by making time for it is life-affirming. What do I know for sure about beauty?

- Beauty, like God, is always there; but I am only sometimes aware of it.
- Beauty in nature is a hieroglyphic message, a love note from God.
- I need a space for beauty in my life...time to order my

thoughts, time to be still with my inner teacher, time to ask big questions and notice the answers that are always there.

- Nurturing my inner self matters. It's like the flight attendant's direction to put on my oxygen mask first. Taking care of myself is a necessary prerequisite to taking care of anyone else I love. When I practice self care, I invite others to consider caring for themselves, too. When I choose to work hard all night and all day, choose not to sleep much, choose not to eat well, and choose not to exercise, I don't honor my inner or outer self; and I suggest by my example that these life-sapping choices are ones people might be expected to make. Writing helps me have more clarity about the choices I'm making and the alternatives that I can consider choosing.
- Beauty is a portal.
- Beauty invites presence in the moment, and presence in the moment opens the portal to beauty. Maybe this is the first point for the list. Maybe it is the only point.

Janet writes: What does my inner self know for sure about beauty? Get out of my head and into my heart. A small insight from yoga—when I feel pain or discomfort in my yoga poses, that is telling me that I am not bringing the beauty of my natural alignment to that part —if I support it with the rest of my muscles and bones, it eases, and the pose become beautiful and restful. So the sand in the oyster of my experience— when I feel discomfort— can be a helpful teacher if I balance the intelligence of the head—what hurts and why—with the wisdom of the heart—how can I love myself into wholeness and create a pearl from this irritating sand? Create. Improvise. Express myself without any words. Let my being and my doing meet each other. Go to the kitchen and roast a tray of curried cauliflower. Paint the front door turquoise. Walk in the snowstorm and notice how my friend's coat shouts a joyful splash of red against the white. Make sketches of portals. Call a friend who needs comfort and who can comfort me.

MOVE THE WAY LOVE MAKES YOU MOVE

Writing as a way of slowing down, paying attention, and being present is an open invitation to you. You may want to revisit the invitations in this chapter to see how what you know about the beauty you love develops and changes. We keep moving forward in our awareness, and you will, too. Your insights and the ways you currently have of "kneeling and kissing the ground" or celebrating and honoring beauty will evolve as you notice, name, and nurture them.

Sometimes just ten minutes of reflective writing will help you move within to beauty. We also encourage you to plan for a day away at a beautiful place, perhaps with your writing partner, to spend a longer time writing your way through some of these invitations.

We wish you beauty on your own personal path of truth as you continue to find ways to "take down a musical instrument" and move the way love makes you move.

 Dr. Janet Files and Dr. Sara Sanders have enjoyed collaborating for 24 years, beginning in 1990 as co-directors of the Coastal Area Writing Project and later as CCR facilitators. They have facilitated retreats and workshops that combine Courage principles and writing for a variety of audiences including teachers, hospice workers, and the Franciscan Sisters of Mercy. What travels with them from their Courage experience enlivens the work Janet does for the SC Department of Education with literacy coaches and teachers and shaped Sara's work at Coastal Carolina University as professor of English and Director of the Jackson Family Center for Ethics and Values until her retirement in May 2013. They facilitate Circle of Trust retreats using writing as a practice to deepen inner knowing and are revising their book, *Writing Along the Mobius Strip: A Practice to Set the Heart at Rest*. They would like to hear from you about your experiences with the invitations in this chapter….your comments, suggestions, any writing you are willing to share (janet.files@gmail.com and sara@coastal.edu).

WORDS MATTER: Our Glossary

glos·sa·ry: a collection of textual **gloss**es or of specialized terms with their meanings

(**gloss:** a surface luster or brightness; shine)
--Merriam-Webster Dictionary, 2014

birthright gifts: We come into this world as unique individuals, each with our own **birthright gifts**. They are hard for us to see, because they have always been there. Often if something comes easily for us, such as the gift to see with an artist's eye or the gift to remember poetry or the gift to see how to arrange a room with beauty, we devalue it. **Birthright gifts** are evident from the moment of birth; we only have to pay attention to an infant to understand that. Babies do not show up as raw material to be shaped by their environment and culture; they come fully formed, with the seed of true self. Yes, we are born with identity and integrity, and even as young children, we know what we like and dislike, what we are drawn towards and what we feel resistance to, what makes us feel alive and what drains our energy. But over the next decade or two, as we move through adolescence and schooling, we too often become deformed. We spend the first half of our lives abandoning our **birthright gifts**, Parker Palmer writes in *Let Your Life Speak*, or letting others disabuse us of them. The purpose of education, at its best, is to create the space for each of us to recognize and deepen our unique **birthright gifts**, to honor them and learn to use them in fulfilling our life's purpose.

Circle of Trust®, circle of trust: The **Circle of Trust®** is a registered trademark of the Center for Courage & Renewal, and the programs can only be offered by facilitators prepared by the Center. For a bit more of an explanation, see the embellishment on page 157 or go to the Center's webpage (www.couragerenewal.org). But perhaps even more important, a **circle of trust** could be two people or ten or twenty, who create a safe space for the soul to show up.

276

Although you will find other meanings for a **circle of trust** if you search the Web, the best place to understand the phrase as we use it in this book is in Parker's writing, especially *A Hidden Wholeness*.

Clearness Committee: The **Clearness Committee** has been adapted for the Circle of Trust program from the Quaker tradition. It is a focused microcosm of a larger circle of trust, a safe and trustworthy space, where we have an intense experience of gathering in support of someone's inner journey. For a bit more of an explanation, see the embellishment on page 61.

Deep or double confidentiality: Most of us know the concept of confidentiality, of not sharing anything that is said in a particular setting with anyone outside of those present. **Deep or double confidentiality** is used in the context of the Clearness Committee, meaning that committee members would not only never speak to each other or anyone else about the issue when the Committee ended, but they also would not speak with the focus person about the problem unless she or he requested the conversation.

Hearing into speech: This wonderful way to describe a sacred deep listening that honors silence is credited to theologian Nelle Morton from her experiences in the early 1970's. She writes in *The Journey Is Home*, "If one can be heard to one's own speech, then the speech would be a new speech and the new speech would be a new experience in the life of the speaker – that is, the one heard to speech." She describes this kind of deep listening as "a depth hearing that takes place before speaking – a hearing that is more than acute listening. A hearing that is a direct transitive verb that evokes speech – new speech that has never been spoken before."

Heart: The heart is important in our Courage Work, as it is literally where courage begins. The word courage comes from the Latin word for heart, *cor*. So we are reclaiming the word **heart** from its too-often sentimental use in our culture, to "the core of the self," as Parker writes in *Healing the Heart of Democracy*, " that center place where all of ways of knowing converge – intellectual, emotional, sensory, intuitive, imaginative, experiential, relational, and bodily, among others. The heart is where we integrate what we know in our minds with what we know in our bones, the place where our knowledge can become more fully human."

Hidden wholeness: "There is in all things an invisible fecundity, a dimmed light, a meek namelessness, a hidden wholeness. This mysterious Unity, and Integrity, is Wisdom, the Mother of all, Natura naturans," writes Thomas Merton in *Hagia Sophia*. Courage Work invites individuals who want to live an undivided life into a Circle of Trust, creating a safe space for the soul to show up, to make that hidden wholeness a bit more visible.

Identity and integrity: These two words are at the root of Courage Work, as we talk about creating space where participants can name and claim and nurture their identity and integrity. We share here Parker's beautiful explanation in *The Courage to Teach*: " By *identity* I mean an evolving nexus where all the forces that constitute my life converge in the mystery of self: my genetic makeup, the nature of the man and woman who gave me life, the culture in which I was raised, people who have sustained me and people who have done me harm, the good and ill I have done to others, and to myself, the experience of love and suffering—and much, much more. In the midst of that complex field, **identity** is a moving intersection of the inner and outer forces that make me who I am, converging in the irreducible mystery of being human. By *integrity* I mean whatever wholeness I am able to find within that nexus as its vectors form and re-form the pattern of my life. **Integrity** requires that I discern what is integral to my selfhood, what fits and what does not—and that I choose life-giving ways of relating to the forces that converge within me: do I welcome them or fear them, embrace them or reject them, move with them or against them? By choosing **integrity**, I become more whole, but wholeness does not mean perfection. It means becoming more real by acknowledging the whole of who I am."

Listening, deep listening: The theologian Paul Tillich said the first duty of love is to listen. A kindergartener named Alec carefully explained to Sally that the words **listen** and **silent** have the same letters – just in a different order – and you can't do one without the other. Both listening and silence are essential elements of a Circle of Trust, and that is where deep listening comes in. Deep listening requires the listener to be fully present, with no necessity to respond or to fix. The purpose is to create the space for the speaker to hear his or her own inner truth. Deep listening may include open, honest questions, which are explained below. A result of deep listening is often feeling heard into speech, as explained above.

Mobius strip: The dictionary tells us that the Mobius strip, named for the German mathematician A. F. Mobius, is a one-sided surface made by joining the ends of a rectangle after twisting one end through 180 degrees. Parker Palmer talks about the stages of growing into who we are, of developing our birthright gifts, as growing towards "life on the Mobius strip," a seamless flow of our inner life and our outer world.

Paradox: The ability to understand paradox, to hold two seemingly opposite truths, to embrace both/and rather than either/or, is another important element of the journey toward the undivided life. As the scientist Niels Bohr said, "The opposite of a correct statement is a false statement. But the opposite of a profound truth may well be another profound truth."

Questions; open, honest questions: We have found that questions offer us a much more fertile ground for this journey to living undivided than do answers. The words that Rainer Maria Rilke wrote to a young poet in 1903 still serve as important touchstones for us: "...have patience with everything unresolved in your heart and try to love the questions themselves as if they were locked rooms or books written in a very foreign language. Don't search for the answers, which could not be given to you now because you would not be able to live them. And, the point is to live everything. Live the questions now. Perhaps then, someday far in the future, you will gradually, without even noticing it, live your way into the answer." Honest, open questions have become a practice in our Circles of Trust, one that we learned in the Clearness Committee. Parker defines and teaches the asking of honest, open questions in *A Hidden Wholeness*. He writes that an honest question is one to which the asker cannot possibly know the answer. An open question is one that expands rather than restricts your area of exploration, one that does not push or even nudge towards a particular way of seeing or responding.

Soft eyes: The idea of soft eyes often feels countercultural in a world that emphasizes sharp focus. In our Circles of Trust, we have come to understand that soft eyes are another important practice in the journey toward the undivided life. We encourage participants to see not only each other with soft eyes, but especially, to see themselves that way. Sally often explains soft eyes by sharing a story from her Kellogg fellowship in Bali: "When I asked the Balinese elder who was my mentor while I was there to help me understand the Balinese childrearing practices that result in gentle, compassionate young people, she explained to me that they saw their children with soft eyes. The Balinese consider their children holy. The younger a person is, the closer her soul to heaven and the purer her spirit. Babies have just come from God, so they are not permitted to touch the impure earth before their first birthday and are carried everywhere.

Balinese children are never left alone, nor are they ever physically punished, and rarely are they upset. So, this wise woman told me, we see them with soft eyes, like you would see someone you love... It's not that you don't see the imperfections; you just don't see their sharp edges."

Soul: "Nobody knows what the soul is," writes Mary Oliver in her poem *Maybe,* "it comes and goes/ like the wind over the water." The soul has many names (Thomas Merton calls it true self; the Buddhists, original nature; Quakers, the inner light; Hasidic Jews, the spark of the divine; Humanists, identity and integrity) – and Parker writes in *A Hidden Wholeness* that it doesn't matter *what* we name it, but *that* we name it matters a great deal. We have come to know in our Circles of Trust that the soul is shy, making the creation of safe space very important if we are going to have a chance to hear that inner voice.

Third things: Another important practice in our Circles of Trust is the use of third things so that we don't scare that shy soul away by approaching it too directly. To achieve that indirectionality, we approach topics and themes in our Circles metaphorically, by using a poem or music or art or quote or object that embodies it. Parker names these embodiments as third things – and again, we send you to A *Hidden Wholeness,* if you want more details!

Tragic gap: Parker writes in *A Hidden Wholeness* that "violence of every shape and form has its roots in the divided life." He offers the insight that the heart of nonviolence requires that we acknowledge that we live in a tragic gap – a gap between the way things are and the way we know they might be. In our Circles of Trust, as we learn to embrace paradox, we also learn the practices that allow us to stand faithfully in that tragic gap, holding the tension between reality and possibility.

Ubuntu: This _{Nguni Bantu} word literally means human-ness and is often translated as "humanity towards others." Since Nelson Mandela's presidency in South Africa, the term has spread from that region to other places, often through the writing of Desmond Tutu, who uses it to express the philosophical belief that we are all connected. In our Circles of Trust, as we come to understand the paradox that the inner journey can only be undertaken by an individual, and yet it is too hard to take alone, Tutu's writing on Ubuntu helps us find language for this seemingly counterculture concept, another way to name the idea of solitude in community.

PLACES MATTER TOO

Places matter, too, and there are three that are particularly important to the Writers in our Circle of Trust. The next pages offer a bit about those:

- still learning, inc.
- The Center for Courage & Renewal
- Kirkridge Retreat and Study Center

still learning, inc.

still learning, inc, offers a unique kind of professional development focusing on each person's own identity and integrity.

still learning, inc, is pleased to have created the space for this Writers Circle of Trust. All of the Writers in this book have attended still learning retreats. National CCR facilitator **Sally Z. Hare** is president of still learning and plans and facilitates Circles of Trust in special locations, including the coast of South Carolina and Kirkridge Retreat Center on the Kittatinny Ridge in the Poconos of Pennsylvania. To learn more about upcoming retreats, go to www.stilllearning.org – or email Sally at sally@stilllearning.org

Jim R. Rogers, M. ED., CFLE, is vice president and treasurer of **still learning, inc**. A nationally certified parent and family life educator, Jim has created the ParentsCare curriculum, which deepens and broadens knowledge and resources in parenting and family management education. It invites parents and caregivers to participate in the processes of building and maintaining the best possible relationships with children. Education is the core; education for affirming, healing, prevention, empowerment and developing young children who feel good about who they are and about the environment in which they live. Home is Where the Start is, and healthy knowledgeable parents are the managers of those homes.

Jim is also the author of *The Incredible Importance of Effective Parenting* and *Starts and Stops Along the Way*. You can find Jim at jim@stilllearning.org or 843-238-9291.

I am still learning.

--- Michelangelo at age 90

CENTER FOR
Courage
& Renewal

The mission of the Center for Courage & Renewal is to create a more just, compassionate and healthy world by nurturing personal and professional integrity and the courage to act on it.

For such a world, we need people—like the people in this book—who embrace their role and work together to solve pressing, complex problems. Courage & Renewal programs help individuals "lead from within" by acting with courage on their true callings; developing trustworthy relationships; sustaining themselves and others for the long haul; and working together to transform the institutions and communities they serve.

Founded in 1997 by author, activist, and educator Parker J. Palmer, the Center's approach was initially created to renew and sustain educators, and today also reaches those in health care, ministry, and across communities.

Through its network of more than two hundred Courage & Renewal Facilitators across North America and the globe, the Center offers online resources and in-person retreats and programs to cultivate the heart and soul of leadership.

Join this growing movement at www.CourageRenewal.org

Center for Courage & Renewal
1402 Third Avenue, Suite 709
Seattle, WA 98101

206-466-2055
info@couragerenewal.org

Kirkridge, dear friends, innkeepers of the open door,
multitudes shall arise and call you blessed.

– Daniel Berrigan

Since 1942, Kirkridge Retreat and Study Center has been providing a place for rest and renewal for people along life's journey. Kirkridge's emphasis from the beginning was the integration of inner contemplation with the outward call to action for justice.

Kirkridge is located on the beautiful Kittatinny Ridge of Eastern Pennsylvania near the Delaware Water Gap and Pocono Mountain region.

KIRKRIDGE

RETREAT AND STUDY CENTER
2495 Fox Gap Road, Bangor, PA 18013-6028

www.kirkridge.org

THE CLOSING CIRCLE

As we move into with our Closing Circle, we invite each Writer to share what's in her or his heart as we complete the Writers Circle of Trust that has resulted in our quilting of this book. The closing circle in every Circle of Trust is an important time of reflection, of solitude in community.

Janet Files: Sara and I have been in Circles of Trust with 16 of the authors in this book, and 11 have been participants in "Writing to Set the Heart at Rest" retreats we've facilitated. Being part of this circle of writers exploring the beauty we love feels like a homecoming. Writing our story for this book has been deeply satisfying, generative and transformative, leading us to more clearness about what we value and find beautiful in the connection between writing and the principles and practices of Circles of Trust.

Sara Sanders: We hope our readers will find that our invitations to uncover the beauty they love will awaken provocative inner questions they want to live into. We hope they will trust the urgings of their hearts and be brave enough to follow what rings true to them on their journey toward wholeness. Writing the chapter for this book has been a joyful continuation of our own experience of doing just that—asking "What is the Beauty I love and how does it make me move in the world?" Janet and I love collaborating, and we are profoundly grateful to our co-facilitators and co-editors, Sally and Megan, for asking us to join the voices in this book to sing the Beauty we love.

Marian R. David: This writing process was wonderful, cathartic, validating, and amazing in that I found myself revealing much more of me than I imagined, but it all flowed, so I went with it.

Marcie Ellerbe: This Writers Circle of Trust has helped me gain clarity about how I define meaningful work. It has reminded me that my work is a very large part of my life and given me the courage to say that this is OK.

Carolyn Ellis: The Writers Circle of Trust has helped me discover again the value of writing in order to articulate who I am.

Caroline Fairless: Reflecting on the process of writing for this book, I am remembering it was hard to find the place to begin, and so I chose to begin in the middle. I feel honored to be a part of a Writers Circle of Trust. I love to imagine what shape and form the other narratives are taking. I am eager to know the others of the Circle ever more deeply.

John Fox: I enjoyed honing raw materials into the threads of what is true and then weaving those fibers into the stories I shared for this co-creation of the Writers Circle of Trust.

Wanda Freeman: Writing for this book has peeled away the restricting layers and set into motion what I need to pick up and continue the journey to unfailing courage I started almost 20 years ago. With intention, I seek myself to share myself. In a couple of years, I will retire from Forestbrook Middle School, a much better person than when I fell into the teaching profession.

Veta Goler: Being part of this Writers Circle of Trust has clarified and given me words for what I already knew in my heart.

Megan LeBoutillier: When invited to co-edit this book and to contribute a chapter of my own, I knew immediately I wanted to be involved. So, when I realized that the chapter I would write required a level of vulnerability I do not relish, I had to lean into the trust I feel for Courage Work and know all is for the best. I am aware that where I think I am headed is frequently not where I wind up. At least I appreciate the journey, even if I am not a great navigator.

Morgan Lee: Being in this Writers Circle of Trust, being in a community where I know that "my people" are out there while I am considering my own stories, was different and refreshing. For me, storytelling is primal and it is at the heart of my life and my work. To be invited to write some of my story in such a way touched my heart and my soul.

Sandie Merriam: Being a Writer in the Circle of Trust has enabled me to see the common threads/ stepping stones of my own life for the first time. Before this opportunity I saw my life in pieces/ scattered... With the encouragement and mirroring that I received in the writing process, I have begun to see myself and my life's journey as having had much more congruence than I realized as I lived what seemed like chaos when I was in the middle of it!

Pat Mulroy: Writing has helped me to publicly claim myself: digging deep inside my own story, saying it out loud, hoping that my life can inspire someone else to feel the courage that living authentically brings.

Jean Richardson: Writing for this book is a true exercise of trust. Like much of Courage work, it has been a gift, to speak the truth of my life and honor my walk toward wholeness.

Anna Marie Robinson: Writing for this book has been a very personal journey. It has given me an opportunity to reflect upon the spiritual energies surrounding me at home and at work. Equally, the process of writing for this book has helped me to value the work ethic of my sister who writes professionally.

Jim R. Rogers: Writing my story has created a loud crash through my protective cover, not wanting anyone to know about the personal and private struggles, pretending that if I don't tell anyone, no one will know, and I won't feel embarrassed or weak or wrong.

Sue E. Small: This Writers Circle of Trust has been a metaphor for my life's experiences: accepting an invitation to commit, taking the first steps of trying to do/write something new, reviewing and (second-guessing), reflecting, revising, and re-writing again and again, finding the faith to finish or stop writing, and letting it go… as it is, trusting that it is enough for now.

Debbie Stanley: What has the process of writing for our book felt like for me? Delightful and energizing. Allowing a part of my life journey to spill out onto paper was refreshing, baffling, and sobering. It was an awesome way to have a self-made clearness committee. My writing self was the focus person; meaning, clarity, and voice made up my committee.

Jackie Stanley: This process of writing for our book was extremely difficult for me. It required admitting some life truths that have been buried. It required embracing, naming and claiming some experiences that I thought were better left unsaid….and especially not shared. I am better for sharing and I understand that the journey of life is Beautiful… Together Light AND shadow = Beauty.

289

Kay Stewart: As I reflect on the wonders of being part of this Writers Circle of Trust, Anne Lamott's three simple prayers come to mind: Help, Thanks, and Wow! What a gift to be invited into this sacred space of deep listening and affirmation of the Beauty I love.

Sally Z. Hare: I see myself as a Reader, not a Writer, so even deciding to write a book was hard, but it seemed a way to honor my commitment to going public in order to notice and name and nurture Courage Work in the world – and its importance in my life. When I listened to myself about the Beauty I love -- my passion for reading and for creating space for others to hear themselves, I had this realization: "I don't have to write a book! I just need to invite others to join me in a Writers Circle of Trust!" So I did – and it's been a time of joy and intense learning for me – and constant surprise. I think the biggest surprise has been the appreciation and gratitude from the Writers for the way accepting this invitation was another step in their own journeys to the undivided life.

At noon, Fear is nowhere to be found
As shadows stretch, danger finds a place to hide
In night's darkness. Fear grips us tightly
Faith loosens the grip to set us free

---Ruby Sue Tootser

CPSIA information can be obtained at www.ICGtesting.com
Printed in the USA
BVOW05s2112160414

350573BV00003B/21/P